First World War
and Army of Occupation
War Diary
France, Belgium and Germany

GUARDS DIVISION
Headquarters, Branches and Services
Adjutant and Quarter-Master General.
29 August 1915 - 30 April 1919

WO95/1197/1

The Naval & Military Press Ltd
www.nmarchive.com
Published in association with The National Archives

Published by

The Naval & Military Press Ltd

Unit 10 Ridgewood Industrial Park,

Uckfield, East Sussex,

TN22 5QE England

Tel: +44 (0) 1825 749494

www.naval-military-press.com

www.nmarchive.com

This diary has been reprinted in facsimile from the original. Any imperfections are inevitably reproduced and the quality may fall short of modern type and cartographic standards.

© **Crown Copyright**
Images reproduced by permission of The National Archives, London, England, 2015.

Contents

Document type	Place/Title	Date From	Date To
Heading	1915-1919 Guards Division. "A" & "Q" Branch Aug 1915-Apl 1919		
Heading	1915 Diaries After		
War Diary		29/08/1915	31/08/1915
Miscellaneous	Guards Division. Fighting Strength for week ending 27th August, 1915.		
Miscellaneous	A. 124th Co. A.S.C.		
Miscellaneous	141st, 142nd Field Ambulance		
Miscellaneous	Grenadier Guards. Roll of Officers by Battalions who are Serving with the Expeditionary Force.		
Miscellaneous	2nd Battalion, Grenadier Guards.		
Miscellaneous	3rd Battalion, Grenadier Guards.		
Miscellaneous	4th Battalion, Grenadier Guards.		
Miscellaneous	First Battalion Coldstream Guards.		
Miscellaneous	Second Battalion Coldstream Guards.		
Miscellaneous	Third Battalion Coldstream Guards.		
Miscellaneous	Fourth Battalion Coldstream Guards (Pioneers).		
Miscellaneous	Roll of Officers serving with the 1st and 2nd Battalions Scots Guards in the Expeditionary Force.		
Miscellaneous	Officers of 1st Battalion Irish Guards.		
Miscellaneous	List of Officers serving with the 2nd Battalion Irish Guards, British Expeditionary Force.		
Miscellaneous	Welsh Guards. Roll of Officers with the Expeditionary Force. 1st. Battalion.	29/08/1915	29/08/1915
Heading	Guards Divn (A & Q) Oct 15 Vol III		
War Diary		01/10/1915	31/10/1915
War Diary		01/11/1915	30/11/1915
Miscellaneous	Guards Div. A. & Q. September 1915.		
War Diary		01/09/1915	30/09/1915
Miscellaneous	Sheet No.2		
Miscellaneous	G "Branch"	30/09/1915	30/09/1915
Miscellaneous			
Miscellaneous	Appendix A. Drafts for week ending September 4th, 1915.		
Miscellaneous	Drafts for week ending Sept. 4th. Appendix A.		
Miscellaneous	Drafts for week ending Sept 11th: Appendix B		
Miscellaneous	Drafts for week ending September 11th, 1915. Appendix B		
Miscellaneous	Drafts for week ending September 19th, 1915. Appendix C.		
Heading	74th Division Engineers CRE. Field Coys Signals September 1918		
Heading	Guards Division Headquarters (A & Q) Guards Division Vol I. 29 July to 31 Aug. 15		
Miscellaneous	Guards Division		
Heading	War Diary Dec 1915 Till July 1916		
Heading	H.Q. Cav. Div. (A & Q) Dec Vol. V		
War Diary		01/12/1915	31/12/1915
Heading	H.Q. A. & Q. Guards Div Jan Vol VI		
War Diary	La Gorgue.	01/01/1916	31/03/1916

Type	Description	Start	End
Miscellaneous	Routine After Order by Major-General G.P.T. Feilding. D.S.O. Commanding Guards Division. App 521	05/03/1916	05/03/1916
War Diary		01/04/1916	31/07/1916
Heading	A.A. & Q.M.G. Guards Division August 1916. Box 1197. August 25th to 31st transferred to WO 154/17		
War Diary		01/08/1916	31/08/1916
Heading	Diaries Sept 1916 V March 1918		
War Diary		01/09/1916	30/09/1916
War Diary	Belloy	01/10/1916	30/01/1918
War Diary	Arras.	01/02/1918	21/03/1918
War Diary	Bretoncourt.	22/03/1918	31/03/1918
Heading	April 1918 V April 1919		
Heading	War Diary A. & Q. Guards Division April 1918 Casualty Return 20th March to 17th April		
War Diary	Bretoncourt.	01/04/1918	14/04/1918
War Diary	Bavincourt	14/04/1918	24/04/1918
War Diary	Humbercamp.	25/04/1918	29/04/1918
Heading	Casualties From 20 March to 17 April 1918		
Miscellaneous	The Brigade Major, Brigade of Guards, Carlton House Terrace, London. S.W.	21/04/1918	21/04/1918
Miscellaneous	Total Casualties from Noon, 20th, March, 1918 to Noon, 17th. April, 1918.		
Miscellaneous	Oct 1915. a/c of opnns Br Gen J Ronsonly-2 Gds Bn d/9 Octr		
War Diary	Humbercamp.	01/05/1918	28/05/1918
War Diary	V.27.c.7.7. (Sheet 51c. S.E.) La Bazeque Wood.	07/05/1918	07/05/1918
War Diary	Bavincourt	10/05/1918	06/06/1918
War Diary	W.3.d.4.5.	07/07/1918	31/08/1918
Miscellaneous	Guards Division Administrative Instructions, No.1. Appendix 1	19/08/1918	19/08/1918
Miscellaneous	Total Casualties From Noon 20/8/18 to Noon 31/8/18		
Miscellaneous	List of Officer Casualties in the Division from 20th. to 29th. August. 1918.		
War Diary	W.3.d.4.5.	01/09/1918	03/09/1918
War Diary	A.11.b.8.7. Hamelincourt.	04/09/1918	05/09/1918
War Diary	B.17.a.8.8	06/09/1918	06/09/1918
War Diary	L'Homme Mort	07/09/1918	10/09/1918
War Diary	B.17.a.8.8.	11/09/1918	15/09/1918
War Diary	Lagnicourt.	16/09/1918	30/09/1918
Miscellaneous	Guards Division Administrative Instructions Reference G.D. Order No.218 of 5/9/18.	05/09/1918	05/09/1918
Miscellaneous	SSO SAA Sec APM Div. Train		
Miscellaneous	The following amendments to Guards Division Administrative Instructions No.11, issued under this office No.1089/94/A of 24/9/18, are issued for information:-	26/09/1918	26/09/1918
Miscellaneous	Guards Division Administrative Instruction No.11	24/09/1918	24/09/1918
Miscellaneous	Schedule "A". Roads, Tracks, and Canal Crossings, Available for use by the Guards Division.		
Heading	War Diary Administrative Staff. Guards Division October 1918.		
War Diary	Lagnicourt.	01/10/1918	07/10/1918
War Diary	Flesquieres	08/10/1918	10/10/1918
War Diary	Boussieres	11/10/1918	01/11/1918
War Diary	Vertain	02/11/1918	04/11/1918
War Diary	Villers Pol	05/11/1918	07/11/1918

War Diary	Mecquigny	08/11/1918	10/11/1918
War Diary	Mecquigny Maubeuge	11/11/1918	11/11/1918
War Diary	Maubeuge	12/11/1918	19/11/1918
War Diary	Binche	20/11/1918	20/11/1918
War Diary	Charleroi	21/11/1918	25/11/1918
War Diary	Fosse	26/11/1918	28/11/1918
War Diary	Assesse	29/11/1918	04/12/1918
War Diary	Ochain	05/12/1918	11/12/1918
War Diary	Grande Halleux	12/12/1918	13/12/1918
War Diary	Hellenthal	14/12/1918	16/12/1918
War Diary	Zulpich	17/12/1918	18/12/1918
War Diary	Cologne	19/12/1918	24/12/1918
War Diary	Lindenthal	25/12/1918	09/03/1919
War Diary	Cologne	10/03/1919	10/03/1919
War Diary	Germany	11/03/1919	30/03/1919
War Diary	Lindenthal Cologne Germany	30/03/1919	30/03/1919
War Diary	Lindenthal Cologne	01/04/1919	23/04/1919
War Diary	Duren, Germany	24/04/1919	24/04/1919
War Diary	Antwerp	25/04/1919	27/04/1919
War Diary	Tilbury	29/04/1919	29/04/1919
War Diary	Whitehall, London, SW	30/04/1919	30/04/1919

1915-1919
GUARDS DIVISION

'A' & 'Q' BRANCH

AUG 1915 - APL 1919

1915
Diaries & notes

Army Form C. 2118

WAR DIARY
or
INTELLIGENCE SUMMARY
(Erase heading not required.)

"A"

War Diary
Gds. Div. Formation
Aug. 1915.

Instructions regarding War Diaries and Intelligence Summaries are contained in F. S. Regs., Part II. and the Staff Manual respectively. Title Pages will be prepared in manuscript.

Place	Date	Hour	Summary of Events and Information	Remarks and references to Appendices
	1915.			
	July 29th.		3rd Battalion Grenadier Guards arrive at ESQUERDES and come under G.H.Q.Troops.	
	August 5th.		1st Battalion Grenadier Guards arrive at WIZERNES and come under G.H.Q.Troops.	
	August 7th.		Household Cavalry Divisional Squadron arrive from HAVRE and go into billets at ESQUERDES. Squadron found from 1st Life Guards.	
	August 9th.		2nd Battalion Scots Guards arrive at WIZERNES and come under G.H.Q.Troops.	
	August 14th		Household Cavalry Cyclist Company drawn from Royal Horse Guards and 2nd Life Guards arrive at ST.MARTIN-au-Laert and come under G.H.Q.Troops. Captain C.M.HEADLAM, Bedfordshire Yeomanry and 2nd Lieutenant O.LYTTLETON join as Aides-de-Camp to the General Officer Commanding.	
	August 15th		Brigadier General F.G.HEYWORTH,C.B., D.S.O., arrives to take over command of the Division temporarily. Major F.G.ALSTON, Scots Guards arrives as D.A.A & Q.M.G.	
	August 16th		Major (Temp.Lt.Col) W.H.V.DARELL, D.S.O., Coldstream Guards arrives as A.A.& Q.M.G. No: 46 Mobile Veterinary Section joins the Division.	
	August 17th		Guards Division ceases to be under G.H.Q.Troops Head Quarter Office is opened at 16 Rue St.BERQUIN, ST.OMER. Captain G.E.C.RASCH, D.S.O., Grenadier Guards arrives as G.S.O.3.	
	August 18th		Colonel (Temp.Major-General) F.R.Earl of CAVAN, G.B., M.V.O., arrives at ST.OMER having inspected Units of the Guards Division in ENGLAND. Guards Pioneer Battalion (late 4th Battalion Coldstream Guards) detrain at LUMBRES and move into billets at WAVRANS and ELNES. 4th Battalion Grenadier Guards detrain at ST.OMER and move into billets at BLENDECQUES. No.16 Divisional Signal Company arrive at LUMBRES and detrain, remaining at Divisional Head Quarters at LUMBRES. 19th Infantry Brigade Supply Column from 19th Infantry Brigade arrive and move to billets at ST.MARTIN. Divisional Supply Column arrive and move to billets at ST.MARTIN.	

Army Form C. 2118.

WAR DIARY
or
INTELLIGENCE SUMMARY

(Erase heading not required.)

Instructions regarding War Diaries and Intelligence Summaries are contained in F.S. Regs., Part II. and the Staff Manual respectively. Title Pages will be prepared in manuscript.

Place	Date	Hour	Summary of Events and Information	Remarks and references to Appendices
	1915. August 18.		Lieutenant Colonel G.S.McLOUGHLIN, C.M.G.,D.S.O., Royal Army Medical Corps arrives as A.D.M.S., to the Division. Major B.N.BROOKE, D.S.O., Grenadier Guards arrives to take over duties of Brigade Major, 2nd Guards Brigade. Captain A.F.N.THORNE, Grenadier Guards arrives as D.A.Q.M.G., to the Division. M.MILLERAND, French Minister of War, inspects the undermentioned Battalions on the Royal Flying Corps ground at 5 p.m.:- 1st Battalion, Grenadier Guards. 3rd -do- -do- -do- 2nd -do- Scots Guards. Lord KITCHENER and Sir JOHN FRENCH were present. The parade was commanded by Colonel M.A.L.CORRY, D.S.O., 3rd Battalion Grenadier Guards. Brigadier General HEYWORTH attended as Divisional Commander. The 3 Battalions received M.MILLERAND with a General Salute and marched past in half companies. No.45 Sanitary Section detrain at LUMBRES and join Head Quarters at LUMBRES. Major W.W.BLADES, D.S.O., Army Ordnance Department arrives as D.A.D.O.S., to the Division. Captain E.C.T.WARNER, Scots Guards takes over duties of Staff Captain, 3rd Guards Brigade. Major F.C.O'RORKE, Army Veterinary Corps, reports as A.D.V.S.	
	August 19.		Divisional Head Quarters move to LUMBRES opening at 2 p.m. and closing in ST.OMER at the same hour. 2nd Battalion Irish Guards detrain at LUMBRES and move into billets at ACQUIN. Captain A.V.Earl of CLANWILLIAM, Royal Horse Guards, R of O., arrives as Assistant Provost Marshal to the Division. 4th Guards Brigade move to HAM - NORRENT FONTES area en route to join Guards Division, and are visited by the Divisional Commander. No.4 Field Ambulance and Section of 2nd Divisional Train moves with 4th Guards Brigade.	
	August 20.		1st Battalion Welsh Guards detrain at ST.OMER and move into billets at ARQUES. 4th Guards Brigade move to area ARQUES - RENESCURE.	
	August 21.		4th Guards Brigade march through ST.OMER and are inspected on the march by the Commander-in-Chief in the GRANDE PLACE, ST.OMER. The Brigade moves into billets in the area MOULLE - HOULLE - EPERLECQUES. The 4th Guards Brigade becomes the 1st Guards Brigade.	

Army Form C. 2118

WAR DIARY
or
INTELLIGENCE SUMMARY
(Erase heading not required.)

Instructions regarding War Diaries and Intelligence Summaries are contained in F. S. Regs., Part II. and the Staff Manual respectively. Title Pages will be prepared in manuscript.

Place	Date	Hour	Summary of Events and Information	Remarks and references to Appendices
	1915. August 22.		Orders received for 1st Guards Brigade to vacate their present area on 24th instant and move to billets S. of WAVRANS. D.A.A & Q.M.G., reconnoitres the new area. Rear party of Welsh Guards 3 Officers and 125 men arrive.	
	August 23.		4th Battalion Grenadier Guards carried out experiment of embarking in barges on the Canal at ARQUES. Brigadier General H.C.LOWTHER, C.V.O., C.M.G., D.S.O., reports. Lieutenant Colonel J.C.BLACK reports as Officer Commanding Train and Major A.W.JOHNS as Senior Supply Officer, and Captain H.E.STANDAGE as Adjutant.	
	August 24.		Head Quarter Company and Nos: 3 & 4 Companies of the Divisional Train arrive - Head Quarter Company remained at LUMBRES. No: 3 Company to 3rd Brigade. No: 4 Company to 2nd Brigade. 61st F.A.Brigade (Howitzers) detrain at LUMBRES and ST.OMER and move to billets at and around BAYENGHEM. 1st Battalion Scots Guards move to CAMPAGNE and 1st Battalion Coldstream Guards to HERBELLE en route to join the Division. Captain T.D.G.HOWELL, Royal Army Medical Corps reports as D.A.D.M.S., to the Division. Major R.S.TEMPEST, Scots Guards arrives to take over duties of Brigade Major, 3rd Guards Brigade. First Guards Brigade move to billets as under:- Head Quarters and 1st Irish Guards............THIEMBRONNE. 2nd Grenadier Guards............CAMPAGNE-LEZ-BOULONNAIS. 2nd Coldstream Guards............VERCHOCQ. 3rd Coldstream Guards............CLETY. 4th Field Ambulance............RUMILLY. No:3 Company Divisional Train....WILLIAMETZ. Guards Divisional Ambulance Workshop arrives at LUMBRES.	
	August 25.		Remainder of 61st F.A. Brigade arrive. 75th Field Company, Royal Engineers detrain at LUMBRES and march to their billets at EQUIRE in First Brigade Area. 1st Battalion Coldstream Guards move to LUMBRES. 1st Battalion Scots Guards move to TATINGHEM.	

Army Form C. 2118

WAR DIARY
or
INTELLIGENCE SUMMARY
(Erase heading not required.)

Instructions regarding War Diaries and Intelligence Summaries are contained in F. S. Regs., Part II. and the Staff Manual respectively. Title Pages will be prepared in manuscript.

Place	Date	Hour	Summary of Events and Information	Remarks and references to Appendices
	1915. August 25.		6 Wolseley Cars arrive for the Division from HAVRE, specially sent out from the War Office. Lieutenant Colonel Hon.W.P.HORE-RUTHVEN, C.M.G., D.S.O., arrives and takes over duties of G.S.O.1.	
	August 26.		3rd Field Ambulance arrive and move into billets in 3rd Brigade Area near HALLINES and are attached 3rd Brigade. Divisional Ammunition Sub-Park arrives and takes up its position along the main road to E. of AFFRINGUES. 76th Field Company, Royal Engineers arrives and moves into billets at QUELMES. Detraining at ST.OMER 95th Field Company, Royal Engineers. 17 men Military Mounted Police arrive detraining at LUMBRES and are attached to Head Quarters. Divisional Commander holds a Tactical Exercise for the Divisional Squadron and Cyclist Company. Lieutenant Colonel J.E.VANRENEN, Royal Engineers arrives and takes over duties as Commanding Royal Engineer to the Division. Brigadier General J.PONSONBY, C.M.G., D.S.O., assumes command of 2nd Guards Brigade.	
	August 27.		Major (Temp.Lieut-Colonel) J.McG.STEELE, vacates command of 2nd Battalion Coldstream Guards and proceeds to 7th Division to command 22nd Infantry Brigade. 95th Field Company, Royal Engineers arrive at ST.OMER and move into billets at LONG PONT and WINS in 3rd Brigade area. Lieutenant Colonel J.V.CAMPBELL, D.S.O., assumes command of the 1st Infantry Brigade during the absence on leave of Brigadier General G.P.T.FEILDING,D.S.O.. Lieutenant Colonel R.S.de HAVILLAND is attached to Divisional Head Quarters on a visit under G.H.Q.instructions.	
	August 28.		Railhead is moved to LUMBRES. 9th Field Ambulance arrives and moves into billets at BOISDINGHEM.	
	August 29.		Divisional Ammunition Column begins to arrive. Ordnance Travelling Workshop arrives to be attached temporarily for repair of cartswater-carts, wagons, etc. Captain Prince AYMON de FAUCIGNY-LUCINGE reports as Officer de liaison.	
	August 30th		Remainder of Divisional Ammunition Column arrive and move into billets No.1 & 2 Sections at	

Army Form C. 2118

WAR DIARY
or
INTELLIGENCE SUMMARY
(Erase heading not required.)

Instructions regarding War Diaries and Intelligence Summaries are contained in F.S. Regs., Part II. and the Staff Manual respectively. Title Pages will be prepared in manuscript.

Place	Date	Hour	Summary of Events and Information	Remarks and references to Appendices
	1915.			
	August 30.		at AFFRINGUES. No: 3 Section at SEINGHEM. 74th Brigade, Royal Field Artillery arrive at ST.OMER and LUMBRES and move into billets at NIELLES. Lieutenant Colonel R.S de HAVILLAND returns to ENGLAND. 95th Field Company, Royal Engineers march into 1st Army Area to join 7th Division and to relieve the 55th Field Company, Royal Engineers detailed to join this Division. Colonel (Temp.Brigadier General) C.E.GOULBURN, D.S.O., arrives to take over duties of Commanding Royal Artillery. The Staff of the Head Quarters Divisional Artillery arrive. Ordnance Store and Travelling Workshop moves to WAVRANS. Divisional Supply Column moves from ST.MARTIN to LUMBRES.	
	August 31.		The Divisional Commander proceeded to MAIZIERES and was decorated by General JOFFRE with the Cross of Commander of the Legion d'honneur. The Officer Commanding, Machine Gun School at WISQUES gave a day's instruction to Brigadiers, Battalion Commanders and Machine Gun Officers in the employment of Machine Guns. Major N.R.DAVIDSON, Royal Artillery arrives and takes up his duties as G.S.O.2 to the Division.	APPENDIX "A"

Strength of Division (Infantry) for week ending August 27th 1915.

2nd September, 1915.

C. Dall Lt Col.
AA & QMG
for Major-General,
Commanding Guards Division.

GUARDS DIVISION.

FIGHTING STRENGTH FOR WEEK ENDING 27TH AUGUST, 1915.

UNIT.	Fighting Strength.		Details.	
	Officers	Other ranks	Officers	Other ranks
1st GUARDS BRIGADE.				
2nd Grenadier Guards	21	1058	....	31
2nd Coldstream Guards	23	977	5	20
3rd Coldstream Guards	24	1019	2	7
1st Irish Guards	26	951	....	19
2nd GUARDS BRIGADE.				
3rd Grenadier Guards	25	988	....	19
1st Coldstream Guards	21	976	1	6
1st Scots Guards	19	1008	1	69
2nd Irish Guards	25	1008	2	4
3rd GUARDS BRIGADE.				
1st Grenadier Guards	22	1012	8 *(12)*	120 *(52)*
4th Grenadier Guards	24	1003	1	3
2nd Scots Guards	18	964	2	34
1st Welsh Guards	29	999	....	13
4th Coldstream Guards	21	998	....	....
Divisional Cavalry Squadron.	6	155	....	....

I inspected today by verbal orders
from Sect. of State.

A. 124th C: A.S.C.
B. 168t " } at SHOREHAM.
C. 436t "

A require.   2 limbered wagons
              7 Revolvers.

B require   4. G.S. Wagons.
              2 limbered.
              1 water cart
              24 sets double harness.
              Equipment for men { Bandoliers
                                 { Waterbottles
                                 { Haversacks

C require -   Everything except
              men & horses.

A B & C require clothing for men —

Horses excellent —

[signature]

1. Inspected today the
141st } Field Ambulances
142nd }
              at CROOKHAM.

They are ready & complete in all
particulars except a few Army
tools.
Their period of training has been
short but the horses are very good
& material excellent.

                    Cavan, Maj Gen.

Wizernes

GRENADIER GUARDS.

ROLL OF OFFICERS BY BATTALIONS WHO ARE SERVING WITH THE EXPEDITIONARY FORCE.

1st Battalion Grenadier Guards.

Major.G.F.Trotter,M.V.O.,D.S.O.,Commanding Battalion.

Captain.J.S.Hughes.
- " C.Greville.
- " M.E.Maitland.
- " F.L.V.Swaine.
- " W.E.Nicol.
- " W.S.Pilcher.

Lieutenants.O.Wakeman.
- " Lord.F.C.Stanley.
- " R.le.P,Trench.
- " Earl of Dalkeith.
- " Sir.A.L.M.Napier.

R.Wolrige-Gordon.
- " Viscount Lascelles.

2nd Lieutenants. F.E.H.Paget.
- " A.A.Moller.
- " P.K.Stephenson.

G.T.H.J.Villiers.
- " E.Heneage.
- " C.Leeke.

Quartermaster.and Hon: Lieut.J.Teece.

Machine Gun Officer. 2nd Lieut.E.H.J.Duberly.

2nd Battalion, Grenadier Guards.

Lieutenant-Colonel.G.D.Jeffreys.Commanding Battalion.

Major.Lord H.Seymour. Senior Major.

Captain.R.H.V.Cavendish.M.V.O.

Major. C.R.Champion.de.Crespigny.

Captain.I.St.C.Rose.

"   A.de.P.Kingsmill.

"   Hon:W.R.Bailey. Adjutant.

Lieutenants.E.H.Noble.

"   A.K.S.Cuninghame..Transport Officer.

"   J.L.Buchanan.

"   A.F.R.Wiggins.

"   J.C.Craigie.

"   H.A.Clive.

2nd Lieutenants. W.H.Beaumont-Nesbitt.

"   L.St.L.Hermon-Hodge.

"   I.H.Ingleby.

M.Knatchbull-Hugesson.

"   E.W.M.Grigg.

"   H.F.C.Crookshank.

"   E.R.M.Fryer.

"   H.G.W.Sandeman.

Hon:W.A.D.Parnell.

Hon:A.V.G.Agar-Robartes.

Hon:Lieutenant.and Quartermaster.W.E.Acreman.

2nd Lieutenant.D.Abel.Smith.   Machine Gun Officer.

3rd Battalion, Grenadier Guards. *Esquadts*

Colonel. N.A.L.Corry, D.S.O., Commanding Battalion.

Major. G.Molyneaux-Montgomerie. Senior Major.

Captains. E.G.H.Powell.
" W.R.C.Murray.
" G.N.Vivian.
" C.F.A.Walker.

Lieutenants. G.G.B.Nugent. Adjutant.
" C.S.Rowley.
" C.M.C.Dowling.
" Sir.R.M.Filmer.Bart.
" E.H.J.Wynne.
" G.P.Bowes-Lyon.
" G.G.Gunniss
" Hon: FO.H.Eaton.
" F.Anson.
" A.Anson.
" G.F.R.Hirst.

2nd Lieutenants. H.D.Vernon.
" A.T.A.Ritchie.
" C.F.E.Crabbe.
" Hon:A.G.Agar-Robartes.
" T.C.Higginson.
" F.D.Lycett-Green.
" R.W.Phillips.

Hon:Lieutenant and Quartermaster. G.H.Wall.

2nd Lieutenant. R.Williams. Machine Gun Officer.

4th Battalion, Grenadier Guards. *Blendyn*

Major G.C.Hamilton, D.S.O., Commanding Battalion.
   "   Hon: C.M.B.Ponsonby, M.V.O., Senior Major.
Captain. T.F.J.N.Thorne.   Adjutant.
   "   E.D.Ridley.
   "   J.A.Morrison.
   "   H.L.Aubrey-Fletcher, M.V.O.,
   "   Sir G.Houston-Boswall.Bart.
Lieutenants. R.S.Lambert.   Transport Officer.
C.L.Blundell-Hollinshead-Blundell.
   "   Hon: E.W.Tennant.
   "   C.R.Britten.
   "   C.E.M.Ellison.
   "   G.E.Shelley.
   "   P.Malcolm.
   "   E.F.Penn.
2nd" Lieutenants. M.H.Macmillan.
   "   B.C.Layton.
   "   R.W.Leigh-Pemberton.
   "   E.R.D.Hoare.
   "   G.A.Ponsonby.
   "   M.A.T.Ridley.
   "   A.H.Tompson.

2nd Lieutenant and A/Quartermaster. E.Ludlow.
Lieutenant M.G.Williams.   Machine Gun Officer.

FIRST BATTALION COLDSTREAM GUARDS.

Major A.G.E.Egerton.	Commanding Officer.	
	Senior Major.	
Lieut.M.B.Smith.DSO.,	Adjutant.	
	M.G.Officer.	
Hon.Captain J.Boyd.	Quartermaster.	

Captain G.M.Darell.
 "   R.C.Feilding; S.R.
 "   E.B.G.Gregge-Hopwood.DSO.
Tem.Cap.Hon.T.C.R.Agar-Robartes. S.R.

Lieut. C.J.M.Riley.
 "   Hon.M.H.D.Browne.
Temp.Lt.Hon.E.K.Digby.
 "   " R.Peake.
 "   " N.E.P.Sutton. S.R.

2nd Lt. O.G.Style.   S.R.
 "   " J.R.Woods.   S.R.
 "   " R.F.Pratt-Barlow.   S.R.
 "   " R.M.Wright.   S.R.
 "   " R.T.Philipson.   S.R.
 "   " Visct.Holmesdale.
 "   " G.Barry.

Temp.Lt.Hon.C.H.F.Noel.   Base.
2nd Lt. F.M.Fisher.   Hospital.
 "   " C.E.P.Green.   ---do---
 "   " G.L.I.Smith.   S.R.)
 "   " J.C.Fair.   ) Posted to Expeditionary Force but
 "   " L.C.Smith.   S.R.) not yet joined Battalion.
 "   " A.N.Howard.   S.R.)

-*-*-*-*-*-*-*-*-*-*-*-*-

SECOND BATTALION COLDSTREAM GUARDS.

Tem.Lt.Col. J.M.Steele.   Commanding Officer.
Major P.A.Macgregor, DSO.,   Senior Major.
Temp.Capt. L.M.Gibbs.   Adjutant.
Temp.Lt. B.Birkbeck.   M.G.Officer.
Hon.Lieut.W.T.Brotherton.   Quartermaster.

Captain A.Leigh-Bennett, DSO.,
   "   H.D.Bentinck.
   "   W.T.Towers-Clark.
Temp.Capt.H.C.Loyd.
   "   " H.W.Verelst.
   "   " S.G.F.Taylor.

Lieut. A.H.M.Ramsay.
   "   W.G.Shaw-Stewart.
Tem.Lt.C.J.W.Darwin.

2nd Lt. E.St.L.Bonvalot.   S.R.
  " " R.J.Pinto.   S.R.
  " " Viscount Gage.
  " " C.H.Wilkinson.   S.R.
  " " W.E.C.Baynes.   S.R.
  " " A.J.H.Smith.   S.R.
  " " G.P.Fildes.   S.R.
  " " H.H.Burn.
  " " E.J.W.Smyth.
  " " C.W.Janson.   S.R.

Lieut. A.H.E.Ashley.   Hospital.
Tem.Lieut.O.W.H.Leese.   Hospital.

2nd Lieut.A.W.Kirk. S.R.   )Posted to Expeditionary Force but
   "   "   W.G.Bulteel. S.R.   )not yet joined Battalion.

THIRD BATTALION COLDSTREAM GUARDS.

```
Major J.V.Campbell, DSO.          Commanding Officer.
                                  Senior Major.
Temp.Capt.A.F.Smith.              Adjutant.
                                  M.G.Officer.
Hon.Captain F.T.Prichard.         Quartermaster.

Captain  G.E.Vaughan.
   "     C.B.Gunston.       S.R.
T. "     F.Longueville.
T. "     H.A.Cubitt.
T. "     J.C.Wynne Finch.

Lieut.   C.S.Jackson.
   "     G.F.N.Palmer.
Tem.Lt.  D.Campbell.
  " "    A.O.J.Hope.
  " "    C.E.Tufnell.
  " "    F.P.Acland Hood.
  " "    W.T.Legge.          S.R.

2nd Lieut.J.E.H.Platt.       G.R.
   "  "   H.P.Meakin.        S.R.
   "  "   B.R.Jackson.       S.R.
   "  "   R.N.Dilberoglue.
T. "  "   B.Butler-Stoney.
   "  "   D.G.Rooke.         G.R.
   "  "   J.S.Wilmot-Sitwell.
   "  "   R.O.Hambro.        S.R.
T. "  "   M.Dorman.

Captain P.R.B.Lawrence.   Bde M.G.Officer 4th (Guards) Brigade.
Lieut.  R.Bingham.        Attached.

2nd Lieut. J.R.Blacker.  S.R. ) Posted to Expeditionary Force but
   "   "   C.M.Pearce.   S.R. ) not yet joined Battalion.
```

FOURTH BATTALION COLDSTREAM GUARDS (PIONEERS).

Temp.Lt.Col.R.C.E.Skeffington-Smyth. R of O.	Commanding Officer.
Major Hon.G.V.Baring, R of O.	Senior Major.
Captain G.J.Edwards.	Adjutant.
Temp.Lt. J.S.Coats.	M.G.Officer.
2nd Lieut.W.E.Hutchinson.	Acting Quartermaster.

Captain R.B.J.Crawfurd.
"   G.A.O.Lane, R of O.
"   Hon.E.M.Pakenham. R of O.

2nd Lieut.	R.Sharpley.	S.R.
" "	D.J.C.Glass.	S.R.
" "	H.C.St.J.Thompson.	S.R.
" "	G.J.M.Hardy.	S.R.
" "	Q.S.Greene.	S.R.
" "	J.M.Peto.	
" "	H.J.R.Brierly.	
" "	J.C.Piggott.	S.R.
" "	P.A.Shaw.	S.R.
" "	W.F.Hoblyn.	S.R.
" "	A.H.Dickinson.	S.R.
" "	G.Furze.	S.R.
T. " "	E.Blundell.	

Lieut. Lord Petre.   ) Posted to Expeditionary Force but not
2nd Lt. J.S.Heathcote.S.R.) yet joined Battalion.

Roll of Officers serving with the 1st and 2nd
Battalions Scots Guards in the Expeditionary Force.

1st Battalion Scots Guards	2nd Battalion Scots Guards.
Lieut.Colonel S.H.Godman D.S.O.	Lieut.Col.A.B.E.Cator D.S.O.
Captain N.A.Orr-Ewing D.S.O.	Captain G.J.Bagot Chester.
" Sir V.A.F.Mackenzie Bt.M.V.O.	
" A.V.Poynter D.S.O.	Captain W.J.M.Hill.
" J.H.Cuthbert D.S.O.	" A.R.Orr.
" J.S.Thorpe.	" J.A.Stirling.
" M.Barne.	" F.H.Ballantine-Dykes.
Lieut.A.M.Jones.	Lieut.W.H.Wynne Finch.
" H.Hammersley.	" C.H.Seymour.
" J.A.E.Drury Lowe.	" N.Lechmere.
" N.Fergusson.	" J.Balfour.
" C.Bartholomew	" W.A.Boyd.
2nd Lt.C.S.Armstrong.	2nd.Lt.E.S.Clarke.
" D.H.Brand.	" S.H.Broadwood
" C.E.Trafford.	" A.F.Purvis.
" A.B.Rochfort.	" R.L.McDonald.
" D.W.Ellis.	" F.Ward.
" C.Mackworth Praed.	" R.E.Warde.
Lieut.A.J.Thompson,Adjutant	" Hon.C.T.Mills.
Captain D.Kinlay,Quartermaster.	" E.F.W.Arkwright.
	Captain E.C.T.Warner,A.Adjt.
	Lieut.T.Ross,Quartermaster.

[signature] Colonel,
Commanding Scots Guards.

OFFICERS OF 1ST BATTALION IRISH GUARDS.

Commanding Officer - Lieut-Colonel R. Le N. Lord Ardee. C.B.
Second in Command - Major G.H. Madden (Commanding temporarily)
Adjutant - Captain Lord Desmond FitzGerald.

Captain	T. M. D. Bailie.
"	M. V. Gore-Langton.
"	V. C. J. Blake.
Lieutenant	J.S.N. Fitzgerald.
Lieutenant	R. G. C. Yerburgh.
"	P. H. Antrobus.
"	~~C. D. Wynter.~~
"	L. R. Hargreaves.
"	~~A. J. H. Hamilton.~~
"	S. E. F. Christy.
"	~~R. H. Witts.~~
"	C. Pease.
"	R. Rankin.
Second Lieutenant	R. H. W. Heard.
"	A. F. L. Gordon.
"	N. F. Durant.
"	K. E. Dormer.
"	L. C. Whitefoord.
"	P.J. H. Close.
"	Hon. H.B. O'Brien.
"	R. J. P. Rodakowski.
"	C. R. Tisdall
"	K.W. Hogg.
"	H. F. d'a. S. Law.
"	~~T. H. Langrishe.~~ T.H. Langrishe / T.K. Walker

Quartermaster - Hon. Lieut. & Quartermaster H. Hickie.

List of Officers serving with the 2nd
Battalion Irish Guards, British Expeditionary
Force.

Commanding Officer - Lieut-Col. Hon. L. J. P. Butler.
Adjutant - Captain Hon. T. E. Vesey.
Acting Quartermaster - 2nd Lieut. J. Brennan.

    Captain Hon. H. R. Alexander.
        "   J. B. Bird.

Lieut. A. J. R. Hamilton. sick.
  "   C. J. H. Moore.
  "   D. C. Parsons.
  "   C. D. Wynter
  "   G. N. Hubbard.
  "   F. H. Witts
  "   J. G. Magill (R.A.M.C. attached).

2nd Lieut. J. B. Keenan.
    -do-   G. Y. L. Walters.
    -do-   A. Pym.
    -do-   C. F. Purcell.
    -do-   T. P. Law.
    -do-   J. Kipling.
    -do-   W. F. J. Clifford.
    -do-   R. Hannay.
    ~~-do-~~   ~~T. N. Langrishe.~~
    ~~-do-~~   ~~T. K. Walker.~~
    -do-   R. E. Sassoon.
    -do-   G. F. B. Hine.
    -do-   B. B. Watson.
    -do-   T. F. Tallents.
    -do-   R. H. Grayson.
    -do-   R. E. Coxon.

WELSH GUARDS.

Roll of Officers with the Expeditionary Force.

1st. Battalion.

Lieut-Colonel.W.Murray-Threipland.

Capt.A.P.Palmer,D.S.O.
Capt.G.W.F.Phillips.
Capt.R.G.W.Williams-Bulkeley.
Capt.O.T.D.Osmond-Williams. D.S.O.
Capt.J.H.Bradney.
Capt.Rhys Williams.
Capt.H.Dene.
Capt.M.O.Roberts.

Lieut.H.E.Wethered.
Lieut.W.H.J.Gough.
Lieut.R.W.Lewis.
Lieut.J.J.P.Evans.
Lieut.K.G.Menzies.
Lieut.E.G.Mawby.
Lieut.J.Randolph.
Lieut.G.C.L.Insole.
Lieut.H.J.Sutton.
Lieut.B.T.V.B.Hambrough.
Lieut.J.A.Dyson Perrins.

2nd.Lieut.H.T.Rice.
2nd.Lieut.G.C.H.Crawshay.
2nd.Lieut.H.A.Evan-Thomas.
2nd.Lieut.W.A.L.Fox-Pitt.
2nd Lieut.Hon.P.G.J.F.Howard.
2nd Lieut.F.A.V.Copland-Griffiths.
2nd Lieut.N.G.Wells.
2nd Lieut.R.Smith.

Lieut & Quartermaster.W.B.Dabell.

Lieut.W.E.Picton Phillips.R.A.M.C.

F.W.E.Blake Major for Colonel,
Commanding Welsh Guards.

WELSH GUARDS.

Roll of Officers with the Expeditionary Force.

1st. Battalion.

Lieut-Colonel. W. Murray-Threipland.

Capt. A.P. Palmer, D.S.O.
Capt. G.W.F. Phillips.
Capt. R.G.W. Williams-Bulkeley.
Capt. O.T.D. Osmond-Williams, D.S.O.
Capt. J.H. Bradney.
Capt. Rhys Williams.
Capt. H. Dene.
Capt. M.O. Roberts.

Lieut. H.E. Wethered.
Lieut. W.H.J. Gough.
Lieut. R.W. Lewis.
Lieut. J.J.P. Evans.
Lieut. K.G. Menzies.
Lieut. E.G. Mawby.
Lieut. J. Randolph.
Lieut. G.C.L. Insole.
Lieut. H.J. Sutton.
Lieut. B.T.V.B. Hambrough.
Lieut. J.A. Dyson Perrins.

2nd. Lieut. R.T. Rice.
2nd. Lieut. G.C.H. Crawshay.
2nd. Lieut. H.A. Evan-Thomas.
2nd. Lieut. W.A.L. Fox-Pitt.
2nd. Lieut. Hon. P.G.J.F. Howard.
2nd. Lieut. F.A.V. Copland-Griffiths.
2nd. Lieut. N.G. Wells.
2nd. Lieut. R. Smith.

Lieut & Quartermaster. W.B. Dabell.

Lieut. W.E. Picton Phillips. R.A.M.C.

F.W.E. Blake Major for Colonel,
Commanding Welsh Guards.

121/7449

Cannabis Sativa (A + O)

Oct '15

Vol III

WAR DIARY
or
INTELLIGENCE SUMMARY
(Erase heading not required.)

Army Form C. 2118

Instructions regarding War Diaries and Intelligence Summaries are contained in F.S. Regs., Part II. and the Staff Manual respectively. Title Pages will be prepared in manuscript.

Place	Date	Hour	Summary of Events and Information	Remarks and references to Appendices
	October	1.	NOEUX-LES-MINES becomes Guards Division railhead. The 13 battalions of the Division commenced to refit, and were issued with smoke helmets, iron rations, boots and other requirements to make up for losses and consumption. G.O.C. held a conference.	
		2.	Refitting of the battalions continued. The G-in-C, (Field Marshal Sir JOHN FRENCH, G.C.B., etc., etc.,) rode through 2nd and 3rd Gds. Brigade areas, and visited the G.O.C. 2000 picks and 2000 shovels drawn from railhead to make up deficiencies.	
		3.	The reposting of officers in the different battalions of each regiment, rendered necessary by the recent heavy casualties took effect. The picks and shovels drawn yesterday were issued to battalions. The Guards Division relieved the 2nd Division in the front line. For return of sick and injured animals for week ending Septr. 30th, see Appendix.	
		4.	The following drafts have arrived since Octr 1st:- 1st G.G. 2 O.R. 1st C.G. 5 O. 99 O.R. 1st S.G.126 O.R. 1st I.G.1 O. 42 O.R. 1st W.G. 1 O. 2nd G.G. 1 O.R. 2? G.Nil. 2nd S.G. 7 O.R. 2nd I.G.1 O. 200 O.R. 104 O.R 3rd G.G.115 O.R. 3? ? 4 O.R. 4th G.G. 92 O.R. A Divisional bomb, grenade and T.M. ammunition store was formed in the brewery VERMELLES.	
		6.	Divisional and Advanced Headquarters established in the Chateau des Pres, SAILLY-LABOURSE. Bomb store in dug outs N.E. of this village taken over from 28th Division. Divisional Train moved to VERQUIGNEUL. 4th Field Ambulance to VERQUIGNEUL. 3rd and 9th Field Ambulances to SAILLY-LABOURSE.	
		7.	Railhead moved to BETHUNE. Reinforcements:- 2nd C.G. 1 O. 40 O.R. 3rd C.G. 16 O.R. 1st C.G. 2 O. 190 O.R. 1st S.G. 2 O. 265 O.R. 1st G.G. 1 O. 50 O.R. 1st I.G. 30 O.R.	

WAR DIARY
or
INTELLIGENCE SUMMARY

(Erase heading not required.)

Army Form C. 2118

Place	Date	Hour	Summary of Events and Information	Remarks and references to Appendices
	October 8.		9000 Mills' Hand Grenades expended in resisting and defeating German attack. This expenditure was met by 6000 Mills' from 46th Division.	
			Reinforcements:-	
			3rd G.G. 1 O. 3rd G.G. 5 O. 150 O.R. 2nd S.G. 1 O.R.	
			1st G.G. 2 O. 1st S.G. 1 O. 62 O.R. 2nd I.G. 2 O. 130 O.R.	
			3rd G.G. 5 O.} 4th G.G. 4 O. 290 O.R. 4th C.G. 2 O. 2 O.R.	
			150 O.R.}	
	9.		A further dump of 5000 Mills' Hand Grenades received.	
			Issue of 1 blanket per man ordered from G.H.Q.	
	10.		Reinforcements:-	
			2nd G.G. 1 O. 1 O.R. R.E. 75th Field Coy. 2 O.	
			2nd C.G. 2 O. 2 O.R. 76th " " 1 O.	
			2nd S.G. 3 O. 3 O.R. 9th Field Ambulance.(M.T., A.S.C.) 3 O.R.	
	11.		Reinforcements:-	
			3rd G.G. 100 O.R.	
			3rd G.G. 65 O.R.	
			German aeroplane brought down in Guards Division area.	
	12.		The Division relieved in the trenches by 46th Division. The Bdes. were billetted as follows:-	
			1st Guards Brigade at VERQUIN and HESDIGNEUL.	
			2nd Guards Brigade at DROUVIN and VAUDRICOURT.	
			3rd Guards Brigade at SAILLY-LABOURSE and VERQUIGNEUL.	
			Pioneer Battalion at FOUQUIERES.	
			No 9 Field Ambulance moved to HESDIGNEUL.	
			Divisional Train moved to BETHUNE-NOEUX-LES-MINES road.	
			Bomb store at VERMELLES, handed over to 46th Division.	
			The relief was not completed till after midnight.	
	13.			

Army Form C. 2118

WAR DIARY
or
INTELLIGENCE SUMMARY
(Erase heading not required.)

Instructions regarding War Diaries and Intelligence Summaries are contained in F.S. Regs., Part II. and the Staff Manual respectively. Title Pages will be prepared in manuscript.

Place	Date	Hour	Summary of Events and Information	Remarks and references to Appendices
	October 13.		G.O.C. visited the 3 Brigade Headquarters. Reinforcements:- 3rd Guards Brigade 64 O.R. 82 steel splinter proof helmets issued to the Division for trial. 1st G.Gds. and 1st W.Gds. moved to VERMELLES. 4th G.Gds. and 2nd S.Gds. moved from VERQUIGNEUL and took over the billets thus vacated at SAILLY-LABOURSE. Sir DOUGLAS HAIG (commanding 1st Army) and 11th Corps Commander visited G.O.C.	

	14.		H.Q. and remaining 2 batts. of 3rd Guards Brigade moved to VERMELLES. Reinforcements:-
			  2nd C.G. 40 O.R. 1st G.G. 40 O.R. 1st S.G. 1 O. 31 O.R.
			  3rd C.G. 64 O.R. 4th C.G. 1 O. 2nd S.G. 50 O.R.
			  1st C.G. 25 O.R. (Pioneers) 1 O.R. 2nd I.G. 1 O. 50 O.R.
			                     1st W.G. 26 O.R.
			 Greatcoats belonging to 1st Guards Brigade, which had been stored at the Base, during the summer, were sent up; some of these were in a bad condition and consequently returned.	

	15.		H.Q. and 4 Battns. of 2nd Guards Brigade moved to VERMELLES to take over a section of the line. H.Q. and 2 Battns. of 1st Guards Brigade moved from VERQUIN to SAILLY-LABOURSE. The other 2 Battns. of this Brigade at HESDIGNEUL moved and billeted in VERQUIGNEUL. No 9 Field Ambulance moved back to SAILLY-LABOURSE, and Divisional Train to VERQUIGNEUL. Reinforcements:- 3rd G.G. 2-0. 1st S.G. 1-0. 2nd Lieut. O. LYTTLETON, G.G. (A.D.C.) returned to duty with 3rd Battn. G. Gds. as acting Adjutant.	
	16.		2nd Lieut. H.A. RYAN-THOMAS, W.Gds. appointed Divisional bomb supply Officer, and put in charge of the bomb stores at VERMELLES and SAILLY-LABOURSE. To return to the normal system of supply, i.e., column loaded—sections empty, the Divisional supply Column loaded at railhead, but there was no refilling.	
	17.		Two shells landed in the bomb store at VERMELLES, and some boxes of ball grenades were exploded During the night of the 16/17th 15000 Mills' bombs were expended in the line. The 2 Battns. of 1st Guards Brigade at SAILLY-LABOURSE moved up to VERMELLES, the billets thus vacated being taken over by the 2 Battns. at VERQUIGNEUL, which also moved.	

WAR DIARY or INTELLIGENCE SUMMARY

Army Form C. 2118

(Erase heading not required.)

Place	Date	Hour	Summary of Events and Information	Remarks and references to Appendices
	October 17.		(continued) Normal system of supply in force; supply lorries dumped at 6.00 a.m. and train wagons refilled at 9.00 a.m. Lorries then reloaded at railhead and remained full during the night.	
	18.		Reinforcements:- 2nd C.G. 2 O.s 4th C.G. 2 O.s 3rd C.G. 2 O.s	
	19.		H.Q. and remaining 2 Battns. of 1st Guards Brigade moved to VERMELLES, the billets thus vacated at SAILLY-LABOURSE being taken over by H.Q. and 2 Battns. 3rd Guards Brigade, on relief. Reinforcements:- 2nd G.G. 1 O. 2nd C.G. 8 O.R. 1st S.G. 9 O.R. 3rd G.G. 1 O.R. 3rd C.G. 8 O.R. 1st I.G. 5 O.R. 1st G.G. 1 O.R. 4th C.G. 4 O.R. 1st W.G. 52 O.R. (Pioneers)	
	20.		Reinforcements:- 2nd G.G. 1 O.R. 1st G.G. 1 O. 68 O.R. 1st C.G. 1 O.R. 1st W.G. 1 O. 2nd C.G. 1 O.R.	
	2		28th Division Artillery, which has been covering the front of the Guards Division, was withdrawn from the line to entrain with the Infantry of 28th Division for MARSEILLES.	
	21.		1 Battn. 3rd Guards Brigade moved back to ANNEQUIN. 2 Companies 4th Coldstream Guards (Pioneers) also moved to ANNEQUIN, and 2 Companies to LABOURSE. All came back from VERMELLES. Reinforcements:- 2nd G.G. 40 O.R. 2nd C.G. 89 O.R. 1st I.G. 1 O. 61 O.R. 3rd G.G. 26 O.R. 3rd C.G. 1 O.R. 4th C.G. 30 O.R. 2nd S.G. 43 O.R. 2nd I.G. 1 O. 35 O.R. (Pioneers)	
	23.		3rd Guards Brigade relieves 2nd Guards Brigade on night of 23/24th, and return to rest billets.	
	24.		Lieut. Col. Lord ESMEE GORDON LENNOX arrives to take over command of 1st Battn. Scots Guards. Band of Grenadier Guards - 1 Officer and 32 Other ranks - arrive. Draft of 1 Officer and 25 Other ranks arrive for 2nd Bn. Scots Guards. 35 " " " " " " " 2nd Bn. 8 Irish ".	

Army Form C. 2118

WAR DIARY
or
INTELLIGENCE SUMMARY
(Erase heading not required.)

Instructions regarding War Diaries and Intelligence Summaries are contained in F. S. Regs., Part II. and the Staff Manual respectively. Title Pages will be prepared in manuscript.

Place	Date	Hour	Summary of Events and Information	Remarks and references to Appendices
	October 25.		2nd Guards Brigade and Pioneer Battn. relieved by 12th Division, and are railed from BETHUNE to LILLERS, moving into billets in area ST.HILAIRE-HAM-NORRENT-FONTES. Draft of 48 men arrive for 2nd Bn. Grenadier Guards. 2 Officers and 95 O.R. for 3rd Bn. Grenadier Guards. 1 " " 45 " " 2nd Bn. Irish " 1 " " for 2nd Bn. Coldstream Guards.	
	26.		Band plays at Divisional Headquarters, in the morning, and to the Reserve Brigade of the 12th Division in the afternoon at LABOURSE.	
	27.		On the night of 26/27th remainder of Division is relieved and moves into billets :- 1st Brigade at HESDIGNEUL and LAPUGNOY. 3rd Brigade at ALLOUAGNE and CANTRAINE. R.E. at BAS RIEUX. Divisional Squadron at FONTENELLE FARM. Cyclists at HAUT RIEUX. Orders received to draw Lewis Guns up to 4 per Battalion.	
	28.		Troops started to march to parade ground at HAUT RIEUX for Inspection by his Majesty the King. Owing to a fall from his horse his Majesty was unable to carry out his inspection, and troops returned to billets. Weather very bad.	
	29.		G.O.C. goes on leave and Brig-Gen· HEYWORTH assumes command of the Division.	
	30.		House to house search for derelict equipment commenced in area. Baths to open at AUCHEL and RAIMBERT. 19 cyclists arrive as reinforcements.	
	31.		Drafts:- 2nd Scots Gds. 1 Off. 62 O.R. 1st Grenadier Gds. 130 O.R. 3rd Grenadier Gds. 10 O.R. 1st Coldstream Gds. 35 O.R. 1st Scots Gds. 1 Off. 2nd Irish Gds. 50 O.R.	

WAR DIARY or INTELLIGENCE SUMMARY

Army Form C. 2118

Place	Date	Hour	Summary of Events and Information	Remarks and references to Appendices
	October 1st		NOEUX-LES-MINES becomes Guards Div. railhead. The 1.3 battalions of the Div. commenced to refit, & were issued with smoke helmets, iron rations, boots & other requirements to make up for losses & consumption. The ~~General~~ (Major) Field Marshal Sir J~~ohn French~~ visited the ~~Div~~. G.O.C. held a conference.	
	October 2nd		Refitting of the battalions continued. The C. in C. (Field Marshal Sir John French, G.C.B. etc etc) & G.O.C. 3rd Cav. Bde. arr. and d visited the G.O.C. 2000 picks & 2000 shovels drawn from railhead to make up for deficiencies.	
	October 3rd		The reporting of officers on the different battalions of each regiment, rendered necessary by the recent heavy casualties took effect. The picks & shovels drawn yesterday were issued to batts. The Guards Div. relieved the 2nd Div. on the front line. For return of sick & injured animals for week ending Sept. 30th see Appendix.	
	October 4th		The following drafts have arrived since Oct. 1st:- 1st G.G. 2nd G.G. 3rd G.G. 1st C.G. 2nd C.G. 3rd C.G. 1st S.G. 2nd S.G. 1st I.G. 2nd I.G. 1st W.G. 2.O.R. 10.R. 115.O.R. 92.O.R. 3ff. 99.O.R. 4.O.R. 136.O.R. 7.O.R. 1ff.42.O.R. 1ff. 200.O.R. 1ff/10.O.R. A divisional bomb, # grenade & T.M. amm. & store was formed on the Armoury at VERMELLES.	
	October 5th			

Army Form C. 2118

WAR DIARY
or
INTELLIGENCE SUMMARY
(Erase heading not required.)

Instructions regarding War Diaries and Intelligence Summaries are contained in F. S. Regs., Part II. and the Staff Manual respectively. Title Pages will be prepared in manuscript.

Place	Date	Hour	Summary of Events and Information	Remarks and references to Appendices
	October 6th		Divisional Advanced Headquarters established in the Chateau des Pres, SAILLY-LABOURSE. Bomb Store in dug-outs N.E. of the village taken over from 28th Div. Div. Train moved to VERQUIGNEUL. 4th Field Ambulance to VERQUIGNEUL. 3rd & 9th Field Ambulances to SAILLY-LABOURSE.	
	October 7th		Railhead moved to BETHUNE. Reinforcements: 2nd C. Gds. 10. OR. 40.OR. 3rd C.Gds. 15.OR. 1st I.Gds. 30.OR. 1st C.Gds. 20. 190.OR. 1st S.Gds. 20. 263 OR. 1st G.Gds. 10. 50.OR	
	October 8th		9,000 Mills Hand Grenades expended in resisting & defeating German attack. This expenditure was met by 6,000 Mills [illegible] 1.O. 3rd G. Gds. 10. 150.OR. Reinforcements: 3rd C.Gds. [illegible] 3rd G.Gds. 30. 130.OR. , 1st S.Gds. 10. 62.OR. 2nd I.Gds. 20. 130.OR. 1st G.Gds. 20. 4th G.Gds. 40. 290.OR. 2nd S.Gds. 40. 1.OR. 4th C.Gds. 20. 2 OR.	
	October 9th		A further dump of 5,000 Mills Hand Grenades received. Some of 1/klankuh for man ordered from G.H.Q.	
	October 10th		Reinforcements: 2nd G.Gds. 10. 1.OR. 2nd C.Gds. 20. 20R. 2nd S.Gds. 30. 3.OR. R.E. 7th Field Coy. 20. 76. 10. 9th Field Ambulance (M.T. ASC.) 3 OR.	

WAR DIARY
or
INTELLIGENCE SUMMARY

(Erase heading not required.)

Army Form C. 2118

Place	Date	Hour	Summary of Events and Information	Remarks and references to Appendices
	October 11th		Reinforcements:- 3rd C.Gds. 100 O.R. 3rd G.Gds. 63 O.R. German aeroplanes brought down in Guards Div. area.	
	October 12th		The Div. relieved in the trenches by 16th Div. The Bdes. were billeted as follows 1st Gds. Bde. at VERQUIN & HESDIGNEUL 2nd Gds. Bde. at DROUVIN & VAUDRICOURT. 3rd Gds. Bde. at SAILLY-LABOURSE & VERQUIGNEUL. Pioneer Batt. at FOUQUIÈRES. No 9 Field Ambulance moved to HESDIGNEUL. Div. Train moved to BETHUNE-NOEUX-LES-MINES road. Bomb Store at VERMELLES handed over to 46th Div. The Relief was not completed till after midnight G.O.C. visited the 3 brigade Headquarters. Reinforcements:- 3rd G.Gds. 66 O.R. Steel splinter proof helmets issued to the Div. for trial.	
	October 13th		8 AM. G.Gds. & 1st W.Gds. moved to VERMELLES. 5th G.Gds. & 2nd S.Gds. moved from VERQUIGNEUL & took over the billets then vacated at SAILLY-LABOURSE. General Sir Douglas Haig (Commanding 1st Army) & 11th Corps commander visited G.O.C.	

WAR DIARY
or
INTELLIGENCE SUMMARY

Army Form C. 2118

(Erase heading not required.)

Place	Date	Hour	Summary of Events and Information	Remarks and references to Appendices
	October 14th		H.Q. & remaining 2 batts. of 3rd Gds. Bde. moved to VERMELLES. Reinforcements :- 2nd C. Gds. 400.R, 3rd C. Gds. 64 o.R. 1st C. Gds. 400.R, 3rd C. Gds. 64 o.R. 2 G. Gds. 25 o.R, 1st S. Gds. 10. 30 o.R. 2nd I. Gds. 10. 50 o.R. 1st G. Gds. 400.R 2nd S. Gds. 500.R. 1st W. Gds. 26 o.R. 4th C. Gds. (Pioneers) 10. 10.R. Greatcoats belonging to the 1st Gds. Bde. which had been stored at the base during the summer were sent up & some of these were in a bad condition & consequently returned.	
	October 15th		H.Q. & 4 batts. of 2nd Gds. Bde. moved to Vermelles to take over a section of the line. H.Q. & 2 batts. of 1st Gds. Bde. moved from VERQUIN to SAILLY-LABOURSE. The other 2 batts. of this bde. at HESDIGNEUL moved & billeted in VERQUIGNEUL. No 9 Field Ambulance moved back to SAILLY-LABOURSE, & DIV. Train to VERQUIGNEUL. Reinforcements : 3rd G. Gds. 2 officers, 1st S. Gds. 1 officer. 2nd Lt. O. by Wicton F. Gds. (A D C) returned to duty with 3rd Batt. G. Gds. as acting adjutant. (N. Gds.)	
	October 16th		2nd Lt H.A Evan-Thomas appointed divisional bomb supply officer, & put in charge of the bomb stores at VERMELLES & SAILLY-LABOURSE. To return to the normal system of supply i.e. column loaded, sections empty, the above Div. Supply column loaded at railhead but these were no refilling.	
	October 17th		Two shells landed in the bomb store at VERMELLES & some boxes of bell grenades were exploded. During the night of the 16/17th 15,000 Mills bombs were expended in the line. The 2 batts. of 1st Gds. Bde. at SAILLY-LABOURSE moved up to VERMELLES the lullets thus vacated being taken over by the 2 batts. at VERQUIGNEUL, which also moved. Normal system of supply in force ; supply lorries dumped at 6.00.A.M. & train wagons refilled at 9.00. Lorries then returned at railhead & was remained full during the night.	

WAR DIARY
or
INTELLIGENCE SUMMARY
(Erase heading not required.)

Army Form C. 2118

Place	Date	Hour	Summary of Events and Information	Remarks and references to Appendices
	October 18th		Reinforcements: 2nd C. Gds. 2 officers. 3rd C. Gds. 2 officers. 4th C. Gds. 2 officers.	
	October 19th		H.Q. & remaining 2 batts. of 1st Gds. Bde. moved to VERMELLES, the billets thus vacated at SAILLY-LABOURSE being taken over by H.Q. & 2 batts. 3rd Gds. Bde. on relief. Reinforcements: 2nd G. Gds. 1 officer. 2nd C. Gds. 20 OR. 3rd C. Gds. 6 OR. 1st I. Gds. 5 OR. 3rd G. Gds. 1 OR. 1st S. Gds. 9 OR. 1st G. Gds. 1 OR. 1st W. Gds. 52 OR. 4th C. Gds. (Pioneers) 4 OR.	
	October 20th		Reinforcements: 2nd G. Gds. 1 OR. 2nd C. Gds. 1 OR. 1st C. Gds. 1 OR. 1st G. Gds. 1 officer. 10 OR. 1st W. Gds. 1 officer. 28th Div. artillery, which has been covering the front of the Guards Div. was withdrawn from the line to entrain with the infantry of 28th Div. for MARSEILLES.	
	October 21st		1 batt. 3rd Gds. Bde. moved back to ANNEQUIN; 2 coys. 4 C. Gds. (Pioneers) also moved to ANNEQUIN & 2 coys. to LABOURSE. All came back from VERMELLES. Reinforcements: 2nd G. Gds. 60 OR. 2nd C. Gds. 29 OR. 3rd C. Gds. 1 OR. 1st I. Gds. 1 officer. 61 OR. 3rd G. Gds. 26 OR. 2nd I. Gds. 1 officer. 35 OR. 2nd S. Gds. 43 OR. 4th C. Gds. (Pioneers) 30 OR.	

WAR DIARY
or
INTELLIGENCE SUMMARY

Place	Date	Hour	Summary of Events and Information	Remarks and references to Appendices
	October 22nd			
	Oct 23.		3rd Guards Brigade relieve 2nd Guards Brigade on night of 23/24 and return to rest billets.	
	Oct 24.		Lt. Col. Lowrie Geddes Sermon arrives to take over command of 1st Bn Scots Guards. Band of Grenadier Guards 1 officer and 32 other ranks arrive. Draft of 23 other ranks arrive for 2nd Scots Guards. 35 " " " 2nd " "	
	Oct 25.		2nd Guards Brigade and Pioneer Battalion relieved by 12th Division and are railed from BETHUNE to LILLERS marching into billets in area ST HILAIRE - HAM - NORRENT-FONTES. Draft of 48 men arrive for 2nd Bn Grenadier Guards. 2 officers and 95 O.R. for 3rd " " " 1 " " 45 " " " 2nd " Irish " 1 " " for 2nd Bn Coldstream Guards	

WAR DIARY
or
INTELLIGENCE SUMMARY
(Erase heading not required.)

Place	Date	Hour	Summary of Events and Information	Remarks and references to Appendices
	Oct 26		Band plays at Divisional Head Quarters in the morning and to the Reserve Brigade of the 12th Division in the afternoon at LA BOURSE.	
	Oct 27		On the night of 26/27 march of Division is relieved and moves into billets 1st Bde at HESDIGNEUL and LAPUGNOY 3rd " at ALLOUAGNE and CANTRAINE. R.E. at BAS RIEUX Div. Squadron at FONTEVELLE Farm " Gel. to at HAUT RIEUX Orders received to draw Lewis guns up to 4 per Battalion.	
	Oct 28		Troops started to march to parade ground at HAUT RIEUX for inspection by his Majesty the King. Owing to a fall from his horse his Majesty was unable to carry out his inspection and troops returned to billets. Weather very bad.	
	Oct 29		G.O.C. goes on leave and B.G. Heyworth assumes command of the Division.	

Place	Date	Hour	Summary of Events and Information	Remarks and references to Appendices
	Oct 30		Have to have search for derelict Equipment commenced in Area.	
	Oct 31		Baths to open at AUCHEL and Raimbert. 19 Gal. & arrived as reinforcements.	
			Drafts 2nd Scots Guards 1 Off 62 mes O.R	
			1st Grenadier Gds. 130 O.R	
			3rd " 10 O.R	
			1st Coldm " 35 O.R	
			1 Scots " 1 Off	
			2 Irish Guards 50 O.R	

Army Form C. 2118

WAR DIARY
or
INTELLIGENCE SUMMARY

(Erase heading not required.)

Instructions regarding War Diaries and Intelligence Summaries are contained in F. S. Regs., Part II. and the Staff Manual respectively. Title Pages will be prepared in manuscript.

Place	Date	Hour	Summary of Events and Information	Remarks and references to Appendices
	Nov.1		Leave arrangements change, new system via HAVRE inaugurated. Bomb school under directions of Major Baden Powell formed at H.Q. for the instruction of men of Household Cavalry Divisional Squadron and Cycle Company.	
	Nov.2		Nos. 64 & 67 T.M. Batteries handed over to 12th Division. D.A.A. & Q.M.G & G.S.O 2 attend conference at Corps Head Quarters with reference to move to new Area etc. Conference held at this Head Quarters of representatives of Units and Brigades to collect evidence to refute charges of loss of stores which the 12th Division denied having received on relief. sufficient evidence collected to clear the Division of this loss, and forwarded to the Corps.	
	Nov.3		D.A.A & Q.M.G & G.S.O 1 visit Lahore Division to see about billets, and arrangements for the coming move of the Division. Lt.Col. Jeffreys returned to take over command of his Battalion again after having acted temporarily as Brigadier to the 35th Brigade. Reported rendered to Corps regarding alleged loss of Steel Helmets.	
	Nov.4		Colonel Gubbins R.F.A proceeds to England and Major KINSMAN R.H.A takes over command of 76th Bde. R.F.A. 2nd Lt. J.E.H. PLATT 3rd Coldstream Guards reports to Corps as officer i/c Claims. Instructions issued for distribution of Transport for Machine Gun Companies and Lewis guns throughout the Division.	
	Nov.5		D.A.A & Q.M.G goes round the new Area for Artillery etc. Orders received to take over 27 Lewis Guns that had been on loan to 12th Division. An additional 5 Lewis Guns still remain on loan to 46th Division. Shortage of about 2000 nosebags in the Division which base seem unable to make up.	
	Nov.6		The Army Commander decorates the following with French Decorations at Corps Headquarters:— Lieut N.E.R. SUTTON, C.Gds., Captain H.A. CUBITT, C.Gds., Drill Sergt. OAKLEY 2nd G.Gds. Drill Sergt. HUGHES 1st G.Gds., Sergt. FINCH 2nd C.Gds., Sergt. VANT 3rd C.Gds., Sergt. A.LAMOND 1st G.Gds.	

Army Form C. 2118

WAR DIARY
or
INTELLIGENCE SUMMARY
(Erase heading not required.)

Instructions regarding War Diaries and Intelligence Summaries are contained in F.S. Regs., Part II. and the Staff Manual respectively. Title Pages will be prepared in manuscript.

Place	Date	Hour	Summary of Events and Information	Remarks and references to Appendices
	Nov.7		The following also received decorations, but were not present, Sergt-Major BARNHAM 1st C.Gds. and Cpl. J.GREEN 2nd S.Gds. Divisional Commander returns. 6 Lewis guns in bad order received from 12th Division remainder of 27 promised tomorrow. Brigadier General R. SCOTT-KERR C.B.,M.V.O,D.S.O joined the Division for temporary attachment.	
	Nov.8		The PRINCE DE LUCINGE, officer de Liaison, is taken away from the Division. M. de la CHESNAYE officer interpreter is posted in his place. Corps Commander goes on leave and Lord CAVAN assumes command of the Corps. Brigadier General FEILDING assumes command of the Division. The 76th Bde.R.F.A move to billets in Area near LE SART. 2nd Guards Brigade move to billets at LA GORGUE. HQRS, 3rd Bn. Gren. Gds., 1st Bn.Cold.Gds. 2nd Bn. Irish Gds.and 9th Field Ambulance and Machine Gun Company in LA GORGUE. 1st Bn. Scots Guards in Farms Square L26 & L27. HQRS. Divisional Train to South of MERVILLE squares K35d and Q5b. Divisional Cavalry and Cyclists to Square R.2. 55th Field Coy. R.E. to Square M14a. 76th " " " " M19b. 75th " " " " MERVILLE. 4th Bn. Coldstream Guards (Pioneers) to R22b, R16b & c, R11e.	
	Nov.9		3rd Gds. Bde. move into billets in the neighbourhood of MERVILLE. 45th Sanitary Section moves to LA GORGUE.	
	Nov.10		Divisional H.Q. established at LA GORGUE, Q office opened up in the forenoon. 1st Gds. Bde. move North to billet West of LESTREM.	
	Nov.11		A conference was held at Divisional H.Q. to discuss the Winter programme which was attended by the acting G.O.C. Brigadiers, Bde. Majors, C.R.A. C.R.E. A.D.M.S., A.D.V.S., O.C. Div. Train and the Divisional Staff. The Division took over the Indian Corps baths which will be run by Lt. PEARSON (O.C.45th Sanitary Section)	

Army Form C. 2118

WAR DIARY
or
INTELLIGENCE SUMMARY
(Erase heading not required.)

Instructions regarding War Diaries and Intelligence Summaries are contained in F. S. Regs., Part II. and the Staff Manual respectively. Title Pages will be prepared in manuscript.

Place	Date	Hour	Summary of Events and Information	Remarks and references to Appendices
	Nov.12		Div. Ammn. Column moved into billets at LESTREM. The exchange of mules for horses commenced, the mules being handed over to the Lahore Div.	
	Nov.14		2nd & 3rd Guards Bdes. relieved the 46th and 20th Divs. in the trenches. 1st Guards Bde. moved into LA GORGUE (H.Qrs. 2nd G.Gds. and 3rd C.Gds) MERVILLE. (2nd C.Gds. & 1st Irish Gds.). Div. Cavalry Squad. moved to billets E. of MERVILLE.	
	Nov.15		New positions of Divisional refilling points on the LA GORGUE - MERVILLE Rd. between BEAUPRE farm at Beet factory used for the first time. A meeting of transport officers was held at Divisional H.Q.	
	Nov.17		Lord CAVAN returned to the Division as G.O.C. on the expiration of leave of 11th Corps Commander. Brig. Gen. Fielding resumed his duties as G.O.C. 1st Gds.Bde. Authorisation for the issue of rum to the amount of a daily issue to troops in the trenches, and an issue of three times a week to troops resting. Conference held at 11th Corps H.Q. on the subject of a hutting scheme, attended by A.A. & Q.M.G., D.A.A & Q.M.G. & Adjutant, Div.R.E.	
	Nov.18		Col. N.A.L.CORRY (Commanding 3rd Grenadier Gds.) takes over the command of 2nd Guards Bde. in the absence of Brig. Gen. Ponsonby on leave. 99 remounts arrived for the Div. at MERVILLE Station where a distribution was made to units requiring them.	
	Nov.19		A barge with a cargo of shale came alongside the quay near the PONT DE LA MEUSE in LA GORGUE for the use of the Division, and units requiring shale sent wagons to fetch it. A ration of rum was issued to all troops of the Division.	
	Nov.20		1st Guards Bde. relieved 2nd Guards Bde. in the trenches. Battalions of 2nd Gds. Bde. being billeted as follows:- 3rd G.Gds. and 2nd I. Gds. in LA GORGUE. 1st C.Gds. and 1st S. Gds. in MERVILLE. The Rt. Hon. W.S. CHURCHILL arrived with the Division to be attached.	

Army Form C. 2118

WAR DIARY
or
INTELLIGENCE SUMMARY
(Erase heading not required.)

Instructions regarding War Diaries and Intelligence Summaries are contained in F.S. Regs., Part II and the Staff Manual respectively. Title Pages will be prepared in manuscript.

Place	Date	Hour	Summary of Events and Information	Remarks and references to Appendices
	Nov.21		Railhead changed from BETHUNE to MERVILLE. Div. Supply Column moved to billets W. of MERVILLE. The Rt. Hon. Sir J.REDMOND M.P. visited the Division and inspected 1st & 2nd Batts. Irish Guards with the G.O.C.	
	Nov.22		The G.O.C. visited the billets of D.A.C. Train, Cavalry, Cyclists, 1st Coldstream Gds. & 1st Scots Gds. The Corps Commander also visited the D.A.C. and rest billets of the two battalions of 2nd Gds. Bde. in LA GORGUE.	
	Nov.23		4th Field Ambulance moved to REGNIER LE CLERG.	
	Nov.24		2000 Loveband socks issued to the baths, for distribution to troops. Pioneer Bn. moved into LAVENTIE, also 75th Field Company R.E.	
	Nov.26		2nd Guards Bde. relieved 3rd Guards Bde. in the trenches, the latter brigade taking over the billets thus vacated in LA GORGUE & N. & S. of MERVILLE. The following drafts arrived at railhead for the Division, all "other ranks":- 20 for 2nd G.Gds. 25 for 1st I. Gds. 35 for 3rd G.Gds. 25 for 1st S. Gds. 25 for 2nd I. Gds. 60 for 1st G.Gds. 30 for 4th G.Gds. 25 for Pioneers (4th C.Gds.)	
	Nov.27		The G.O.C. presided at a divisional conference held in Headquarters, and attended by the "G" & "Q" Staffs, Brigadiers, C.R.A., C.R.E. etc. Gymnasium vacated by 9th Field Ambulance, taken over as recreation room.	
	Nov.28			
	Nov.29		Staff officers of 38th Div. attached to Guards Div. for instruction. Leave allowance increased to all officers and men of the Division proceeding on leave to travel via BOULOGNE.	
	Nov.30		G.O.C. gave a lecture on the organisation of the B.E.F. to the officers of the 3rd Gds. Bde.	

Typed [WAR DIARY] Guards Div.

A. & Q.

September 1915.

The Original M.S. Diary for September 1915 (kept by, and in the handwriting of H.R.H. The Prince of Wales) was abstracted and taken away by M⁵ H.A. Cordery in October 1939, while the Section was still at Audit House, E.C.4.

S. Woolgar
i/c Docts in Basement.

WAR DIARY
or
INTELLIGENCE SUMMARY

(Erase heading not required.)

Instructions regarding War Diaries and Intelligence Summaries are contained in F. S. Regs., Part II. and the Staff Manual respectively. Title Pages will be prepared in manuscript.

Place	Date	Hour	Summary of Events and Information	Remarks and references to Appendices
	1915.			
	September 1.		55th Field Coy. R.E. arrived from 7th Division, and moved into billets at LONG PONT, and a Field day was held for the Infantry, Cavalry, Cyclists, and Signal Coy. of the Division. Major General Sir Francis Lloyd, K.C.B., C.V.O., D.S.O. was present. Lieut. H.R.H. Prince of Wales, Grenadier Guards, and Lieut. Lord Claud Hamilton, Grenadier Guards, arrived as extra Staff Officers. It is notified that Guards Division became part of XIth Corps on 30/8/15.	
	2.		61st Brigade R.F.A.(Hows) and 74th Brigade R.F.A. march at 9.00 a.m. to join Meerut & Lahore Divisions for practice in shooting. These brigades billet for the night of 2nd/3rd in G.H.Q. area, and are supplied from Guards Divisional Railhead.	
	3.		Heavy rain fell during the night of 2nd/3rd and continued until noon. Lorries with supplies for 61st and 74th Brigades R.F.A. are detached full and sent to rendezvous at MERVILLE. Lorries to be attached when empty to Meerut & Lahore Divisional Supply Columns. Draft of 48 men arrive for 1st Battn. Irish Guards, and 2 men for 2nd Battn. Coldstream Guards.	
	4.		Arrival of 75th Brigade R.F.A. moving to billets at MERCK-ST-LIEVIN, and 76th Brigade R.F.A. moving to billets at OUVE-WIRQUIN. M.G. Carrier used by 4th Battn. Grenadier Guards, adopted by the Division, and Ordnance Officer ordered to procure material. Captain G.H.GREVILLE, Grenadier Guards, appointed to command the Divisional Bombing School, which is in process of formation. Application to issue an extra ½ lb. of vegetables refused.	
	5.		The Corps Commander, (Lieut.General R.HAKING, C.B.,) visits Divisional Headquarters. For drafts for week ending Septr. 4th, see Appendix A.	

Instructions regarding War Diaries and Intelligence
Summaries are contained in F.S. Regs., Part II.
and the Staff Manual respectively. Title Pages
will be prepared in manuscript.

INTELLIGENCE SUMMARY

(Erase heading not required.)

Place	Date	Hour	Summary of Events and Information	Remarks and references to Appendices
	September 6.		75th Brigade R.F.A. goes to 20th Division for practice. 3rd Guards Brigade had a Field day in the neighbourhood of BLENDECQUES, which was attended by the G.O.C.	
	7.		76th Brigade R.F.A. moves to Indian Corps area, to join Meerut Division temporarily for practice. Guards Divisional Sub-Park split up, 1 part going to 3rd Ammunition Park, and the other part to Indian Ammunition Park. This move was temporary and in connection with the practice shooting of 75th and 76th Brigades R.F.A.	
	8.		G.O.C., attended a Field day in which the 4 battalions of 2nd Guards Brigade took part. 4 Lewis guns received for instructional purposes, and distributed amongst units.	
	9.		Corps Commander spent the afternoon in the Divisional area and visited 1st Battn. Coldstream Guards in billets, 9th Field Ambulance, Divisional Supply and Ammunition Columns. G.O.C. attended a Field day carried out by 1st Battn. Irish Guards in the neighbourhood of THIEMBRONNE; he also visited the D.A.C.	
	10.		G.O.C. visited 3rd, 4th, and 9th Field Ambulances.	
	11.		2nd Lieut.P.C.H. de SARGE arrives and takes over the duties of French Interpreter at H.Q. of the Division, vice 2nd Lieut. Comte de BRETEUIL, transferred to CALAIS. The D.A. & Q.M.G. of 11th Corps visited the refilling points of the Divisional H.Q. troops of 3rd Guards Brigade.	
	12.) 13.)		For drafts for week ending Septr. 11th, see Appendix B.	
	14.		G.O.C. accompanied by Brig-Gen. R.A., and G.S.O.s 1 and 2, attended a demonstration of gas bombs at the trench mortar school at St. VENANT. 74th Brigade R.F.A. returned from Indian Corps and went into billets at BAYENGHEM. 17 remounts arrived.	

1875 Wt. W503/826 1,000,000 4/15 I.B.C. & A. A.D.S.S./Forms/C. 2118.

INTELLIGENCE SUMMARY

(Erase heading not required.)

Place	Date	Hour	Summary of Events and Information	Remarks and references to Appendices
	September 15.		The Corps Commander, accompanied by the G.O.C. attended a Field day of the 1st Guards Brigade, in the neighbourhood of MERCK-ST-LIEVIN, and addressed all the officers of this Brigade at the conclusion of the operations. He subsequently addressed the officers of 2nd Guards Brigade at LUMBRES, and 3rd Guards Brigade at WIZERNES.	
	16.		G.O.C. inspected 2nd Guards Brigade on parade at LUMBRES, with Lt. Col.(Temp. Brig-General) J. PONSONBY, C.M.G., D.S.O., in command. Later he attended a conference at 11th Corps H.Q. at TILQUES.	
	17.		G.O.C. inspected 3rd Guards Brigade on parade at ARCQUES, with Lt. Col. W.MURRAY-THREIPLAND in temporary command. D.D.R. 1st Army, visited the Division to inspect horses to be cast; 31 horses were cast. 61st (Howitzer) Brigade, and 76th Brigade R.F.A. return from Indian Corps and billet at NIELLES LEZ-BLEQUIN and OUVE-WIRQUIN respectively.	
	18.		G.O.C. attended a Field day in the neighbourhood of SELQUES, in which operations 2nd Guards Brigade and 55th Field Coy. R.E. were engaged.	
	19.		G.O.C. accompanied by Sub-Chief G.S. inspected 1st Guards Brigade Machine Gun Coy. at THIEMBRONNE. Orders received for Division to move on night of 22nd/23rd.	
	20.		G.O.C. visited 76th Brigade R.F.A. in their billets at OUVE-WIRQUIN.	
	21.		Field Marshal Earl KITCHENER, K.G., accompanied by G.O.C. inspected 1st Battn. Irish Guards at THIEMBRONNE. G.O.C. attended 3rd Guards Brigade Field day in the neighbourhood of ARCQUES.	

Instructions regarding War Diaries and Intelligence Summaries are contained in F.S. Regs., Part II and the Staff Manual respectively. Title Pages will be prepared in manuscript.

INTELLIGENCE SUMMARY

(Erase heading not required.)

Place	Date	Hour	Summary of Events and Information	Remarks and references to Appendices
	September 22.		86 remounts arrived from Base remount depot for the Division. The 3 Brigade groups moved during the night to 3 Brigade areas East of FAUQEMBERGUES-WIZERNES road. H.Q. group remained at LUMBRES.	
	23.		H.Q. group moved to NORRENT-FONTES. The other 3 groups moved by night to new Divisional area South of AIRE. Guards Divisional Supply Column moved to ST. HILLAIRE.	
	24.		Divisional Railhead changed to LILLERS.	
	25.		Guards Divisional Headquarters moved to PERNAY. Advanced Headquarters established at NOEUX-LES-MINES. The Division moved up into the area vacated by 21st Division, with the head of the column at NOEUX-LES-MINES and the tail at LABUISSIERE. Last troops did not reach their billets till 2.00 a.m. The 4 groups of the train refilled at BURBURE.	
	26.		The 3 brigades moved in to the front lines in the afternoon, and the Artillery came into NOEUX-LES-MINES and billeted in the area vacated by the 1st Guards Brigade. Divisional Headquarters at NOEUX-LES-MINES and Advanced Headquarters established at SAILLY-LABOURSE. The train moved to a point S.E. of NOEUX-LES-MINES after refilling at HAILLICOURT. D.A.C. moved from MARLES-LES-MINES to HAILLICOURT.	
	27.		The Supply Section of the train dumped at SAILLY-LABOURSE, refilled at the NOEUX-LES-MINES - BETHUNE road, and returned full to its billets at NOEUX-LES-MINES. The cookers of each battn. came back to SAILLY-LABOURSE to replenish, and returned to their 1st line transport which was brigaded and situated as follows:- 1st Guards Brigade at 45 B. S.E. corner. 2nd Guards Brigade at L 11 C. N.E. corner. 3rd Guards Brigade at G 14 C. N.W. corner. Pioneers at L 11 C. N.E. corner. D.A.C. moved to distillery S.W. of NOEUX-LES-MINES.	

INTELLIGENCE SUMMARY

(Erase heading not required.)

Instructions regarding War Diaries and Intelligence Summaries are contained in F. S. Regs., Part II. and the Staff Manual respectively. Title Pages will be prepared in manuscript.

Place	Date	Hour	Summary of Events and Information	Remarks and references to Appendices
	September 28.		Refilling of Supply Sections of the train as on 27th, and replenishing of battalion cookers took place at the 4 different points where the 1st line transport is brigaded separately. Guards Divisional Railhead moved from LILLERS to CHOCQUES.	
	29.		Refilling and replenishing as on 28th. The Divisional Artillery and Pioneer Battalions of 21st and 24th Divisions attached to the Guards Division. The Pioneer batts. to collect all salvage.	
	30.		LABOURSE becomes Guards Divisional Headquarters for both G branch and 2nd Echelon. On relief 3rd Guards Brigade marched into close billets at LABOURSE. 12 tons of coal were brought from FOSSE No. 8, de VERQUIN, and dumped in the centre of Brigade areas; coal at 38 francs a ton. 1st Guards Brigade billeted at MAZINGARBE and 2nd Guards Brigade at VERQUIGNEUL, on return from the front line after relief. 16 remounts arrived from Base.	

Shoot No.2.

3rd Battalion Coldstream Gds.

Capt. LAWRENCE. (See Staff).

4th Battalion Coldstream Gds.

Capt. L.G.C.Lord PETRE.   W.O.

1st Battalion Scots Guards.

Lt.-Col. S.H.GODMAN.   W.O.
Major N.A. ORR-EWING.   W.O.
Capt.Sir V.A.F. MACKENZIE.BT.
                             W.O.
Capt. A.V.POYNTER.   W.O.
Capt. J.H. CUTHBERT.   M.W.O.
Lieut. E.D.MACKENZIE.   W.O.
Lieut.N.M.FERGUSSON.   W.O.
Lieut.A.M.JONES.   W.O.
2nd Lt.G.S. ARMSTRONG.   M.W.O.
2nd Lt. E.W. ELLIS.   W.O.
2nd Lt. V.H. BRAND.   W.O.
2nd Lt. G.S.DAWKINS.   W.O.
CAPT. J.S.THORPE. (W.on duty)

2nd Battalion Scots Guards.

Lieut. C.A.M.CATOR.   W.O.

1st Battalion Irish Guards.

2nd Lt. J.G.MAJOR.   K.O.

2nd Battalion Irish Guards.

Capt.Hon.T.E.VESEY.   W.O.
Capt.C.D.WYNTER.   W.O.
2nd Lt. W.B. STEVENS.   W.O.
2nd Lt. J. KIPLING.   M.O.
2nd. Lt. W.F. CLIFFORD.   B.K.O.
2nd Lt. T.P.LAW.   W.O.
2nd Lt. R.S.H. GRAYSON.   M.O.
2nd Lt. R.E.SASSOON.   W.O.

4th Battalion Grenadier Guards.

Lt.-Col.G.C.HAMILTON.   G.O.
Capt.H.L. AUBREY-FLETCHER.   W.O.
Capt.Sir G.R.HOUSTON-BOSWALL.BT. W.
Lieut.P.MALCOLM.   W.O.
2nd Lt. A.H. THOMPSON.   W.O.
Major Hon.C.M.B. PONSONBY. W. M.O.
  (Died on battlefield at 9 a.m. 30th)
2nd Lt. M.A.T.RIDLEY.   W.O.
2nd Lt. E.R.D.HOARE.   W.O.
2nd Lt. M.H.MACMILLAN.   W.O.
Capt. T.F.J.N.THORNE.   W.M.O.
Lieut. G.E.SHELLEY.   W.O.

1st Battalion Welsh Guards.

Capt. A.P. PALMER.   K.O.
Capt. G.W.F. PHILLIPS.   W.O.
Capt. O.T.D.OSMOND-WILLIAMS.   W.O.
Capt. R. WILLIAMS.   W.O.
Lieut. E.G. MAWBY.   B. K.O.
2nd Lt. J.W.L. CRAWSHAY.   W.O.
2nd. Lt. Hon. P.G.J.F.HOWARD.   W.O.
Lieut. J. RANDOLPH.   B.K.O.
2nd Lt. R. SMITH.   B.K.O.
2nd Lt. F.A.V.COPLAND-GRIFFITHS.
                          W.O. at Duty.
Lieut. H.J. Sutton.   W.M.O.

=================================

STAFF.

Capt.P.R.B.LAWRENCE.
  (B.M.G.O. 2nd Gds.Bde.)   W.O.

76th FIELD COMPANY.

Major M.O.C. TANDY.   W.O.
Lieut.R.C. BAILE.   W.O.
                             at Duty.

G 'Branch'

Herewith lists as far as are known up to date

    W = wounded
    O = Official
    M = Missing

            W. Dadell Lt Col.

30. 9. 15.
12. 20 pm

            GOC
            London District

This is later than my letter of this date & is more certainly correct.

30th Sept
            Cavan M.G.
            Guards Div.

46.

1st Scots Guards. 13	2nd Irish Guards. 8	1st Grenadiers. 5	4th Grenadiers. 11	2nd Scots. 1	1st Welsh. 11	4th Coldstream. 1
Lt.Col.S.H.GODMAN, W.O.	Capt.Hon.T.E. VESEY. W.O.	2nd Lt.G.J.T.H. VILLIERS W.O.	Lt.Col.G.C. HAMILTON. G.O.	Lieut.C.A.M. CATOR. W.O.	Capt.A.P.PALMER. K.O.	Capt.Lt.G.C. LORD PETRE. W.O.
Major N.A.ORR-EWING. W.O.	Capt.C.D. WYNTER. W.O.	Maj. Nicol W.O.	Capt. H.L.AUBREY-FLETCHER. W.O.		Capt.G.W.F. PHILLIPS. W.O.	
Capt. Sir V.A.F. MACKENZIE, Bart. W.O.	2nd Lt.W.B. STEVENS. W.O.	Capt Sir. A.L.M. NAPIER. Bt W.O.	Capt. Sir G.R. HOUSTON-BOSWALL, Bart. W.		Capt.O.T.D.OSMOND-WILLIAMS. W.O.	
Capt. A.V.POYNTER. W.O.	2nd Lt.J. KIPLING. M.O.		Lieut.P.MALCOLM. W.O.		Capt.R.WILLIAMS. W.O.	
Capt. J.H.CUTHBERT. M.W.O.	2nd Lt.W.F. CLIFFORD. B.K.O.		2nd Lt. A.H. THOMPSON. W.O.		Lieut.E.G.MAWBY. B.K.O.	
Lieut. E.D. MACKENZIE. W.O.	2nd Lt.T.P. LAW. W.O.		MajorHon.C.M.B. PONSONBY. W.& MO		2nd Lt.J.W.L. CRAWSHAY. W.O.	
Lieut. N.M. FERGUSSON, W.O.	2nd Lt.R.S.H. GRAYSON. M.O.		2nd Lt. M.A.T. RIDLEY. W.O.		2nd Lt.Hon.P.G.J.F. HOWARD. W.O.	
Lieut. A.M.JONES W.O.	2nd Lt.R.E. SASSOON. W.O.		2nd Lt. E.R.D. HOARE. W.O.		Lieut.J.RANDOLPH. B.K.O.	
Wnd Lt. G.S. ARMSTRONG. M.W.O.			2nd Lt. M.H. MACMILLAN. W.O.		2nd Lt. R. SMITH. B.K.O.	
2nd Lt. D.W.ELLIS. W.O.			Capt. T.F.J.N. THORNE. W.& M.O.		2nd Lt.F.A.V. COPLAND-GRIFFITHS W.O. (at duty)	
2nd Lt. D.H.BRAND. W.O.			Lieut.G.E.SHELLEY. W.O.		Lieut.H.J.SUTTON. W.&-M.O.	
2nd Lt. G.S. DAWKINS. W.O.						
Capt. J.S.THORPE. W. (on duty).						

x died on battlefield at 9 a.m. 30=.

2nd Grenadiers.	2nd Coldstream.	3rd Coldstream.	1st Irish.	3rd Grenadiers.	1st Coldstream.
1	-	-	1	8	13
2nd Lt.C.CROSLAND. W.O.		Capt. LAWRENCE. (on staff)	2nd Lt. J.G.MAJOR. K.O.	Capt.G.N.VIVIAN. W.O.	Captain G.M.DARELL, W.O.
				Lieut.C.M.&C. DOWLING. W.	2ndLt.J.S.HEATHCOTE W.O.
				2ndLt.A.T.AYRES-RITCHIE. W.O.	Capt.HON.T.C.R.AGAR-ROBARTES. W.O.
				2ndLt.F.D.L. GREEN. W.O.	2nd Lt.J.J.A.ViscountHOLMESDALE. W.O.
				Lieut.C.S.ROWLEY. M.O.	2nd Lt.G.BARRY. W.O.
				Lieut.C.T.E. CRABBE. M.O.	Lieut.C.J.M.RILEY. W.O.
				Lieut.F.ANSON. W.O.	2nd Lt.O.G.STYLE. M.O.
				Capt.W.R.C. MURRAY. W.O.	2nd Lt.J.R.BLACKER. M.O.
					2nd Lt.G.L.I.SMITH. M.O.
					2nd Lt.J.C.FAIR. M.O.
					2nd Lt.R.F.PRATT-BARLOW. W.O.
					Lieut.Col.A.G.E.EGERTON. K.O.
					Lieut.Hon.M.H.D.BROWNE. K.O.

Staff.	76th Field Coy.
Capt.P.R.B. LAWRENCE. (B.M.G.O.2nd Gds.Bde) W.O.	Major M.O'C.TANDY. W.O. Lieut.R.C.BAILE. W.O. on duty.

APPENDIX A.

Drafts for week ending September 4th, 1915.

1st Grenadier Guards...........25 Other ranks.
3rd Grenadier Guards........... 1 Officer.
1st Coldstream Guards...........5 Officers.
2nd Coldstream Guards...........2 Officers.
                                              2 Other ranks.
2nd Scots Guards................43 Other ranks.
1st Irish Guards................48 Other ranks.

Appendix A.

Drafts for week ending Sept. 4th:—

1st Grenadier Gds. 25 other ranks.
3rd   "   "   1 officers.
1st Coldstream Gds. 5 officers.
2nd   "   "   2 officers. 2 other ranks.
2nd Scots Gds.   43 other ranks.
1st Irish Gds.   48 other ranks.

Appendix B.

Drafts for week ending Sept. 11th:-

2nd Bn. Grenadier Gds.		1 officer.
3rd Bn. Grenadier Gds.		1 officer.
1st Bn. Coldstream Gds.		20 other ranks.
2nd " " "		4 other ranks.
3rd " " "		1 officer.
4th " " "		35 other ranks.
1st " Scots. Gds.		1 officer.
2nd " Irish Gds.		3 officers.

APPENDIX B.

Drafts for week ending September 11th, 1915.

2nd Grenadier Guards.............1 Officer.

3rd Grenadier Guards.............1 Officer.

1st Coldstream Guards..........20 Other ranks.

2nd Coldstream Guards...........4 Other ranks.

3rd Coldstream Guards...........1 Officer.

4th Coldstream Guards..........35 Other ranks.

1st Scots Guards................1 Officer.

2nd Irish Guards................3 Officers.

APPENDIX C.

Drafts for week ending September 19th, 1915.

1st Grenadier Guards............3 Officers.
                                2 Other ranks.

3rd Coldstream Guards...........2 Officers.
                                5 Other ranks.

1st Scots Guards................4 Officers.

2nd Scots Guards................3 Officers.
                                1 Other ranks.

74TH DIVISION
ENGINEERS
C.R.E. Field Coys Signals
SEPTEMBER 1918

121/6695.

Guards Division

HeadQuarters (A & Q) Guards Division

Vol I

29 July 15 to 31 Aug. 15

Guards' Division.

The composition of the Division is in the Appendix –

Notes re the Brigade & Artillery command.

~~Notes~~ The Brigadiers who were commanding Guards Brigades & had been doing so for some time were very properly selected for the 3 Brigades – Feilding – Lowther – Heyworth –
On 20th Aug I heard that Lowther was selected for the Military Secretaryship to the C in C vice Lambton – I hoped for Pereira but it was decided that Brigadiers already employed had better not be moved – ~~It was~~ ~~intimated that Steele was next on the list~~ ~~for promotion & that so good a soldier was~~ ~~available~~ Ponsonby was appointed to succeed Lowther & Steele given the 22nd Brigade.

* Ponsonby was senior to Steele & I wrote M/S to advise Ponsonby being appointed.

The question of the command of the Artillery much exercised the Chief of the General Staff – He thought it very important that we should have some young man who had the experience of this campaign. The guns were those of the new 16th Division with some RS Officers in command & varied experience. They had shot at LARKHILL but had very little training – The material appeared to be excellent. I saw them at Larkhill on 16th Aug –

In conversation with the CGS & MS on 20th Aug I asked for L¹ Col¹ Boyd who was originally in the 41st Brigade R.F.A. – & whose brilliant exploits in Oct-Nov. 1914 near YPRES endeared him to my old Brigade –

I look on it as vitally important to the future success of the Division to have the very best of Artillery Advisers – The infantry are so good that nothing but the closest & best Artillery support will be good enough –

Brig Gen Davidson was app¹ᵈ

The Staff –

By His Majesty's wish HRH the Prince of Wales was attached to the General Staff – I am very proud of the honour done to the Division – The rest are good & well tried officers, all known to me – & all Guardsmen except the CRA Davidson in whom I have every

Concentration

Confidential.

The area was a large one with ample room for everybody to be quite comfortable. Divisional H.Qrs. at LUMBRES on the main S. OMER – BOULOGNE road. & the whole Division in villages a few miles West of S. OMER – but widely scattered.

On Aug. 21 orders were received to move the 1st Brigade (Feilding) further South so as to make room for the new Divisions coming out.

On Sunday Aug 22 Col: Montgomerie came to see me from GHQ & told me I was to command the XIth Corps temporarily – that the Guards Divn. wd. form part of it but that finally it wd. come under Genl. Haking –
We decided to have an Office in S. Omer –

The 1st Gds. Brigade (Feilding) moved on Aug. 24. a very hot day to a new area to the South about THIEMBRONNE. They halted 2 hours for dinner just beyond LUMBRES: Our Howitzers arrived.

On Aug 31. at a Review of the 3rd French Corps I received from General Joffre the cross of a Commander of the Legion of Honour. & was congratulated by Generals Foch & d'Urbal.

On Sept 1 the first concentration of the Infantry of the Guards Division took place at & near WISMES – under a simple tactical scheme. Maj Genl. Sir Francis Lloyd K.C.B who was the guest of the C in C. saw all 3 Brigades on the march – Some battalions had marched over 17 miles in the day, but not one single man in the Division fell out.

HRH the Prince of Wales joined the Staff from leave. I arranged with him that he shd. keep the War Diary & make himself thoroughly au fait with every unit of the Division & assist the Q branch –

Sept. 1.

The Howitzer Brigade & the 74th F.A. Brigade marched up to have a week's experience with the First Army.

I pointed out to Brig. Genl. Gordon who had come out from England as C.R.A. that I did not think that a man who had left the army for 14 years & had no experience of this war could do either himself or the Division full justice. He concurred. I therefore asked for his immediate relief before we went to the front.

I said much the same to Major Colvin of the 1st L.G.ds who had come out in command of the Divisional Mounted Troops. He went further than Gordon & wrote a letter asking to be relieved on the ground of inexperience.

It is in my opinion far kinder to tell a man at once that he is not fitted for a position than to let him try on until he commits himself. Mistaken they can be rectified on the field of battle — but cannot be postponed if not avoided, by placing the best men, before the Division is engaged —

I had to give very strict instructions that H.R.H. the Prince of Wales was never to be out after dark unless attended by an officer. An orderly was not sufficient.

*. An officer whose name it wd. not be fair to write was referred to me as "eccentric, excitable & contentious". I interviewed him & told him that had I not known him to be a gallant gentleman I sh. have sent him home — but that as I believed him to be a man who would very likely bring credit on the Regiment he belonged to, if given the chance, I was prepared to give him the chance, but if further trouble arose, I sh. have him sent home on the clear understanding that he was "too insubordinate to serve with men".

*. This Officer got the Military Cross on Dec. 20.

4.

On Sept 15. Capt Commander L.Gen: Hacking saw a Field Day of the 1st Brigade & expressed his high approval. He afterwards addressed the Officers of the 1st, 2d & 3d Brigades & told them how much depended on platoon leaders - & that we sh'd go up somewhere behind the 1st Army ready to fill up any hole made in the crust of German defences -

On Sept 16 & 17 I reviewed the 2nd & 3rd Brigades. They were drawn up in Mass - The march past, the handling of arms, & the general appearance were at that high *a most proper* (standard) for all Guardsmen under all & every condition -

I was very particularly impressed with Brig Genl. Ponsonby's word of command - with the marching of the Left Flank Co. of the 1st Batt: Scots Guards & the 4th Batt: Grenadier Guards - & with the exact timing of the motions of the "present" & the "slope" throughout both Brigades.

I am convinced that for Ceremonial purposes the word of command sh'd be given to the whole Brigade by the Brigadier & not by a couple of the second files Pans & other devices for soldiers with poor voices -

I have already spoken of the excellent march of Brig Genl Ponsonby's word of command & the 3rd Brigade - under Lt.Col: Murray Threipland (B/P. Heyworth was in leave) also presented arms with splendid precision -

On Sept 18 the 2nd Brigade were exercised with their affiliated Brigade of Artillery. All the guns & many officers have been sent up to the front to study the ground for future operations.

Brig Genl. Wardrop. R.A. was appointed CRA to my very complete satisfaction.

Sept 21.   This was an important day. The bombardment preliminary to offensive operations began. Orders were received for the Guards Division to move forward by 2 night marches, starting on night of 22/23 to an area due South of AIRE behind the 21st & 24th Divisions & in front of the Cavalry Corps.

Lord Kitchener inspected the 1st Bn. Irish Guards. He thanked them for their fine services & told them they wd shortly have opportunity to show that they cd do the same again.

Lt-Col. Madden was in command.

The 3rd Brigade were exercised with the 76th Bde. R.F.A.

The guns of the bombardment cd be very clearly heard the wind being East.

Our Opn Order No. 1 attached

Sept. 23.   The Division moved forward to an area about LILLERS by night.

L. Genl. Hakeing gave all Divisional, Brigade, Battalion & R.A. Commanders a very good lecture on the tactical situation – in LILLERS.

I issued the following General Order –

"On the eve of the biggest battle in the World's History the G.O.C Guards Division wishes his troops God speed.

He has nothing to add to the stirring words uttered by the Corps Commander this morning but he wishes to impress upon all ranks two things.

(i) that the fate of future generations of Englishmen hangs on the issue of their fight.

(ii) that great things are expected

of the Guards Division.
As a Guardsman of over 30 years standing the G.O.C. knows that he need say no more—"

Sept 24 & 25) Moved forward to NOEUX les MINES.
Battle began well.

26. Ordered at 10 a.m. to move up Division to old line of British trenches between VERMELLES — HULLUCH road on left & LOOS on right. Later to relieve 21st & 24th Divisions during night.

27. Feilding Brigade on left. Ponsonby on right relieved 21st & 24th as ordered — putting out posts some 600ˣ in front of our most advanced line.
Heyworth's Brigade in reserve along the railway just in front of VERMELLES.

Corps Commander at 1 p.m. gave me verbal orders for an attack to begin at 4 p.m.—
The details are covered in War Diary—
I s[h]ould to say that the advance covered by the smoke cloud on its left or N.E. exposed flank was admirably carried out, & that Heyworth handled his Brigade with great skill over the very heavily shelled area just N of LOOS—
The O.C. 2 Scots Guards made a wise decision on Hill 70. to dig in just on reverse side of crest & not at furthest point gained; altho' this entailed a sacrifice of some of our wounded in between

Sept 28. It was to have an task complete but I
ordered the 2 Brigade to attack PUITS 14 bis &c.
this day. but my plan was, partly in the light
of knowledge gained since of enemy position
in that our Artillery preparation was too
much centered on what we believed to be
the strong points - whereas they were about
100ᵈ to 200ᵈ further East.

The 1st London made a splendid effort
& did get there but c'd not hold it -

29th The loss of Ingleton & his Adj by one big shell
next day was a very severe one *

The shelling of the CHALK PIT was very heavy
indeed all day & also of LOOS. but good
digging proved once more that bombardments
are not to be much feared.

30th On night of 30/1 Oct we were all relieved by
XIIth Division & have got - big fires & good hot
food & 2 complete nights rest about
LA BOURSE till night of 3/4 Oct when we
were ordered forward again -

Oct. 4 My instructions were to take the "Quarries".
& Gen Feilding was given the task with 1st Brigade
helped by covering fire from 3rd Brigade -
2nd Brigade in reserve -

Oct. 5. This order was cancelled - & 12th Divⁿ took
over that bit of our line opposite the Quarries
& we held the left - & extended to Auchy Rd

Oct. 8: The enemy bombarded our trenches & Vermelles from 11 to 3.15 & then launched an attack against the south face of Hohenzollern & the point held by the 8th Brigade.

This attack partly by bomb & partly by assault mainly & was completely repulsed. The full story of it has gone to London.

The 3. C. G. & 2. C. G. really saved the day.

The losses were [illegible] attached in Appendix.

Oct. 26. The Division was relieved by the 12th Division & went into rest billets about ALLOUAGNE — ~~HESDIGNEULS~~. We had been 28 ~~18~~ days in the trenches. Had taken two pieces of the Hohenzollern Fort & dug a new line over 1500 yards long with all its necessary accessories — & communication trenches under very difficult conditions. Some of it was only 25 yards from the enemy & a very large number of corpses had to be removed & reburied.

The casualties of the Division in this period were

O. 19. killed   OR. killed 333   Total.
34. wounded   wounded 1224   =   1752
1. missing   missing 137
                       ~~prisoners~~ 4

In my opinion the 2nd Battn. Scots Guards did their lion share of this work both in fighting & digging, but the whole achievement was good & we handed over to our successors a safe & good line.

Commenced —

Period Oct 4. 26.
I noticed a little tendency to treat the Division especially the divisional Staff, as if we were all a family party of Guardsmen & that the restraint necessary when writing official documents was not always observed — I therefore wrote somewhat sharply to two of the three Brigadiers who immediately apologized —

An action taken by my CRA was highly disapproved by the Corps Commander & myself. He however acted with frank candour, saw his mistake & in my presence of his own wish apologized to those he had wrongly found fault with — this no doubt strengthening rather than weakening his disciplinary control —

Oct 28
The Division had a great disappointment. We were all ready to parade for Inspection by His Majesty — in mass in a very big field of stubble & plough near LILLERS — At 12.30 p.m. we heard of the King's accident & all engagements cancelled. I was to have had the honour of dining with the King that niche — but that was of course also cancelled —

at 29
I came Home on leave. Saw O.C Grenadier Guards & GOC London District, gave them my opinion of the Division & its one weak spot & why it was weak

namely that Col: M. Cary was not well enough to command the 3rd Bn. Grenadier Guards properly -

I was very glad of a chance at home for altho' I lay no claim to share the bodily fatigues & trials of those actually in trenches, there is a wearing strain of the ceaseless responsibility for the welfare of the Division & the safety of our Line —

Nov. 6 Returned — to find I was temporarily in command of the XIth Corps & was ordered to hie with it. General Stockwell came out to stay —
Guards Division moved up to an area about LA GORGUE marching by Brigades on 8th 9th 10th — preparatory to taking over the line from just north of NEUVE CHAPELLE to FAUQUISSART —
A real boggy bad line & no summer preparation for a winter sojourn — Optimism rampant!

Nov. 19. Was summoned by telegram to see C in C. He asked me if I wd take Winston Churchill to train with my Division — I said certainly — & W.C. came to lunch next day & then into trenches with Mr a Jeffreys —
Sir John French also asked me my views as to the proper employment of the Guards Division in Winter. I told him I felt that good troops were being wasted in the Bog — & that we wd do better work for the Army by training behind: Keeping the men well & happy & ready for big efforts later on. He was much pleased that I took that view & told me that on return of the Chief of the Staff he wd order it.
Great changes in European situation however prevented this from being carried out —

Nov. 19th to Dec 13	Sniping continues of an active sort on our sides. Our Artillery good. On Dec 11. 4th Guards carried out a surprise attack. See Appendix. The drainage of our line was all done by the RE but as usual repairs after frost & much rain took up all the time of the men & little if any new work c'd be carried out except on Strongpoints at back.
Dec 13 to Dec 22	Much as above. Various other enterprises carried out — & DCM & Mil[itary] Cross awarded.

On 22nd I received a letter from Mil: Sec: to say I had been appointed to command XIV Corps. Much honoured & flattered but dread leaving Guards' Division.

Dec 23 On 23: I held a conference — chiefly to impress Brigadiers with necessity of having no truce or any fraternization with Enemy on Xmas day. These orders were correctly given out. but to my utter dismay I heard on return from Church that Germans & our men had met between the lines & had an informal truce. The Battalions concerned were
   1. Bn Coldstream
   1. Bn Scots —
   2. Bn Scots —

I ordered Court of Inquiry at once — & wrote my opinion on it myself & when received took it to Corps Commander on night of 26th. The papers are now at G.H.Q. & we await the verdict.
It was the only blow I have had since the Division was formed — & to my mind it was inexcusable as it was flagrant disobedience. I stopped all leave in the 3 Battalions pending decision from above.
Whatever that may be I s[houl]d like to record that I think the Officers who did not do all they ought to have done were —   (1st Ramsay
   Capt Barne 1 Scots Gds.   1. Coldstream.
   Capt de Teissier. 1. Scots Gds.
   Capt Sir I. Colquhoun 1 Scots Gds.

Dec 25. Xmas day — I went round every unit in the Division — & told them of my appointment to the XLV Corps — & my intense sorrow at leaving them —

Dec 27 — At 11.55 a m on return from an Inspection of our forward posts I received a Private letter from the Sec[retary] of the General Staff worded as follows.

"Congratulations on getting a Corps & on taking your Division with you"

This was more than I had dared to hope & was one of the moments worth living for.

On Jan 1. I was recommended by Corps Comd. to go home on leave & did so till Jan 11 when I joined H.Q XIV Corps at DOULLENS & spent a long day motoring round seeing 2 Divisional & 5 Brigade Commanders —

III Army Commander (Allenby) in command —

He told me he did not expect any big offensive now till May at earliest, as it was advisable to wait for Russia to be really ready —

XIV Corps consists of { Guards Division
Ulster Division. (36)
W. Lancs Division T. (55)

War Diary
Dec 1915
Till
July 1916

H.S. Gandan (A.+9)
Sec / Vol V

Army Form C. 2118

WAR DIARY
or
INTELLIGENCE SUMMARY
(Erase heading not required.)

Instructions regarding War Diaries and Intelligence Summaries are contained in F. S. Regs., Part II. and the Staff Manual respectively. Title Pages will be prepared in manuscript.

Place	Date	Hour	Summary of Events and Information	Remarks and references to Appendices
	Dec. 1st		The A.A. & Q.M.G. gave a lecture to the Officers of the 3rd Guards Brigade on the system of Supply of the B.E.F. in the Field.	
	Dec. 2nd		A barge with a cargo of coal arrived at LA GORGUE for the use of the Division. 3rd Guards Brigade relieved 1st Guards Brigade in the trenches, the Battalions of 1st Guards Brigade being billeted as follows :- 3rd Coldstream Guards & 1st Irish Guards in LA GORGUE. 2nd Grenadier Guards & 2nd Coldstream Gds. N.&S. of MERVILLE. Capt. G.E.C.RASCH, D.S.O., Grenadier Guards, assumed the duties of Brigade Major, 2nd Guards Brigade in succession to Major B.N.SERGISSON BROOKE, D.S.O., appointed G.S.O.2.5th Corps.	
	Dec. 3rd		Lieut. (Temp.Captain) A.F.SMITH, Coldstream Guards assumed the duties of G.S.O.3. Major R.N.V.KELLY, R.A., A.O.D. succeeds Major W.W.BLADES, D.S.O., A.O.D. as D.A.D.O.S., on the latter's appointment as D.A.D.O.S. of 46th Division. Soldiers Clubs at LA GORGUE and LAVENTIE opened for the first time.	
	Dec. 4th		G.O.C. held a Conference at Divisional Headquarters for 1st Guards Brigade.	
	Dec. 5th		A Meeting was held at Divisional Headquarters, presided over by the D.A.A. & Q.M.G. to discuss the formation of Soldiers Clubs at LA GORGUE and LAVENTIE. It was attended by the 2nd in command of each Battalion of the Division and several Chaplains.	
	Dec. 6th			
	Dec. 7th			
	Dec. 8th		1st Guards Brigade relieved 2nd Guards Brigade in the trenches, Battalions being billeted as follows :- 3rd Grenadier Guards & 2nd Irish Guards in LA GORGUE; 1st Coldstream Guards and 1st Scots Guards N. & S. of MERVILLE.	
	Dec. 9th			

1875 Wt. W593/826 1,000,000 4/15 J.B.C. & A. A.D.S.S./Forms/C. 2118.

Army Form C. 2118

WAR DIARY
or
INTELLIGENCE SUMMARY

(Erase heading not required.)

Instructions regarding War Diaries and Intelligence Summaries are contained in F.S. Regs., Part II. and the Staff Manual respectively. Title Pages will be prepared in manuscript.

Place	Date	Hour	Summary of Events and Information	Remarks and references to Appendices
	Dec. 10th		The following drafts arrived :- 3rd Coldstream Guards 30 O.R. 1st Irish Guards 25 O.R. 1st Coldstream Guards 20 O.R. 1st Scots Guards 20 O.R. 2nd Irish Guards 20 O.R. 2nd Scots Guards 1 Officer. 4th Coldstream Guards 25 O.R.	
	Dec. 11th			
	Dec. 12th		Captain Hon. P.W.LEGH, Grenadier Guards, reported arrival on appointment as A.D.C. to G.O.C.	
	Dec. 13th		Bathing installation at PONT DU HEM opened for use of 2 Battalions of right brigade, in brigade reserve. 3 truck loads of Shale arrived at FOSSE for the use of Guards Division.	
	Dec. 14th		2nd Guards Brigade relieved 3rd Guards Brigade in the trenches, 3rd Guards Brigade Battalions being billeted as follows :- 1st Grenadier Guards & 1st Welsh Guards in LA GORGUE. 4th Grenadier Guards & 2nd Scots Guards N. & S. of MERVILLE.	
	Dec. 15th			
	Dec. 16th			
	Dec. 17th			
	Dec. 18th			
	Dec. 19th		Field Marshall SIR JOHN FRENCH was succeeded by General SIR DOUGLAS HAIG as Commander-in-Chief of the British Expeditionary Force in France. G.O.C. held a Conference attended by the 3 Brigadiers, O.R.A., C.R.E. etc.	
	Dec. 20th		3rd Guards Brigade relieved 1st Guards Brigade in the trenches, the Battalions being billeted as follows :- 2nd Coldstream Guards & 1st Irish Guards in LA GORGUE. 2nd Grenadier Guards & 3rd Coldstream Guards N. & S. of MERVILLE. 2nd London R.F.A. Brigade, 1st London R.F.A. Division arrived for attachment. 2 truck loads of Shale and 1 of Metal arrived at FOSSE for the use of Guards Division.	

1875 Wt. W593/826 1,000,000 4/15 I.R.C. & A. A.D.S.S./Forms/C. 2118.

Army Form C. 2118

WAR DIARY
or
INTELLIGENCE SUMMARY
(Erase heading not required.)

Instructions regarding War Diaries and Intelligence Summaries are contained in F. S. Regs., Part II. and the Staff Manual respectively. Title Pages will be prepared in manuscript.

Place	Date	Hour	Summary of Events and Information	Remarks and references to Appendices
	Dec.	21st		
	Dec.	22nd		
	Dec.	23rd		
	Dec.	24th	There were 2 Refillings; 1st Refilling with train wagons as usual. 2nd Refilling 2 hours later with wagons from reserve park and baggage wagons. Guards Division Railhead changed from MERVILLE to LA GORGUE. Leave alloted as follows :- 1st Guards Brigade 20. 2nd and 3rd Guards Brigades 10 each. R.A. 4. Pioneers 2. R.E. 2. Train, Supply Column, Squad, Cyclists 1 each.	
	Dec.	25th	Xmas Day. G.O.C. visited all Units of the Division except the 4 Battalions in the trenches.	
	Dec.	26th	1st Guards Brigade relieved 2nd Guards Brigade in the trenches, the 4 Battalions relieved being billeted as follows :- 1st Coldstream Guards and 1st Scots Guards in LA GORGUE. 3rd Grenadier Guards and 2nd Irish Guards N. & S. of MERVILLE.	
	Dec.	27th		
	Dec.	28th	Refilling points moved into Station Yard at LA GORGUE. New system of Refilling adopted. Pack train arrived at railhead and wagons load from 4 dumps composed of contents of pack train, 1 and 2 groups refill 1 hour before 3 and 4. Captain H.V. HESKETH-PRICHARD delivered a lecture on the Art of Sniping in LA GORGUE, which was attended by the Corps Commander, G.O.C., Brigadier and Officers of 2nd Guards Bde.	
	Dec.	29th	Following drafts arrived :- 3rd Grenadier Guards 2 O.R. 1st Scots Guards 1 O.R. 2nd Irish Guards 3 O.R. 1st Grenadier Guards 1 O.R. 4th Grenadier Guards 4 O.R.	

1875 Wt. W593/826 1,000,000 4/15 J.B.C. & A. A.D.S.S./Forms/C.2118.

Army Form C. 2118

WAR DIARY
or
INTELLIGENCE SUMMARY
(Erase heading not required.)

Instructions regarding War Diaries and Intelligence Summaries are contained in F. S. Regs., Part II. and the Staff Manual respectively. Title Pages will be prepared in manuscript.

Place	Date	Hour	Summary of Events and Information	Remarks and references to Appendices
	Dec.	30th	D.A. & Q.M.G. delivered a Lecture on the Supply of an Army in the Field to the Officers of the 2nd Guards Brigade.	
	Dec.	31st	G.O.C. deleivered a Lecture on "The Great Chapter 7". Following drafts arrived :- 2nd Grenadier Guards..23 O.R. 2nd Irish Guards......25 O.R. 1st Grenadier Guards.. 3 O.R. 4th Grenadier Guards..25 O.R. 2nd Scots Guards.....50 O.R.	

H.Q. A. & Q. Guards Div
Jan/18 Vol VI

Army Form C. 2118

WAR DIARY
or
INTELLIGENCE SUMMARY
(Erase heading not required.)

Instructions regarding War Diaries and Intelligence Summaries are contained in F. S. Regs., Part II. and the Staff Manual respectively. Title Pages will be prepared in manuscript.

Place	Date	Hour	Summary of Events and Information	Remarks and references to Appendices
LA GORGUE.	1916. Jan. 1st.		G.O.C. went on leave. Brigadier General F.J.HEYWORTH,C.B.,D.S.O.,(G.O.C.3rd Guards Brigade) assumed temporary command of the Division. 2nd Guards Brigade relieves 3rd Guards Brigade in the trenches, battalions being billeted as follows:- 1st Grenadier Guards and 1st Welsh Guards in LA GORGUE, 4th Grenadier Guards and 2nd Scots Guards North and South of MERVILLE.	
	2nd. 3rd.		Bt.Colonel (Temporary Major-General) G.P.T.FEILDING, D.S.O.,Coldstream Guards takes over the command of the Division vice Major-General The Earl of Cavan, C.B., M.V.O., appointed to command 14th Corps. Captain Hon.P.W.LEGH, Grenadier Guards, left the Division on appointment as A.D.C. to G.O.C., 14th Corps. Bt.Colonel G.D.JEFFREYS,Grenadier Guards, assumes temporary command of 1st Guards Brigade. Captain C.M.HEADLAM, Bedfordshire Yeomanry, left the Division to take over the duties of G.S.O.3,2nd Army.	
	4th.		137 Remounts arrived at MERVILLE Station. 19th Division "FOLLIES" give a performance for the troops in the Recreation Room.	
	5th.		Snow-plough is assembled and ready for trial. 2nd Lieutenant FISHER ROWE, Grenadier Guards, temporarily takes over the duties of Camp Commandant. 114th Infantry Brigade relieves 1st Guards Brigade in the trenches.	
	6th.		Major-General G.P.T.FEILDING,D.S.O.,assumes command of 11th Corps during the absence of the Corps Commander. All steel helmets are transferred from 1st Guards Brigade to 2nd and 3rd Guards Brigade. Captain LEGGE, Coldstream Guards,reports as Temporary A.D.C.	
	7th.		Movement of 114th Infantry Brigade to the trenches,and of 1st Guards Brigade to CALONNE completed.	

1875 W: W593/826 1,000,000 4/15 J.B.C. & A.   A.D.S.S./Forms/C. 2118.

Army Form C. 2118

WAR DIARY
or
INTELLIGENCE SUMMARY

(Erase heading not required.)

Instructions regarding War Diaries and Intelligence Summaries are contained in F.S. Regs., Part II. and the Staff Manual respectively. Title-Pages will be prepared in manuscript.

Place	Date	Hour	Summary of Events and Information	Remarks and references to Appendices
LA GORGUE	1916. Jan. 7th. (Cen)		No.1 Meter Ambulance Convoy Pantomine Company gave a performance in the Recreation Room at LA GORGUE.	
	8th.		Snow-plough handed over to 1st Grenadier Guards and 1st Welsh Guards held a concert in the Recreation Room.	
	9th.		2 truck loads of shale received and handed over to the Artillery. Colonel (Brigadier-General) G.E.PEREIRA arrived to command 1st Guards Brigade.	
	10th.		Colonel CORRY returns to England and gives up command of 3rd Grenadier Guards. A.A & Q.M.G., gives a lecture to the Officers of the 1st Guards Brigade on "The Supply of an Army in the Field". Captain G.M.DARELL, Coldstream Guards, joins Divisional Head Quarters for instruction in Administrative Duties.	
	11th.		Lieutenant KENNERLY RUMFORD gave a concert with a party of the Artists Rifles from G.H.Q. Captain G.H.LODER, Scots Guards and Captain HARCOURT VERNON, Grenadier Guards, report for attachment to Divisional Head Quarters.	
	12th.		G.O.C., inspects the billets of the 2 Reserve Battalions of 114th Infantry Brigade. Captain HARCOURT VERNON is attached to 2nd Guards Brigade.	
	13th.		Horse rations reduced to 6 lbs. of hay a day. Suggestion that wheat straw be mixed with hay.	
	14th. to 16th.		Following drafts arrived from No.7 Entrenching Battalion :- 1st Irish Guards - 1 Officer and 4 Other Ranks. 3rd Grenadier Guards - 30 Other Ranks. 1st Coldstream Guards - 25 Other Ranks. 1st Scots Guards - 1 Officer. 1st Grenadier Guards - 1 Officer. 2nd Scots Guards - 40 Other Ranks.	

Army Form C. 2118

WAR DIARY
or
INTELLIGENCE SUMMARY

(Erase heading not required.)

Instructions regarding War Diaries and Intelligence Summaries are contained in F. S. Regs., Part II. and the Staff Manual respectively. Title Pages will be prepared in manuscript.

Place	Date	Hour	Summary of Events and Information	Remarks and references to Appendices
LA GORGUE.	1916. Jan. 17th.		General Court-Martial held at Divisional Head Quarters, on 2 Officers 1st Bn: Scots Guards relative to festivities in trenches on Christmas Day.	
	18th.		Captain G.M.DARELL, Coldstream Guards, goes to 2nd Guards Brigade to act as temporary Staff Captain. Major B.N.SARGISON BROOKE assumes command of 3rd Bn: Grenadier Guards.	
	19th.		Lieutenant Colonel JEFFREYS leaves to assume command of 58th Infantry Brigade, 19th Division. Members of Artists Rifles gave a concert for the troops. 236 Remounts arrived at LA GORGUE.	
	20th.		Cinematograph Entertainment in Recreation Room.	
	21st.		Following draft arrived :- 4th Grenadier Guards - 26 Other Ranks.	
	22nd.		19th Division "Follies" gave an entertainment in the Recreation Room at LA GORGUE.	
	23rd.		2nd Coldstream Guards moved to PONT DU HEM and 1st Irish Guards moved to RIEZ BAILLEUL. All Corps Troops of 11th Corps in Guards Division billeting area came on to the Divisional feeding strength. Following draft arrived :- 2nd Scots Guards - 5 Other Ranks.	
	24th.		Captain T.R.CLUTTERBUCK, Coldstream Guards, reported as A.D.C., to G.O.C.	
	25th.		2nd Coldstream Guards and 1st Irish Guards relieved 2 Battalions of 115th Infantry Brigade in the trenches. 2nd Grenadier Guards moved up to RIEZ BAILLEUL and 3rd Coldstream Guards to PONT DU HEM, 1st Guards Brigade Head Quarters moved to RUE DE PARADIS.	
	26th.		A.A & Q.M.G., left on a visit to the Guards Divisional Base Depot at HAVRE, and the D.A.G., 3rd Echelon.	

1875 Wt. W593/826 1,000,000 4/15 J.B.C. & A. A.D.S.S./Forms/C. 2118.

Army Form C. 2118

Instructions regarding War Diaries and Intelligence Summaries are contained in F.S. Regs., Part II. and the Staff Manual respectively. Title Pages will be prepared in manuscript.

WAR DIARY
or
INTELLIGENCE SUMMARY
(Erase heading not required.)

Place	Date	Hour	Summary of Events and Information	Remarks and references to Appendices
LA GORGUE	1916. Jan. 26th (Con)		D.A.Q.M.G., attended an inspection of the Divisional Ammunition Column on the march.	
	27th.		2 Officers for 1st Scots Guards and 1 Officer for 2nd Scots Guards arrived.	
	28th.		G.O.C. takes over temporary command of 11th Corps in the absence of the Corps Commander. Brigadier-General F.J.HEYWORTH, C.B.,D.S.O., assumes temporary command of the Division. G.O.C., attends funeral of Captain Sir R.FILMER, Bart.,4th Grenadier Guards, at MERVILLE. A.A.& Q.M.G., returns from the Base. Following drafts arrived :- 3 Officers and 20 Other Ranks for 1st Coldstream Guards. 25 Other Ranks for 1st Scots Guards. 25 Other Ranks for 2nd Irish Guards. 25 Other Ranks for 1st Grenadier Guards. 1 Officer for 4th Coldstream Guards (Pioneers).	
	29th.		The Coldstream Band gave their first concert in the Concert Hall, LA GORGUE, Captain MACKENZIE ROGAN, M.V.O., conducted. Captain G.H.LODER is attached to the "Q" Branch for Instruction.	
	30th.		Captain ARTHUR F.SMITH leaves Guards Division, and Lieutenant E.W.M.GRIGG is posted as G.S.O.3 in his place.	
	31st		A Variety Entertainment was given by the "MERVILLE MAGS" in the Concert Hall, LA GORGUE.	

Edward Lt.
for Brigadier-General,
Commanding Guards Division.

Army Form C. 2118

WAR DIARY
or
INTELLIGENCE SUMMARY
(Erase heading not required.)

Instructions regarding War Diaries and Intelligence Summaries are contained in F.S. Regs., Part II and the Staff Manual respectively. Title Pages will be prepared in manuscript.

Place	Date	Hour	Summary of Events and Information	Remarks and references to Appendices
	Feb. 1.		3rd Guards Brigade relieved 2nd Guards Brigade in Left Sector.	
	Feb. 2.		Iron Rations - A complete issue of new Iron Rations to take their place.	
	Feb. 3.		Concert by H.M. Coldstream Guards Band. D.D.R., 1st Army inspected horses for casting other than for veterinary reasons.	
	Feb. 4.		10 lbs of hay will arrive at Railhead for issue to H.D. Horses. Coldstream Guards Band will play to the 56th Brigade. Capt. A.L.F.SMITH. (Coldstream Guards) transferred to 11th Corps as G.S.O.3.	
	Feb. 5.		Lieut. E.W.M.GRIGG. (Grenadier Guards) appointed G.S.O.3., Guards Division.	
	Feb. 6.		300 Horses and Mules arrived at LA GORGUE for distribution in the Guards Division.	
	Feb. 7.		Lieut-Colonel DARELL visited the area which the Division will take over in the 2nd Army. 2nd Guards Brigade relieved 1st Guards Brigade in Right Sector.	
LA GORGUE.	Feb. 8.		A Practice Alarm (Gas) in Left Brigade 5-45 a.m. 5000 New Helmets to be issued to replace those used.	
	Feb. 9.			
	Feb. 10.		Artillery Personnel arrived to replace Infantry personnel in 1½" T.M. Batteries. No. 13 and No. 18 T.M. Batteries are now up to strength in Artillery personnel. 5 R.A. Officers reported for attachment to T.M. Batteries; 2 for No. 13 and 3 for No. 18.	
	Feb. 11.		Field Marshall, Earl KITCHENER, K.G., accompanied by General Sir C. MONRO, 1st Army Commander, and 11th Corps Commander, visited the Division, and inspected 1st Guards Brigade on parade near BEAUPRE .arm. Conference held at Divisional Headquarters to discuss the move North the Division is about to make.	

Army Form C. 2118

WAR DIARY
or
INTELLIGENCE SUMMARY
(Erase heading not required.)

Instructions regarding War Diaries and Intelligence Summaries are contained in F.S. Regs., Part II. and the Staff Manual respectively. Title Pages will be prepared in manuscript.

Place	Date	Hour	Summary of Events and Information	Remarks and references to Appendices
	Feb.12.		D.D. of S. & T. (1st Army), D.A. & Q.M.G. (4th Army), visited the Station Yard at LA GORGUE during "refilling".	
	Feb.13.		Lieut-Colonel A.B.E.CATOR, D.S.O., gives up Command of 2nd Battalion, Scots Guards, in order to take over the Command of 37th Brigade, 12th Division. Two Companies Pioneer Battalion move into ESTAIRES.	
	Feb.14.		Remaining 2 battalions and H.Q., 1st Guards Brigade moved into the LES LAURIERS area. H.Q., and two Battalions 58th Brigade took over the billets in LA GORGUE thus vacated. 4th Battalion Coldstream Guards (Pioneers) moved to LES LAURIERS area. Supplies for 1st Guards Brigade dumped in LES LAURIERS area in the afternoon.	
	Feb.15.		1st Guards Brigade, 4th Field Ambulance, and 1 Company Divisional Train moved into the area STEENVOORDE - St.SYLVESTRE - EECKE - GODEWAERSVELDE. 75th Field Company moved to EECKE. A.A. & Q.M.G., visited 2nd Army Headquarters, and attended a conference at 14th Corps H.Q. Supplies for 3rd Guards Brigade for consumption on the 17th dumped at LESTREM Station in the afternoon. Pioneer Battalion moves to HAZEBROUCK Area.	
	Feb.16.		3rd Guards Brigade Group (less 55th Field Company R.E.) move by rail to a Training Area at CALAIS. H.Q., and two battalions 2nd Guards Brigade move to LA GORGUE. D.A.C. and 3 Reserve Batteries. Pioneer Battalion - Move to HAZEBROUCK Area. 9th Field Ambulance to MERVILLE Area. 76th and 55th Field Companies to LES LAURIERS Area. 2nd Guards Brigade move to Rest Area, MERVILLE and LA GORGUE. Brigadier-General C.E.PEREIRA takes Command of the Division.	
	Feb.17.		The following move takes place :- Divisional Headquarters,) Cavalry.) to HAZEBROUCK. Cyclists.) H.Q. Train.	

Army Form C. 2118

WAR DIARY
or
INTELLIGENCE SUMMARY
(Erase heading not required.)

Instructions regarding War Diaries and Intelligence Summaries are contained in F. S. Regs., Part II. and the Staff Manual respectively. Title Pages will be prepared in manuscript.

Place	Date	Hour	Summary of Events and Information	Remarks and references to Appendices
	Feb.17. (Cont.)		1 Battery 61st Brigade R.F.A. moves. 55th Field Company R.E. to HAZEBROUCK Area.	
	Feb.18.		Cavalry and Cyclists move to ARNEKE Area. Supply Column move to WORMHOUDT. Artillery coming out of line concentrate in Area near MERVILLE vacated by the Divisional Ammunition Column.	
	Feb.19.		2nd Guards Brigade Group move to STEENVOORDE Area. Mobile Veterinary Section moves to HAZEBROUCK. 74th and 75th Brigades R.F.A. concentrate in HAZEBROUCK Area. 76th and 61st Brigades R.F.A. concentrate near ARNEKE. 14th Division commence movement by rail from the 14th Corps Area.	
	Feb.20.		Movement of 14th Division by rail continues. Band plays at 11-30 a.m. and 3-30 p.m. in the Market Square at HAZEBROUCK for the benefit of the population.	
	Feb.21.		Artillery less D.A.C. move to new Area ZEGGERS-CAPPEL - RUBROUCK - ESQUELBECQ Station.	
	Feb.22.		2nd Guards Brigade Group move to Area WORMHOUDT - RIETVELD - HERZEELE. Captain G.M.DARELL proceeds to 50th Brigade as Staff Captain.	
	Feb.23.		Headquarters move to ESQUELBECQ. D.A.C. move to Artillery Area. Household Cavalry and Divisional Squadron, and 55th Field Company R.E. move to LEDRINGHEM. Pioneer Battalion moves to HOUTKERQUE. H.Q., Divisional Train to ESQUELBECQ. Mobile Veterinary Section to LEDRINGHEM.	
	Feb.24.		Moves arranged for 1st Guards Brigade to move to CALAIS, and 3rd Guards Brigade to return to WORMHOUDT. Train Companies and Field Ambulances do not change.	

Army Form C. 2118

Instructions regarding War Diaries and Intelligence Summaries are contained in F. S. Regs., Part II. and the Staff Manual respectively. Title Pages will be prepared in manuscript.

WAR DIARY
or
INTELLIGENCE SUMMARY
(Erase heading not required.)

Place	Date	Hour	Summary of Events and Information	Remarks and references to Appendices
	Feb. 25.		1st Guards Brigade commence the move by rail to CALAIS. 3rd Guards Brigade return from CALAIS to WORMHOUDT Area. 2nd Guards Brigade move to Huts W. of POPERINGHE. Owing to frost the roads were very bad, and great difficulty was experienced with wagons. 1 Officer joined 3rd Battalion Grenadier Guards. (Captain E.S. WARD.)	
	Feb. 26.		The above move continues and is completed. Draft of 1 Officer and 30 O.R. arrived for 2nd Battalion Irish Guards. Draft of 20 O.R. joined 1st Battalion Scots Guards. Draft of 20 O.R. joined 4th Battalion Coldstream Guards. Major-General and A.A. & Q.M.G., visit Camps of 2nd Brigade.	
	Feb. 27.		A.A. & Q.M.G., visited POPERINGHE to see Institutes to be handed over by 6th Division.	
	Feb. 28.		Conference at Corps H.Q.; attended by G.O.C., G.S.O., and A.A. Q.M.G. 5-30 p.m. G.O.C. inspects the Artillery in their Rest Area.	
	Feb. 29.		Baths opened at ZEGGERS-CAPPEL and WORMHOUDT. A Company of Pioneer Battalion move to POPERINGHE to be employed on railway work. 200 men 2nd Brigade move to Farm just W. of YPRES (L.5.) to be employed and to be attached to 6th Division. G.O.C. inspects two Companies of the Train. (11 and 436).	

Army Form C. 2118

WAR DIARY
or
INTELLIGENCE SUMMARY

(Erase heading not required.)

G.D.A.
March 16.

Instructions regarding War Diaries and Intelligence Summaries are contained in F.S. Regs., Part II. and the Staff Manual respectively. Title Pages will be prepared in manuscript.

Place	Date	Hour	Summary of Events and Information	Remarks and references to Appendices
	March 1st.		Captain HARCOURT VERNON rejoined from 17th Corps and is attached "Q" Branch under instruction. Brigadier-General WARDROP, C.M.G., to G.O.C., R.A., XIV Corps. Lieutenant-Colonel W. EVANS, D.S.O., to command Guards Divisional Artillery. H.R.H. The Prince of Wales returns to England, Capt. LORD CLAUD HAMILTON accompanies.	
	" 2nd		Captain DUNN and 110 men arrive as draft for the Welsh Guards. Lieutenant J.B. KEENAN, 2nd Irish Guards, and 4 other ranks were wounded at Grenade practice. Orders received that 2nd Guards Brigade would move to CALAIS on the 5th instant.	
	" 3rd		G.O.C. visits Brigade at CALAIS. During Grenade practice at CALAIS, the following casualties occurred. Major Lord DESMOND FITZGERALD killed, Lieut. C.H.R.HANBURY, Lieut. T.E.G.NUGENT, and Rev. R.J.LANE-FOX and one man wounded. Military Secretary visits the Division.	
	" 4th.		Major BADEN POWELL slightly wounded owing to accident with a grenade. Drafts. 19 O.R. 2nd/Scots Guards. 20 O.R. 1st/Coldstream Guards. 20 O.R. 1st/Irish Guards.	
	" 5th.		1st Guards Brigade return from CALAIS. 3rd Guards Brigade move to Huts W. of POPERINGHE. 2nd Guards Brigade to CALAIS. Movement of these Brigades commenced.	
	" 6th.		Movements commenced on March 5th are completed.	
	" 7th.		Lieutenant-Colonel Hon. W.P.HORE-RUTHVEN, C.M.G., D.S.O., to be B.G., G.S. of the 8th Corps, and leaves to take up his appointment. Major (Temporary Lieutenant-Colonel) C.P. HEYWOOD to be G.S.O.1., Guards Division, but not to take up his appointment until March 25th. 9 officers arrive for Coldstream Guards, and one for Scots Guards.	
	" 8th.		Administrative Conference held at Corps Headquarters attended by the A.A. & Q.M.G., Lieutenant H.LLEWELYN, Grenadier Guards joins the Division as assistant instructor at the Divisional Bomb School. One Officer arrived for 1st/Irish Guards (Lt. OGILVY) and one officer for 1st/Grenadier Guards. (2/Lt. HARVARD).	

Army Form C. 2118

WAR DIARY
or
INTELLIGENCE SUMMARY
(*Erase heading not required.*)

Instructions regarding War Diaries and Intelligence Summaries are contained in F. S. Regs., Part II. and the Staff Manual respectively. Title Pages will be prepared in manuscript.

Place	Date	Hour	Summary of Events and Information	Remarks and references to Appendices
	March 9th		Recommendations for honours and awards submitted.	
	" 10th.		A.A. & Q.M.G., attended conference at 2nd Army Headquarters on entraining troops for tactical and other moves. Another bomb accident occurred at CALAIS. Three men were killed, 1 Officer (Lieut.HERMON-HODGE) and 20 men wounded.	
	" 11th.		A party of French Regimental Officers visited the Division.	
	" 12th.		Court of Enquiry on bomb accident in 2nd Guards Brigade received and passed to 14th Corps.	
	" 13th.		Parties of D.A.C. move forward to the new area.	
	" 14th.			
	" 15th.		Cinema Hall at POPERINGHE taken over by the Division. 3rd Guards Brigade move two Battalions to A.30, and two Battalions to YPRES. 1st Guards Brigade move 3 Battalions to Huts W. of POPERINGHE. 55th and 75th Field Companies R.E. move to the Canal Bank and YPRES. No. 4 Field Ambulance relieves a Field Ambulance of the 6th Division.	
	" 16th.		3rd Guards Brigade move into front line trenches and YPRES. 1st Guards Brigade move to A.30 and POPERINGHE. 2nd Guards Brigade commence return from CALAIS and move into billets at OUDEZEELE, WINEZEELE, ARNEKE. Field Companies R.E. relieve those of 6th Division. No. 3 and 9 Field Ambulances relieve those of 6th Division.	
	" 17th.		Move of 2nd Guards Brigade continued and completed. Bt. Lt.Col. G. TROTTER appointed to Command 27th Infantry Brigade. 1st Guards Brigade move up to A.30 Camps and the Canal. No. 3 Field Ambulance moves to PROVEN. Railhead changes to POPERINGHE siding. Refilling direct into Supply wagons. Supply Column is laid up. Following Units attached:—7th Section 2/Bridging Train, R.E., 4th Labour Bn., R.E., 10th Entrenching Bn., 4th Siege Battery, R.F.A.	

Army Form C. 2118

WAR DIARY
or
INTELLIGENCE SUMMARY

(Erase heading not required.)

Instructions regarding War Diaries and Intelligence Summaries are contained in F. S. Regs., Part II. and the Staff Manual respectively. Title Pages will be prepared in manuscript.

Place	Date	Hour	Summary of Events and Information	Remarks and references to Appendices
	March 18th.		Divisional Headquarters move to POPERINGHE. 1st Guards Brigade move up to the Canal Bank and trenches. 2nd Guards Brigade commence their move to POPERINGHE.	
	" 19th.		Divisional Cavalry and Cyclists move into new Divisional Area. 2nd Guards Brigade complete their move, 1 Battalion to POPERINGHE and Camp "B", one Battalion remaining at WINNEZEELE. Remainder of Artillery move to new Area.	
	" 20th.		Remaining Battalion 2nd Guards Brigade and Machine Gun Company move to POPERINGHE and Camp in G.13.b. respectively. Artillery Headquarters moved to POPERINGHE. Leave started again.	
	" 21st.		Army Commander inspects some of the Camps. Lt.Col. C. P. HEYWOOD, Coldstream Guards, reported arrival for duty as G.S.O.I of the Division from G.H.Q.	
	" 22nd.		New Redistribution of French and Belgian Interpreters came into force in consequence of the reduction of their number from 24 to 20 (vide D.R.O.758)	
	" 23rd.		G. in C. visited Divisional H.Q. during the afternoon.	
	" 24th.		Cinema Hall opened by a Concert by Band Coldstream Guards. G.O.C. attended.	
	" 25th.		Corps Commander D.G.M.S., G.H.Q. visited B Camp, the consequence of unfavourable report on sanitation of the camps. As a result, G.O.C. decided to evacuate Camp A on April 1st, Camp C will be handed over on that date. 1st Bn. Coldstream Guards and 1st Bn. Scots Guards (2nd Guards Brigade) relieved 4th Bn. Grenadier Guards and 2nd Bn. Scots Guards (3rd Guards Brigade) in the Right Sector of the trenches.	
	" 26th.		Water Board Conference was held at Div. H.Q. at 10 a.m., Brig-Gen. WILSON, C.E., XIVth Corps, presiding. D.A.Q.M.G., Guards Division and Lt. CONWAY, Cyclists attended as Representatives	

Army Form C. 2118

WAR DIARY
or
INTELLIGENCE SUMMARY
(Erase heading not required.)

Instructions regarding War Diaries and Intelligence Summaries are contained in F. S. Regs., Part II. and the Staff Manual respectively. Title Pages will be prepared in manuscript.

Place	Date	Hour	Summary of Events and Information	Remarks and references to Appendices
	March 26th (contd.)		3rd Bn. Grenadier Guards and 2nd Bn. Irish Guards (2nd Guards Brigade) relieved 1st Bn. Grenadier Guards and 1st Bn. Welsh Guards (3rd Guards Brigade) in Reserve.	
	" 27th		3rd Guards Brigade established its H.Q. in POPERINGHE.	
	" 28th		Instructions received for Major R. H. HERMON-HODGE, M.V.O., R. of O., Grenadier Guards (B.M.98th Inf. Bde.) to take up appointment of D.A.Q.M.G., Guards Division vice Major A.F.A.N.THORNE, Grenadier Guards to Regtl. duty as Second in Command of 1st Battalion Grenadier Guards. Corps Commander, G.O.C.Division and Brigadier 3rd Guards Brigade attended a Concert given by Band Coldstream Guards at Cinema Hall.	
	" 29th		2 N.C.O's and 20 O.R. arrived from T.M.School as personnel for Y.T.M.B., attached to 2nd Guards Brigade, now in process of formation. Major R. H. HERMON-HODGE, M.V.O., R. of O., Grenadier Guards, reported for duty as D.A.Q.M.G. of the Division. Major A.F.A.N.THORNE, D.S.O., Grenadier Guards posted to 1st Bn. Grenadier Guards. The Army Commander visited Divisional H.Q.	
	" 30th		Rev. H. E. HUBBARD, C.F.; C. of E., reported arrival for duty with Divisional Artillery on increase of Establishment.	
	" 31st			

ROUTINE AFTER ORDER
BY
MAJOR-GENERAL G.P.T.FEILDING. D.S.O.
COMMANDING GUARDS DIVISION.
****

Sunday, 5th March, 1916.

No. 698. GRENADES.

All grenades of DUNKIRK manufacture will be withdrawn. No more are on any account to be used in practice.

W.DARELL. Lieutenant-Colonel.

A.A.& Q.M.G.,GUARDS DIVISION.

Army Form C. 2118

WAR DIARY
or
INTELLIGENCE SUMMARY

(Erase heading not required.)

Instructions regarding War Diaries and Intelligence Summaries are contained in F.S. Regs., Part II. and the Staff Manual respectively. Title Pages will be prepared in manuscript.

Place	Date	Hour	Summary of Events and Information	Remarks and references to Appendices
April	1.		Captain Sir J. DYER, Bt., 1st Bn. Scots Guards, ordered to proceed to 2nd Army Headquarters as early as possible for instruction in "A" duties.	
"	2.		5 Officers, 10th Hussars, joined 2nd Brigade for instruction. Lt. Col. C.C.MARINDIN, A.A.& Q.M.G., 51st Division joins Headquarters for attachment.	
"	3.		3rd Guards Brigade relieve 1st Guards Brigade in the line.	
"	4.		Conference 5.30 p.m. to make arrangements for blocking all approaches into YPRES, to endeavour to apprehend certain suspected persons reported to be in the Area. Attended by Heads of Departments. Captain MILLER MUNDY arrives to take over command of the Household Cavalry Divisional Squadron. An Officer of the Roumanian Army visits the Division.	
"	5.		Meeting held at 3 p.m. in "Q" office to discuss division of billets in YPRES attended by members of XIVth and Canadian Corps, Guards Division and Canadian Division. Captain Hon. A. FITZROY hands over command of the Divisional Squadron and returns to England. An Officer of the Russian Army visits the Division and sees a parade of the 1st Bn. Irish Guards	
"	6.		System of contre-espionage comes into force.	
"	7.		-	
"	8.		Following Drafts arrive for the Division.:- The following drafts arrive from the Entrenching Battalion :- 1.G.G. 40. 1.C.G. 20. 1.S.G. 1 Offr. & 58. 2.G.G. 30. 2.C.G. 60. 2.S.G. 1 " 70. 3.G.G. 70. 3.C.G. 35. 4.G.G. 33. 4.C.G. 30 2.I.G. 30. Lecture on Trench Mortars by O.C., 2nd Army Trench Mortar School in POPERINGHE at 11.30 a.m.	
"	9.		Lt. Col. MARINDIN, A.A.& Q.M.G., leaves for attachment to 6th Division.	
"	10.		8 Officers arrived from No.7 Entrenching Bn. as reinforcements :-	

Army Form C. 2118

WAR DIARY
or
INTELLIGENCE SUMMARY

(Erase heading not required.)

Instructions regarding War Diaries and Intelligence Summaries are contained in F.S. Regs., Part II. and the Staff Manual respectively. Title Pages will be prepared in manuscript.

Place	Date	Hour	Summary of Events and Information	Remarks and references to Appendices
April	10. (contd.)		1 G.G. 1. 2 C.G. 1. 1 S.G. 1. 1 I.G. 2. 2 G.G. 1. 2 I.G. 1. 3.G.G. 1. Relief of 2nd Guards Brigade by 1st Guards Brigade commenced.	
April	11.		Billets of Irish Guards in POPERINGHE were shelled and there were the following casualties :- 6 killed, 12 wounded. Relief of 2nd Guards Brigade by 1st Guards Brigade completed.	
"	12.		Lt. B. C. WILLIAMS-ELLIS, Welsh Guards, who had been employed on Intelligence Work with Divisional Headquarters proceeds to report for duty to Intelligence G.H.Q. Leave is stopped from 18th instant.	
"	13.		Captain L. M. GIBBS is attached to Divisional Headquarters under instruction. 2/Lt. CASSY, 2nd Grenadier Guards is attached to Divisional Signal Company under instruction. 5 Officers join the Division - 3 C.G. 1., 2 C.G. 2., 1 S.G. 2. Leave is stopped altogether. All ranks to be back on 18th instant.	
"	14.		1 officer arrived for 2nd Bn. Scots Guards. Army Commander inspects portions of the 2nd Brigade and sees the 1st Bn. Scots Guards on parade and at training.	
"	15.		-	
"	16.		The Bishop of Khartoum preaches to the troops and holds a confirmation. 1 100 Other Ranks joined 1st Bn. Scots Guards. 1 officer joined the Division.	
"	17.		Party of officers go to Corps Headquarters to see experiments made with captured German instrument for picking up signals. 10 officers joined from the Base and Entrenching Bn. 90 O.R. arrived for 2nd Bn. Coldstream Guards.	
"	18.		All officers and men who were on leave are due back with their Units today.	

1875 Wt. W593/826 1,000,000 4/15 J.B.C. & A. A.D.S.S./Forms/C.2118.

Army Form C. 2118

WAR DIARY
or
INTELLIGENCE SUMMARY

(Erase heading not required.)

Instructions regarding War Diaries and Intelligence Summaries are contained in F.S. Regs., Part II. and the Staff Manual respectively. Title Pages will be prepared in manuscript.

Place	Date	Hour	Summary of Events and Information	Remarks and references to Appendices
April	19.		Germans made a raid on WIELTJE on evening of 19th. Two german prisoners were taken. The position was heavily shelled for some time. Our casualties were 4 Officers wounded, including Lt. THEWLIS, 1st Bn. Coldstream Guards. Total Casualties 95. 2nd Guards Brigade relieves 3rd Guards Brigade.	
"	20.		6 Officers joined the Division.	
"	21.		Corps Water Board met in "Q" Office at 10.30 a.m. Meeting at 12 noon with all Transport Officers of the Division to discuss the vacation of fields that could be handed back to the owners for pasturage. Reports on the subject to be sent in by 26th instant.	
"	22.		Captain TOWERS-CLARK gives up his appointment as Staff Captain, 1st Guards Brigade and returns to England as Instructor, Machine Gun School, GRANTHAM. Captain GIBBS becomes acting Staff Captain, 1st Guards Brigade.	
"	23.		49 O.R. draft arrived for 2nd Bn. Scots Guards.	
"	24.		.	
"	25.		Band of the Coldstream Guards left for PARIS to give a concert in aid of the French Red Cross Society, and from PARIS leave for England on the 29th. Captain G. LANE, 4th Bn. Coldstream Guards took up the duties of Camp Commandant temporarily vice Captain R. CLUTTERBUCK, Coldstream Guards, sick in England. Hostile Aeroplanes dropped a few Incendiary and other Bombs on the town this morning at 3.55.	
"	26.		-	
"	27.		G.O.C.2nd Army inspected 2nd Bn. Grenadier Guards in POPERINGHE at 1.45 p.m. and the 3rd Bn. Coldstream Guards in "A" Camp at 2.30 p.m.	
"	28.		G.O.C. inspected the 1st Line Transport, 2nd Guards Brigade at 9.30 a.m.	

Army Form C. 2118

WAR DIARY
or
INTELLIGENCE SUMMARY

(Erase heading not required.)

Instructions regarding War Diaries and Intelligence Summaries are contained in F. S. Regs., Part II. and the Staff Manual respectively. Title Pages will be prepared in manuscript.

Place	Date	Hour	Summary of Events and Information	Remarks and references to Appendices
April (contd)	28		Commander-in-Chief inspected 1st Bn. Irish Guards on parade in "C" Camp at 12.35 p.m. and was to have visited the Bn. Headquarters of the 1st Guards Brigade in POPERINGHE beginning at 3.45 p.m. The latter part of the programme was cancelled. Principal Chaplain (Presbyterian) and Assistant P.C. (R.C.) visited the Division today.	
April	29		POPERINGHE was shelled early this morning.	
"	30		G.O.C. went on leave. Brig.Gen.PERIERA assumed temporary command of Division. POPERINGHE was bombed at 3.45 a.m. today. 2 O.R. 2nd Bn. Coldstream Guards wounded.	

WAR DIARY
or
INTELLIGENCE SUMMARY

(Erase heading not required.)

Army Form C. 2118

HQ ATQ Bde 2a
Vol 10

Place	Date	Hour	Summary of Events and Information	Remarks and references to Appendices
May	1.		Lieut. ARNOLD, 1st Bn. Coldstream Guards, was wounded, also 18 other ranks in the Division and 1 man killed.	
"	2.		Lieut. A. FRIZELLE, 75th Bde., R.F.A., was killed.	
"			3 Officers arrive for 1st Bn. Scots Guards; 11 O.R. for Welsh Guards; 2 O.R. for Cyclist Coy, and 3 for Divisional Squadron.	
"			Casualties 4 killed, 19 wounded.	
"	3.		Lieut. SETON KARR joins Divisional Squadron.	
"			Casualties 6 killed, 18 wounded.	
"			Lt. Col. Hon. L. P. BUTLER gives up command of the 2nd Bn. Irish Guards on being appointed to command the 80th Infantry Brigade.	
"	4.		1st Guards Brigade commence relief of 2nd Guards Brigade.	
"			Casualties - Killed 2, wounded 22 - of which 1 was killed and 8 wounded by an enemy shell they were examining.	
"	5.		Relief of 2nd Guards Brigade by 1st Guards Brigade completed.	
"			Casualties - killed 1, wounded 9.	
"	6.		Brig. General HEYWORTH assumes temporary command of the Division.	
"			Casualties - killed 6, wounded 10.	
"			Lieut. Hon. B. B. PONSONBY wounded on night of 6th/7th.	
"	7.		The Corps Commander visits the Household Cavalry Squadron in their billets.	
"			Casualties - 5 officers wounded - Captain A. H. E. ASHLEY, 2nd Bn. Coldstream Guards. Lieut. Hon. B.B.PONSONBY, 2nd Bn. Grenadier Guards. 2/Lieut. J. W. GRAHAM, 1st Bn. Grenadier Guards. Major R. MARRYAT, 76th Bde., R.F.A. Captain H. T. BULKELEY, 76th Field Coy., R.E.	
"			3 O.R. killed and 66 wounded.	

Army Form C. 2118

WAR DIARY
or
INTELLIGENCE SUMMARY

(Erase heading not required.)

Instructions regarding War Diaries and Intelligence Summaries are contained in F. S. Regs., Part II. and the Staff Manual respectively. Title Pages will be prepared in manuscript.

Place	Date	Hour	Summary of Events and Information	Remarks and references to Appendices
W&V	8.	.	General FIELDING returns from leave. Casualties - Lieut. H.E.C.COLLINS, 4th Bn. Coldstream Guards, slightly wounded and at duty. 2/Lt. H. C. DAVIES, 75th Bde., R.F.A. " O. R. 2 killed, 34 wounded.	" "
"	9.	.	6 Officers joined. Brig. General HEYWORTH and 2/Lt. E. HOARE killed. Lieut. H. G. W. BRADLEY wounded. 2/Lt. E. HOARE killed O.R. killed 6. " wounded 34.	
"	10.	.	Captain MEYNELL, D.A.Q.M.G., 58th Division is attached Headquarters for instruction. Also Lt. Col. PREECE Cmmdg 2/8th Bn. London Regt. Brig. General de WINTON arrives to be attached to 1st Guards Brigade. Casualties - killed 1 O.R. wounded 7 O.R.	
"	11.	.	Temp. Capt. Lord E. STANLEY, 1st Bn. Grenadier Guards wounded. O.R. wounded 19. " killed 3. A shell struck Divisional Headquarters wounding two men. Relief of 3rd Guards Brigade by 2nd Guards Brigade commenced.	
"	12.	.	Lt. Col. PREECE completes his attachment and returns to England. Relief of 3rd Guards Brigade by 2nd Guards Brigade completed. Casualties - wounded 16.) Of which 9 of the 1st Bn. Coldstream Guards were killed killed 9.) and 9 were wounded in billets in POPERINGHE. Divisional Commander inspects the Train.	

1875 Wt. W593/826 1,000,000 4/15 J.B.C. & A. A.D.S.S./Forms/C. 2118.

WAR DIARY
or
INTELLIGENCE SUMMARY

(Erase heading not required.)

Army Form C. 2118

Instructions regarding War Diaries and Intelligence Summaries are contained in F.S. Regs., Part II. and the Staff Manual respectively. Title Pages will be prepared in manuscript.

Place	Date	Hour	Summary of Events and Information	Remarks and references to Appendices
May	13.	.	Casualties - 10 O.R. wounded.	
"	14.	.	" - 1 killed 18 wounded.	
"	15.	.	" - 1 killed 4 wounded.	

"	16.	.	4 Officers reported for attachment to the Division for 3 days :-
			          Lt. Col. H. D. LOWE, 6th Bn. Manchester Regt.
			          Lt. Col. W. J. McCAUSLAND, 74th Bn. Canadian Infantry.
			          Lt. Col. S. G. BECKETT, 75th Bn. Canadian Infantry.
			          Lt. Col. WARNER, 2/1st Kent Cyclists.
			 Casualties - Officers killed 1 :- Capt. H.E.A.PLATT, 1st Bn. Coldstream Guards.
			                wounded 2 :- 2/Lt. E.C.EVERARD (at duty) 3rd Bn. Coldstream Guards.
			                              Lieut. G.B.F.SAMUELSON, 1st Bn. Coldstream Guards.
			              O. R. 1 killed
			                  11 wounded.	

"	17.	.	The Arch-Bishop of Canterbury visited the Division and was taken to YPRES.
			 Casualties - 2 Officers killed :- 2/Lt. J. S. BURTON, 2nd Bn.Grenadier Guards.
			                             2/Lt. J. L. STEWART-RICHARDSON, 2nd Bn. Coldstream Guards.
			               O. R. 1 killed
			                  13 wounded.
			 3rd Guards Bde. M.G. Company moves to HOUTKERQUE.	

"	18.	.	Relief of Division by 20th Division commences, in accordance with movement Table - see General Staff Diary. Casualties - O. R. 2 killed 20 wounded.	

Army Form C. 2118

WAR DIARY
or
INTELLIGENCE SUMMARY
(Erase heading not required.)

Instructions regarding War Diaries and Intelligence Summaries are contained in F.S. Regs., Part II. and the Staff Manual respectively. Title Pages will be prepared in manuscript.

Place	Date	Hour	Summary of Events and Information	Remarks and references to Appendices

May	19.	.	Draft arrived as follows :-
			     2nd Bn. Irish Guards 1 O.R.
			     3rd " Grenadier Gds. 1 O.R.
			     R.F.A. 2 O.R.	

"	20.	.	Casualties - O.R. 6 killed. 17 wounded.	
"	21.	.	4 Officers attached to Division on 16th instant leave for England. Casualties - 2 killed 3 wounded.	
"	22.	.	Headquarters move to ESQUELBECQ and command of front line is handed over. Move is completed. Casualties - 3 killed 8 wounded.	
"	23.	.	Casualties - 1 wounded. 76th Bde., R.F.A. move to train at GRIS NEZ by march route.	
"	24.	.	Sanction given for 1st Guards Brigade to take billets in QUELMES, arrangements to be made with 17th Division.	
"	25.	.	Captain CLUTTERBUCK is appointed Adjutant to 2nd Bn. Coldstream Guards.	
"	26.	.	Capt. CLUTTERBUCK proceeds to 2nd Bn. Coldstream Guards. Capt. Sir JOHN DYER, Bt. is attached to Divisional Headquarters under instruction.	
"	27.	.	Ground examined with a view to hire for training purposes between ESQUELBECQ and WORMHOUDT. 89 O.R. joined 1st Bn. Welsh Guards.	
"	27.	.	Conference at Corps Headquarters attended by A.A.& Q.M.G. to discuss wages paid at Divisional Laundries. Casualties - 6 O.R. wounded.	

Army Form C. 2118

WAR DIARY
or
INTELLIGENCE SUMMARY

(Erase heading not required.)

Instructions regarding War Diaries and Intelligence Summaries are contained in F.S. Regs., Part II. and the Staff Manual respectively. Title Pages will be prepared in manuscript.

Place	Date	Hour	Summary of Events and Information	Remarks and references to Appendices
May	28.	.	Rent Officer No. 2 Area went over ground selected for Training with A.A.& Q.M.G. Drafts arrive as follows :- 2nd Bn. Grenadier Guards 10 O. R. 2nd " Coldstream " 35 " 3rd " " " 4 " 4th " " " 1 " 2nd " Irish " 9 " 1st " Grenadier Guards 24 " 4th " " " 15 " 2nd " Scots " 31 " 1st " Welsh " 7 " H.Q. 2nd Gds. Bde. 1 " 9th Field Ambulance. 1 " (A.S.C.).	
"	29.	.	Correspondence re. hiring of Training area sent to XIV Corps "G". 2nd Bn. Scots Guards commence move to HERZEELE and Pioneer Bn. take over their digging duties in works "L" &c.	
"	30.	.	Exchange between 2nd Scots Guards and Pioneer Bn. completed. Orders received to submit to Corps by 18th June retrospective recommendations for award of the Military Medal.	
"	31.	.	75th Field Coy., R.E. moves by march route from WINNEZEELE to LONGUENESSE. Orders received that ground selected and examined by rent officer between ESQUELBECQ and WORMHOUDT will not be taken for Training Area but that the 2nd Guards Brigade shall train near BOLLEZEELE.	

Army Form C. 2118

WAR DIARY
or
INTELLIGENCE SUMMARY

(Erase heading not required.)

Instructions regarding War Diaries and Intelligence
Summaries are contained in F.S. Regs., Part II.
and the Staff Manual respectively. Title Pages
will be prepared in manuscript.

Place	Date	Hour	Summary of Events and Information	Remarks and references to Appendices
	June 1st.		3rd Guards Brigade move to Camps K.L.M.and N.	
	2nd "		" " " " " : WORMHOUDT Area. Conference at Divisional Headquarters at 5.30 p.m., attended by Brigadiers C.R.A. and C.R.E. 1 O.R., 3rd Bn. Grenadier Guards wounded.	
	2nd.		2nd Guards Brigade move to training area near BOLLEZEELE. 76th Field Company, R.E., also move to this area. D.A.A.& Q.M.G. visits R.E.Park at WIMEREUX to see special works. Lieut. (Temp. Capt.) M.B.SMITH, D.S.O., proceeds to take over duties of Brigade Major, 61st Infantry Brigade temporarily. Captain Sir. John DYER, Bt., returns to Headquarters, 2nd Guards Brigade. The Army Commander is present on the Square at ESQUELBECQ at 8.0 a.m. and the 2nd Guards Brigade march past in Column of Route. 1 O.R. of 55th Field Company, R.E., wounded.	
	3rd.		10 officers joined the Division from No. 7 Entrenching Battalion and 1 from Hospital. List of Honours received.	
	4th.		The band and pipers of the Scots Guards played in the Square at ESQUELBECQ. The Officers of the 11th French Infantry were present also the G.O.C.Brigade. 1 O.R., 4th Bn. Coldstream Guards, wounded.	
	5th.		Major-General inspects the new laundry at WORMHOUDT and inspects the Supply Column. Captain H. C. LOYD, Coldstream Guards, is attached to Divisional Headquarters for instruction in "A" and "Q" work.	
	6th.		Lieut. J. W. LEWIS, 1st Bn. Welsh Guards, killed. 2 O.R. wounded - 1st Welsh Guards, 1 O.R. wounded - 4th Bn. Coldstream Guards.	

Army Form C. 2118

WAR DIARY
or
INTELLIGENCE SUMMARY
(Erase heading not required.)

Instructions regarding War Diaries and Intelligence Summaries are contained in F. S. Regs., Part II. and the Staff Manual respectively. Title Pages will be prepared in manuscript.

Place	Date	Hour	Summary of Events and Information	Remarks and references to Appendices
	June 7th.		1st Guards Brigade and 75th Field Company, R.E., leave the training area at St. OMER and commence movement by road to Camps K.L.M.N., halting for the night in the Area EBLINGHEM - SAN SYLVESTRE CAPPEL. 75th Field Company march to WINNIZEELE.	
	" 8th.		1st Guards Brigade reach Camps K.L.M.& N. 3rd " : " less 4th Bn. Grenadier Guards, move to WORMHOUDT Area. 4th Bn. Grenadier Guards move by road to TATINGHEM en route for 2nd Army School of Instruction at WISQUES.	
	" 9th.		4th Bn. Grenadier Guards moved by road to TATINGHEM as Battalion for 2nd Army School of Instruction at WISQUES.	
	" 10th.		16 N.C.O's went to STEENVOORDE as instructors to the 3rd Canadian Division. Captain G.A.O.LANE, Coldstream Guards, appointed A.D.C. to G.O.C.Guards Division.	
	" 11th.		Captain H. L. AUBREY FLETCHER, Grenadier Guards is attached to Divisional Headquarters for instruction. 1 O.R., 2nd Bn. Coldstream Guards, wounded. 1 Officer joined the 2nd Bn. Scots Guards from the Base.	
	" 12th.			
	" 13th.			
	" 14th.		2nd Guards Brigade moved by bus from the BOLLEZEELE Area to Camps A.B. and G.11.c.	

Army Form C. 2118

WAR DIARY
or
INTELLIGENCE SUMMARY

(Erase heading not required.)

Instructions regarding War Diaries and Intelligence Summaries are contained in F.S. Regs., Part II. and the Staff Manual respectively. Title Pages will be prepared in manuscript.

Place	Date	Hour	Summary of Events and Information	Remarks and references to Appendices
	June 15th		Two Bns. 1st Guards Brigade moved from Camp K & L to the Canal Bank. 4th Bn. Grenadier Guards moved from TATINGHEM to the BAVINCHORE Area. Two Bns. 3rd Guards Brigade moved from WORMHOUDT area to Camps K & L. 2nd Guards Brigade take over the line near HOOGE in the 2nd Canadian Division Area and are detached under the XIV Corps. 2nd Bn. Grenadier Guards - 1 O.R.Killed. 4th Bn. Coldstream " - 2 O.R.Wounded.	
"	16th		2 Bns. 1st Guards Brigade move into the line, the remainder of the Bde. to the Canal Bank or to ELVERDINGHE. 2 Bns. of the 3rd Guards Bde. move from the WORMHOUDT and BAVINCHORE Areas to Camps M & N. 1 officer joined the 2nd Bn. Irish Guards. Capt. LUXMORE BALL 1st Bn. Welsh Guards and Lt. BONHAM-CARTER 1st Bn. Grenadier Guards, Cmndg. 1st Gds. Bde. T.M.Btty and 1 O.R.; 3rd Bn. Coldstream Guards, wounded. 2/Lt. N. S. MONTGOMERY, 2nd Bn. Coldstream Guards, killed.	
"	17th.		2 Bns. 3rd Guards Bde. move from Camps K & L. to the Canal Bank. 2nd Bn. Coldstream Guards 1 O.R. Killed, 6 O.R. wounded. 3rd Bn. " : 2 O.R. : 1 O.R. : 1st Bn. Irish " : - - - : 4 O.R. : 3rd Bn. Grenadier " : - - - : 1 O.R. : 1st Bn. Coldstream" : - - - : 8 O.R. : 2nd Bn. Irish " : - - - : 1 O.R. : 1st Bn. Scots " Killed - Lt. M.N.SCHIFF (16 inst.) 13 O.R. Wounded - Lt. D.H.BRAND. 2/Lt. F.T.MANN. 23 O.R. 75th Coy., R.E. 1 O.R. wounded.	

Army Form C. 2118

WAR DIARY
or
INTELLIGENCE SUMMARY
(Erase heading not required.)

Instructions regarding War Diaries and Intelligence Summaries are contained in F.S. Regs., Part II. and the Staff Manual respectively. Title Pages will be prepared in manuscript.

Place	Date	Hour	Summary of Events and Information	Remarks and references to Appendices
	June	18	Divisional Headquarters move from ESQUELBECQ to St. SIXTE.	
			2 Bns. 3rd Guards Brigade move into the line.	
			2 Bns. 3rd Guards Brigade move to the Canal Bank.	
			Draft of 57 O.R. joined the 4th Bn. Coldstream Guards.	
			2nd Bn. Coldstream Guards 2 O.R.Killed, Lt. C.W.JANSON and 2 O.R.wounded.	
			3rd Bn. " " – – – – – 1 O.R. "	
			1st Bn. Irish " 2 O.R.Killed, Lt. F.H.N.LEE and 4 O.R. "	
			1st Bn. Scots " 1 O.R. " – – – 1 O.R. "	
			2/Gds. Bde. M.G.Coy.	
			1 officer joined 3rd Bn. Coldstream Guards and	
			1 officer – 2nd Bn. Grenadier Guards.	
		19.	2nd Bn. Coldstream Guards – 2 O.R. killed.	
			"X" Gds. T.M.Battery. – 1 O.R. " 4 O.R. wounded.	
			3rd Bn. Coldstream Guards – 1 O.R. " Lt. J. N. MARSHALL and 1 O.R. wounded.	
			1st Bn. Irish " – 2 O.R. " 7 O.R. wounded.	
			1st Bn. Coldstream " – 2 O.R. " 3 O.R. "	
			1st Bn. Scots " – – – 2 O.R. "	
			2nd Bn. Irish " – 1 O.R. killed Capt. P.L.BATTYE and 5 O.R. wounded.	
			1st Bn. Welsh " – – – 4 O.R. wounded.	
			1st Bn. Grenadier " – – – 2 O.R. "	
			75th Field Coy., R.E. – – –	
		20.	2nd Bn. Grenadier Guards – 2 O.R. killed 1 O.R. "	
			2nd Bn. Coldstream " – 1 O.R. " 9 O.R. "	
			3rd Bn. " " – 1 O.R. " –	
			1st Bn. Irish " – – – 2 O.R. "	
			1st Bn. Coldstream " – – – 1 O.R. "	
			1st Bn. Grenadier " – 1 O.R. killed 1 O.R. "	
			1st Bn. Welsh " – – – Lt. H.T.RICE and 9 O.R.wounded.	
			4th Bn. Coldstream " – – – 1 O.R. wounded.	
		21.	Capt. H. L. AUBREY FLETCHER, Grenadier Guards, left D.H.Q. for instruction at XIV Corps H.Qrs.	

WAR DIARY
or
INTELLIGENCE SUMMARY
(Erase heading not required.)

Army Form C. 2118

Instructions regarding War Diaries and Intelligence Summaries are contained in F.S. Regs., Part II. and the Staff Manual respectively. Title Pages will be prepared in manuscript.

Place	Date	Hour	Summary of Events and Information	Remarks and references to Appendices
	June	21	2nd Bn. Coldstream Guards. 3 O.R. killed, 7 O.R. wounded.	
			3rd Bn. " " 2 O.R. ; 2 O.R. ;	
			1st Bn. Irish ; 1 O.R. ;	
			2nd Bn. " ; 3 O.R. killed 3 O.R. ;	
			3rd Bn. Grenadier ; 1 O.R. ; Lt. Hon. H.E.EATON and 3 O.R. wounded.	
			4th Bn. " ; 1 O.R. wounded.	
			1st Bn. Welsh ; 2 O.R. killed 4 O.R. ;	
			61st Bde., R.F.A. 2 O.R. ;	
			74th " " 1 O.R. killed 1 O.R. ;	
			2nd Guards Brigade move from the line near HOOGE in the 2nd Canadian Division area to Camps D.E.O.G. & P.	
	"	22.	2nd Bn. Grenadier Guards 1 O.R. killed 1 O.R. wounded.	
			2nd Bn. Coldstream " 1 O.R. ;	
			3rd Bn. " " Capt. A.O.J.HOPE and 3 O.R. wounded.	
			1st Bn. Grenadier " 4 O.R. wounded.	
			1st Bn. Welsh " 2 O.R. ;	
			4th Bn. Coldstream " 2 O.R. ;	
			76th Bde., R.F.A. 2/Lt. V.L.S.SEARLE and 1 O.R. wounded.	
			Div. Signal Coy., R.E. 1 O.R. wounded.	
	"	23.	10 officers joined the Division from the Entrenching Bn.	
			2nd Bn. Grenadier Guards 1 O.R. wounded.	
			2nd Bn. Coldstream " 1 O.R. ;	
			3rd Bn. " " 2 O.R. killed 6 O.R. ;	
			1st Bn. Irish " 1 O.R. ;	
			1st Bn. Grenadier " 3 O.R. ;	
			4th Bn. " " 10 O.R. ;	
			2nd Bn. Scots " 2 O.R. killed 2 O.R. ;	
			55th Field Coy., R.E., 1 O.R. ;	

Army Form C. 2118

WAR DIARY
or
INTELLIGENCE SUMMARY
(Erase heading not required.)

Instructions regarding War Diaries and Intelligence Summaries are contained in F.S. Regs., Part II. and the Staff Manual respectively. Title Pages will be prepared in manuscript.

Place	Date	Hour	Summary of Events and Information	Remarks and references to Appendices
	June 23. contd.		1st Bn. Welsh Guards 2 O.R. killed Lt. J. L. G. KEARTON and 4 O.R. wounded.	
			61st Bde., R. F. A. — 1 O.R. wounded.	
			75th " " 1 O.R. killed 1 O.R. "	
			76th " " 2/Lt. V.L.S.SEARLE (wounded 22nd) died of wounds.	
			1 O.R. killed 1 O.R. wounded.	
	24.		1 Officer joined the Division from the Entrenching Battalion.	
			2nd Bn. Grenadier Guards. " ; 1 O.R. wounded...	
			2nd Bn. Coldstream " " 6 O.R. "	
			3rd Bn. " " 3 O.R. killed and 5 O.R. "	
			1st Bn. Grenadier " " 1 O.R. "	
			4th Bn. " " 2 O.R. killed 8 O.R. "	
			2nd Bn. Scots " " 1 O.R. "	
			"Z" Gds. T.M.Battery. " " 1 O.R. "	
	25.		2nd Bn. Grenadier Guards. 1 O.R. killed 3 O.R. wounded.	
			1st Bn. Irish " " 2 O.R. "	
			3rd Bn. Coldstream " 1 O.R. killed 11 O.R. "	
			1st Bn. Grenadier " " 3 O.R. "	
			4th Bn. Grenadier " " 1 O.R. "	
			2nd Bn. Scots " 1 O.R. killed 2 O.R. "	
			1st Bn. Welsh " 1 O.R. killed 2 O.R. "	
			3rd Gds. Bde. M.G.Coy. " " 1 O.R. "	
			4th Bn. Coldstream Gds. " " 1 O.R. "	
			Lieut. Viscount GAGE was attached to Divisional Headquarters acting A.D.C.	
	26.		2nd Bn. Coldstream Guards. 1 O.R. killed, 2/Lt. F. BUTLER-THWING and 2 O.R. wounded.	
			3rd Bn. " " 1 O.R. "	
			1st Bn. Irish " " 4 O.R. wounded.	
			1st Bn. Grenadier " " 1 O.R. wounded.	
			2nd Bn. Scots " 4 O.R. killed 6 O.R. "	
			R. F. A. " " 1 O.R. "	
			R. E. " " 1 D.R. "	

WAR DIARY
or
INTELLIGENCE SUMMARY

(Erase heading not required.)

Army Form C. 2118

Instructions regarding War Diaries and Intelligence Summaries are contained in F.S. Regs., Part II and the Staff Manual respectively. Title Pages will be prepared in manuscript.

Place	Date	Hour	Summary of Events and Information	Remarks and references to Appendices
	June	27.	2 Bns. 1st Guards Bde. move from the Canal Bank to Camps in A.30.	
			2 Bns. 2nd Guards Bde. move from Camps in A.30 to Canal Bank.	
			2nd Bn. Grenadier Guards. 2 O.R. wounded.	
			2nd Bn. Coldstream " 2 O.R. "	
			3rd Bn. " " 8 O.R. "	
			1st Bn. Irish " 1 O.R. "	
			1st Bn. Grenadier " 1 O.R. "	
			4th Bn. " " 4 O.R. "	
			2nd Bn. Scots " 1 O.R. "	
			1st Bn. Welsh " "	
		b	Lt. F. L. PUSCH 1st Bn. Irish Guards killed and Lt. R. H. SPINNEY 2nd Bn. Coldstream Guards wounded.	
			Major Viscount Gort, Grenadier Guards, is appointed G.S.O.II, G.H.Q.	
	"	28.	2nd Gds. Bde. less 2 Bns. move from Camps in A.30 to the line relieving 1st Gds. Bde. who move back to Camps in A.30.	
			2nd Bn. Coldstream Guards 9 O.R. wounded.	
			3rd Bn. " " 1 O.R. killed 3 O.R. "	
			1st Bn. Irish " 6 O.R. " 12 O.R. "	
			1st Bn. Grenadier " 1 O.R. "	
			4th Bn. " " 1 O.R. killed 1 O.R. "	
			2nd Bn. Scots " 3 O.R. " 5 O.R. "	
			1st Bn. Welsh " 3 O.R. "	
			3rd Gds. Bde. T.M.Battery (Stokes).. 2 O.R. "	
			4th Bn. Coldstream Guards - S.T. 1 O.R. "	
			55th Field Coy., R.E. 2/Lt./GARDINER killed (27th) and 1 O.R. wounded.	
			75th " " " 1 O.R. killed 10 O.R. wounded.	
			No.9 Field Ambulance 2 O.R. " "	
	"	29.	2nd Bn. Coldstream Guards 1 O.R. wounded.	
			1st Bn. Irish " 1 O.R. killed 4 O.R. wounded.	
			3rd Bn. Grenadier " 1 O.R. "	
			1st Bn. Coldstream " 1 O.R. killed 1 O.R. "	
			1st Bn. Scots " 4 O.R. "	

Army Form C. 2118

WAR DIARY
or
INTELLIGENCE SUMMARY
(Erase heading not required.)

Instructions regarding War Diaries and Intelligence Summaries are contained in F. S. Regs., Part II. and the Staff Manual respectively. Title Pages will be prepared in manuscript.

Place	Date	Hour	Summary of Events and Information	Remarks and references to Appendices
	June 29. contd.		1st Bn. Grenadier Guards 1 O.R. wounded.	
			1st Bn. Welsh " 3 O.R. "	
			75th Field Coy., R.E. 1 O.R. "	
	" 30.		3rd Bn. Grenadier Guards 5 O.R. killed 7 O.R. wounded.	
			1st Bn. Coldstream " " 2 O.R. "	
			1st Bn. Scots " " 5 O.R. "	
			2nd Bn. Irish " " 2 O.R. "	
			1st Bn. Welsh 1 O.R. killed.	
			3rd Gds. Bde. M.G.Coy. 1 O.R. "	
			"X" T.M.Battery. 1 O.R. "	

Army Form C. 2118

WAR DIARY
or
INTELLIGENCE SUMMARY

(Erase heading not required.)

July 1916

Place	Date	Hour	Summary of Events and Information					Remarks and references to Appendices
				Killed.		Wounded.		
				O.R.	O.R.	O.R.	O.R.	
July	1.		3rd Bn. Grenadier Guards.	-	1	-	3	
			1st Bn. Coldstream Guards.	-	-	-	1	
			1st Bn. Scots Guards.	-	-	-	2	
			2nd Bn. Irish Guards.	-	-	-	2	
			2nd Gds. Bde. M.G. Company.	-	-	-	1	
			4th Bn. Grenadier Guards.	-	-	-	1	
			2nd Bn. Scots Guards.	-	-	-	1	
			1st Bn. Welsh Guards.	-	-	-	5	
			Divnl. Signal Coy., R.E.	-	-	-	1	
			D.A.C.	-	-	-	1	
"	2.		1 Officer joined 2nd Bn. Scots Guards.					
				Killed.		Wounded.		
				O.R.	O.R.	O.R.	O.R.	
			3rd Bn. Grenadier Guards.	-	1	-	4	
			1st Bn. Coldstream Guards.	-	-	-	3	
			1st Bn. Scots Guards.	-	-	-	4	
			2nd Bn. Irish Guards.	-	1	-	7	
			1st Bn. Grenadier Guards.	-	-	-	1	
			4th Bn. Grenadier Guards.	-	-	-	3	
			1st Bn. Welsh Guards.	-	4	-	43	2/Lt. G. CRAWFORD-WOOD Killed. Capt. G.C.L. INSOLE Wounded.
			61st Bde., R.F.A.	-	-	-	2	
			55th Field Coy., R.E.	-	-	-	1	
"	3.		3rd Bn. Grenadier Guards.	-	2	-	5	
			1st Bn. Scots Guards.	-	-	-	1	Lt. F.P.H. SYNGE Wounded.
			2nd Bn. Irish Guards.	-	4	-	37	Lt. F.L.M. PYM & 9 O.R. Missing.
			1st Bn. Grenadier Guards.	-	1	-	2	
			4th Bn. Grenadier Guards.	-	-	-	1	
			1st Bn. Welsh Guards.	-	5	-	19	Lt. C. de WIART Wounded. 1 O.R. Missing.
			3rd Gds. Bde. T.M.Btty.	-	1	-	-	

Army Form C. 2118

WAR DIARY
or
INTELLIGENCE SUMMARY

(Erase heading not required.)

Instructions regarding War Diaries and Intelligence Summaries are contained in F.S. Regs., Part II. and the Staff Manual respectively. Title Pages will be prepared in manuscript.

Place	Date	Hour	Summary of Events and Information	Remarks and references to Appendices
July	3.	(cntd)		
			Killed. Wounded.	
			O.R. 2. O.R.	
			61st Bde., R.F.A. - - 1.	
			"Z" Gds. T.M.Btty. - - 3. Lt. H. L. PENFOLD Wounded.	
			76th Field Coy., R.E. - - 3.	
"	4.		3rd Bn. Grenadier Guards. 1 - 2	
			1st Bn. Coldstream Guards. - - 2	
			1st Bn. Scots Guards. - - 2	
			2nd Bn. Irish Guards. 1 - 9	
			1st Bn. Grenadier Guards. 5 - 12	
			4th Bn. Grenadier Guards. - - 3	
			2nd Bn. Scots Guards. - - 4	
			1st Bn. Welsh Guards. - - 2 1 O.R. Missing.	
			3rd Gds. Bde. M.G.Coy. - - 1	
			4th Bn. Coldstream Guards 1 - 1	
			D.A.C.	
			Captain M. B. SMITH, D.S.O. appointed Brigade Major 1st Guards Brigade.	
			Killed. Wounded.	
			O.R. O.R.	
			3rd Bn. Grenadier Guards. - - 1	
			1st Bn. Coldstream Guards. - - 1	
			1st Bn. Scots Guards. - - 1	
			1st Bn. Grenadier Guards. - - ...	
			2nd Bn. Irish Guards. - - ... Lt. G.L.B.JAMES (Att. 2nd Gds. Bde./1	
			T.M.Btty) Wounded (Shell shock).	
			4th Bn. Grenadier Guards. - - 1	
			2nd Bn. Scots Guards. - - 5	
			55th Field Coy., R.E. - - 2	
			Signal Coy., R.E. - - 1	
"	5.		Band of Scots Guards went to Paris.	

Army Form C. 2118

WAR DIARY
or
INTELLIGENCE SUMMARY
(Erase heading not required.)

Instructions regarding War Diaries and Intelligence Summaries are contained in F. S. Regs., Part II. and the Staff Manual respectively. Title Pages will be prepared in manuscript.

Place	Date	Hour	Summary of Events and Information	Remarks and references to Appendices
July	6		2 Bns. 1st Gds. Bde. move from Camps D.E.& O. to Trois Tours and Canal Bank, relieving 2 Bns. 3rd Gds. Bde. who return to Camps D. & E.	
			1st Bn. Coldstream Guards. 1 O.R. Killed. 3 O.R. Wounded.	
			1st Bn. Scots Guards. — " 3 "	
			1st Bn. Grenadier Guards. 1 " — "	
			4th Bn. Grenadier Guards. — " 5 "	
			2nd Bn. Scots Guards. 1 " 11 " 2 O.R. Missing.	
			The Corps Commander inspected 2nd Bn. Grenadier Guards.	
"	7.		2 Bns. 1st Gds. Bde. move from Trois Tours and Canal Bank to the line, relieving 2 Bns. 3rd Gds. Bde. who return to Camps D. & E.	
			1st Gds. Bde. less 2 Bns. move from Camps D. & E. to the Canal Bank and Trois Tours, relieving the 3rd Gds. Bde.	
			4th Bn. Grenadier Guards. 4 O.R. Killed. 20 O.R. Wounded.	Lt.(Temp.Cpt.) M.CHAPMAN Wnded.
			1st Bn. Coldstream Guards. 1 " 2 "	1/Lt.(T.Lt.) W.L.FARNSWORTH "
			2nd Bn. Scots Guards. 1 " 1 "	
			4th Bn. Coldstream Guards. — " 2 "	
			76th Bde., R. F. A. — " 1 "	
			Major M. CRICHTON MAITLAND takes over Command of 1st Bn. Grenadier Guards, vice Lt. Col. St. LEGER GLYN.	
"	8.		2nd Bn. Grenadier Guards. 1 O.R. Wounded.	
			3rd Bn. Coldstream Guards. 3 "	
			3rd Bn. Grenadier Guards. 1 "	
			1st Bn. Coldstream Guards. 1 O.R. Killed. 3 "	
			2nd Bn. Irish Guards. — " 1 "	
			4th Bn. Grenadier Guards. — " 2 "	
			61st Bde., R. F. A. — " 1 "	
			76th " " 1 "	
			1 officer joined 2nd Bn. Irish Guards. and 1 officer joined 2nd Bn. Grenadier Guards.	
			1 " " 3rd Gds. Bde. M.G.Coy.	

Army Form C. 2118

WAR DIARY
or
INTELLIGENCE SUMMARY
(Erase heading not required.)

Instructions regarding War Diaries and Intelligence Summaries are contained in F.S. Regs., Part II. and the Staff Manual respectively. Title Pages will be prepared in manuscript.

Place	Date	Hour	Summary of Events and Information	Remarks and references to Appendices
July	9.		2nd Bn. Grenadier Guards. 3 O.R. Wounded.	
			1st Bn. Irish Guards. 3 " "	
			3rd Bn. Coldstream Guards. 4 O.R. Killed. 16 O.R. Wounded. Lt. J.S.WILMOT-SITWELL Killed. +	
				1 O.R. Missing.
			1st Bn. Scots Guards. - " 1 "	
			4th Bn. Coldstream Guards. 1 " 5 " 2/Lt. H.J. WILLIAMS Killed. X	
			"X" Gds. T.M.Bty. ... ... 2/Lt. B.W.C.A.RENDLE Wounded.	
"	10.		2nd Bn. Grenadier Guards. 6 O.R. Wounded. Capt. A.K.S. CUNINGHAME Slightly wnded & at duty‡	
			2nd Bn. Coldstream Guards. 2 "	
			3rd Bn. Coldstream Guards. 3 "	
			1st Gds. Bde. M.G.Coy. 1 "	
			3rd Bn. Grenadier Guards. 1 2 "	
			1st Bn. Coldstream Guards. 2 "	
			1st Bn. Scots Guards. 1 "	
			2nd Bn. Irish Guards. 1 "	
			A. S. CM	
"	11.		Four Officers & 100 men, composed of 20 men from each Regiment of Foot Guards in the Division, proceeded to PARIS for review under the Command of the H.Q.2nd Bn. Scots Guards (Lt.Col.R.S. TEMPEST). Capt. Sir J. S. DYER; Scots Guards, appointed Staff Capt. of the 2nd Gds. Bde.	
			2nd Bn. Grenadier Guards. 4 O.R. Wounded.	
			3rd Bn. Coldstream Guards. 3 "	
			3rd Bn. Grenadier Guards. 3 O.R. Killed. - "	
			1st Bn. Scots Guards. - " 4 "	
			2nd Bn. Irish Guards. - " 1 "	
			76th Bde., R.F.A. - " 4 "	
			74th Field Coy., R.E. ... ... 2/Lt. R. McLEAN Killed. X	

WAR DIARY
or
INTELLIGENCE SUMMARY
(Erase heading not required.)

Army Form C. 2118

Place	Date	Hour	Summary of Events and Information	Remarks and references to Appendices
July	12.		2nd Bn. Grenadier Guards. 10 O.R. Wounded.	X
			2nd Bn. Coldstream Guards. 2 " "	
			3rd Bn. Grenadier Guards. 1 " "	
			3rd Bn. Coldstream Guards. 7 " "	
			1st Bn. Scots Guards. 2 " "	
			2nd Bn. Irish Guards. 1 " Killed	
			1st Bn. Irish Guards. 1 " " 2 O.R. Wounded. Lt. S.E.F.CHRISTY (11th) killed.	
			75th Field Coy., R.E. - 1 " "	
"	13.		2 officers joined 1st Bn. Grenadier Guards.	
			2nd Bn. Grenadier Guards. 1 O.R. Killed. 17 O.R. Wounded.	
			1st Bn. Irish Guards. 2 " " 1 " "	
			1st Bn. Coldstream Guards. 1 " " 1 " "	
			2nd Bn. Irish Guards. - 9 " "	
			1st Bn. Scots Guards. 2 " " 2 " "	
			4th Bn. Coldstream Guards. 1 " " 2 " "	
			74th Bde., R. F. A. - 2 " "	
			No.3 Field Ambulance. - 1 " "	
			A. S. O.	
			Lt. (T.Cpt.) E.W.M.GRIGG, Grenadier Guards, appointed B.M. 2nd Gds. Bde. vice Cpt. G.E.C.RASCH, D.S.O., Grenadier Guards who returns to Regtl. Duty. Cpt. H.L.AUBREY-FLETCHER, M.V.O., Gren:Gds. appointed G.S.O.III, Gds Divn. vice Lt. (T.Cpt.) E.W.M.GRIGG - To take effect 16/7/16.	
"	14.		2nd Bn. Gren:Gds. 2 O.R. Wounded.	
			2nd Bn. Coldstream Guards. 2 " "	
			1st Bn. Irish Guards. 7 " "	
			3rd Bn. Grenadier Guards. 1 " "	
			1st Bn. Coldstream Guards. 2 " "	
			1st Bn. Scots Guards. 3 " "	
			74th Bde., R. F. A. 1 " "	

Army Form C. 2118

WAR DIARY
or
INTELLIGENCE SUMMARY
(Erase heading not required.)

Instructions regarding War Diaries and Intelligence Summaries are contained in F.S. Regs., Part II. and the Staff Manual respectively. Title Pages will be prepared in manuscript.

Place	Date	Hour	Summary of Events and Information	Remarks and references to Appendices
July	14	contd	Being a French National Fete Day, a review, at which the Detachment from the Guards Division, under Lt. Col. R. TEMPEST, Scots Guards, and the Scots Guards Band were present, took place in PARIS.	
"	15.		Relief of 2nd Guards Brigade by 3rd Guards Brigade commenced night of 13/14 and completed night of 14/15. "G" Camp handed over to Corps Troops. All troops are ordered to leave POPERINGHE. Sanitary Section move to Balloon Camp. Casualties - Lt. J. N. MARSHALL (wounded at duty) 5 O.R. Killed. 9 O.R. wounded.	
"	16.		Band of the Scots Guards return from PARIS. 10 O.R. wounded.	
"	17.		Major BARCROFT (att. D.H.Q. under instruction) ordered to proceed and take up appointment of G.S.O.III 9th Corps, and departs 6.30 a.m. 19th. Camp "P" is handed over to the Division to be completed. Work put in hand. Lt. Hon. A.E.F.YORKE offered appointment of Town Major, YPRES, but prefers to remain as O.C. Salvage Squad. Lt. (Temp.Capt.) J. G. LUMSDEN 2nd Bn. Scots Guards wounded. 2 O.R. Killed - 20 O.R.Wounded.	
"	18.		Lt. S. W. BRIDGE, 12th Bn. Royal Fusiliers joins the Division as Divisional Gas Officer. Casualties 3 O.R. killed. - Lt. Col. FOLLETT and 15 O.R. wounded. Detachment that went to PARIS for the review on July 14th returned.	
"	19.		Casualties - Lt. D. CAMPBELL 3rd Bn. Coldstream Guards and 5 O.R. killed. Lt. M. H. MACMILLAN wounded at duty and 34 O.R. wounded, 22 of which belonged to 4 Bn. Grenadier Guards owing to one shell at Machine Gun Farm. One Company Pioneer Bn. move to BURGOMASTER Farm.	
"	20.		Casualties 6 O.R. killed 11 O.R. wounded.	
"	21.		" 2/Lt. P. GOLD, 2nd Bn. Scots Guards and 1 O.R. killed. Lt. A.L.MAYNARD, 2nd Bn. Scots Guards & 10 O.R. wounded.	

Army Form C. 2118

WAR DIARY
or
INTELLIGENCE SUMMARY
(Erase heading not required.)

Instructions regarding War Diaries and Intelligence Summaries are contained in F.S. Regs., Part II. and the Staff Manual respectively. Title Pages will be prepared in manuscript.

Place	Date	Hour	Summary of Events and Information	Remarks and references to Appendices
July	22.		Casualties - 2 O.R. killed (Lt.(Temp.Capt.) Hon. A.J.P.HOWARD 2/Scots Guards, and 12 O.R. wounded. Lt. R. O. HAMBRO, 3rd Bn. Coldstream Guards, is attached to Divisional Headquarters under instruction.	
"	23.		Wounded - Lt. W.E.C.BAYNES, 2nd Coldstream Guards and 15 O.R. Killed 2 O.R. Orders received for relief of the Division by the 4th Division.	
"	24.		Casualties - killed 6 O.R. wounded 17 O.R. A.A. & Q.M.G., 4th Division came to make arrangements regarding handing over.	
"	25.		Casualties - Wounded Lt. H.T.RICE(at duty) and O.R. 13. Killed O. R. 2. 2 Bns. of 2nd Bde. moved to BOLLEZEELE.	
"	26.		Casualties - 2/Lt. MACLEAR 4th Grenadier Guards and O.R. 4 killed. Cpt. R. V. POLLOK 1st Irish Gds. and 24 O.R. wounded. O.R. 2 Missing. Two Bns. of 2nd Bde. moved to BOLLEZEELE, 2 Bns. of 1st Bde. moved to M.N.Camps.	
"	27.		Casualties - killed 1 O.R. wounded 3 O.R. D.H.Q. moved to ESQUELBECQ. 1/Gds. Bde. to POPERINGHE - HOUTKERQUE - HERZEELE. 3/Gds. Bde. to MILLAIN Area. 55th Fd. Coy.) 75th " ") LEDRINGHEM. 1 Coy. 4/Cold) Guards.	
"	28.		Casualties killed O.R.1 wounded O.R.12. Major DAVIDSON, D.S.O., G.S.O.2 leaves the Division and is appointed G.S.O.1 Royal Naval Division.	

Army Form C. 2118

WAR DIARY
or
INTELLIGENCE SUMMARY

(Erase heading not required.)

Instructions regarding War Diaries and Intelligence Summaries are contained in F.S. Regs., Part II. and the Staff Manual respectively. Title Pages will be prepared in manuscript.

Place	Date	Hour	Summary of Events and Information	Remarks and references to Appendices
July	30.		1st Gds. Bde. railed to St. POL and marched to BOUQUEMAISON & NEUVILLETTE. 2nd Gds. Bde. " " Pt. HOUVIN " LUCHEUX. 3rd Gds. Bde. " " FREVENT " HALLOY. D.H.Q. moved to DOULLENS.	
"	31.		Division completed its move. The Scots Guards band left for England.	

W. Darell Lt. Col.
A.A. & Q.M.G.
for Major-General,
Commanding Guards Division.

A. A. & Q. M. G.

GUARDS DIVISION

AUGUST 1916

Box 1197

Original 25th to 31st transferred to WO 154/17

Army Form C. 2118

WAR DIARY
or
INTELLIGENCE SUMMARY

Administrative Staff,
Guards Division.

(Erase heading not required.)

Place	Date	Hour	Summary of Events and Information	Remarks and references to Appendices
August	1.		1st Guards Brigade moved to SARTON and VAUCHELLES (H.Qrs. at VAUCHELLES-LES-AUTHIE). 2nd Guards Brigade. " BOIS de WARNIMONT (H.Qrs. at AUTHIE). 3rd Guards Brigade " BUS-LES-ARTOIS (H.Qrs. at BUS-LES-ARTOIS). Divisional Headquarters move to BUS-LES-ARTOIS.	
"	2.		Guards Divisional Artillery moved into the area THIEVRES, AUTHIE, St.LEGER-LES-AUTHIE. Casualties. 2nd Irish Guards. Wounded 5 O.R. Capt. E. SEYMOUR, M.V.O., Grenadier Guards, R. of O., joined and took over the duties of G.S.O.II vice Lt.Col.N.R.DAVIDSON, D.S.O., appointed G.S.O.I, 2nd Cavalry Division.	
"	3.		Casualties. 3rd Bn. Grenadier Guards - 2/Lt. M. THRUPP wounded accidentally. 2nd Bn. Irish Guards. - Wounded, Lt. H.R.HORDERN and 10 O.R. Band of Irish Guards arrived this evening and were billeted with 1st Bn. Irish Guards.	
"	4.		Casualties - 2nd Bn. Irish Guards - Wounded 3 O.R.	
"	5.		" - " - Wounded 2 O.R.	
"	6.		" - 4th Bn. Coldstream Guards. - Wounded 1 O.R. 2 Bns and Bde.H.Qrs., 3rd Guards Brigade moved to ARQUEVES. 2 " 2nd Guards Brigade returned from digging and billeted in the BOIS de WARNIMONT The Major-General and A.A.& Q.M.G. went to HARFLEUR, Guards Division Base Depot.	
"	7.		The Major-General and A.A.& Q.M.G. returned.	
"	8.		Band of Irish Guards under Lt. PYM joined Divisional Headquarters.	

Army Form C. 2118

WAR DIARY
or
INTELLIGENCE SUMMARY

(Erase heading not required.)

Instructions regarding War Diaries and Intelligence Summaries are contained in F. S. Regs., Part II. and the Staff Manual respectively. Title Pages will be prepared in manuscript.

Place	Date	Hour	Summary of Events and Information	Remarks and references to Appendices
August	9.		His Majesty visited the Headquarters of the Division. He also saw 2 Bns. of the 3rd Guards Bde. and visited the Headquarters of the 2nd Guards Brigade. The 2nd Guards Brigade relieved the 75th Inf. Bde. (25th Division) in the line - 2 Bns. front line, and 2 Bns. support. Bde.H.Qrs. MAILLY-MAILLET.	
"	10.		D.H.Q. moved to BERTRANCOURT. The 3rd Guards Brigade relieved the 74th Inf. Bde. in the line - 2 Bns. in front line, 2 in support. H.Qrs. at BEAUSSART. 1st Bde. 2 Bns. of the 1st Guards Brigade moved to BERTRANCOURT. G.O.C., Guards Division, took over command of the Division frontage at 6 p.m. Casualties - Wounded 2 O.R.	
"	11.		Casualties - Killed 2 O.R. Wounded 20 O.R. 1st Guards Brigade relieved the 71st Bde. in the line - 2 Bns. front line, 1 Bn. P.18.b., 1 Bn. BERTRANCOURT. 1 Bn., 2nd Guards Brigade moved to BERTRANCOURT. Lord DALKEITH joins D.H.Q. as A.D.C.	
"	12.		Casualties - Killed 3 O.R., wounded 30 O.R., 1 Bn., 3rd Guards Brigade moved back to BUS.	
"	13.		Casualties - Wounded Lt. T.K.BARNSLEY, 1st Bn. Coldstream Guards (Shell shock) & 7 O.R. Killed 3 O.R.	
"	14.		Casualties - Killed 2 O.R., Wounded 17 O.R. 1st Guards Brigade was relieved by a Bde. of the 6th Division and moved to BERTRANCOURT & LOUVENCOURT.	
"	15.		Casualties - Killed 3 O.R., wounded 12 O.R. The 2nd Guards Brigade was relieved by the 6th Division and moved - Bde.H.Qrs. to BUS. 2 Bns. to BERTRANCOURT. 2 Bns. to MAILLY MAILLET.	
"	16.		Casualties - Wounded 3 O.R.	

Army Form C. 2118

WAR DIARY
or
INTELLIGENCE SUMMARY
(Erase heading not required.)

Instructions regarding War Diaries and Intelligence Summaries are contained in F.S. Regs., Part II. and the Staff Manual respectively. Title Pages will be prepared in manuscript.

Place	Date	Hour	Summary of Events and Information	Remarks and references to Appendices
August	16.	contd	1st Guards Brigade relieved a Brigade of the 20th Division in the line. - 2 Bns. front line, 2 Bns. support. Guards Division comes under the command of the 5th Corps.	
"	17.		Casualties - Killed 2 O.R., wounded 4 O.R. D.H.Q. moved to the Chateau at COUIN and relieved 20th Division. 2nd Guards Brigade relieved a Bde. of the 20th Division in the line. Bde.H.Qrs. at SAILLY-au-BOIS.	
"	18.		Casualties - killed 2 O.R., wounded 19 O.R.	
"	19.		Casualties 12 O.R. wounded. The 3rd Guards Brigade was relieved by the 5th Inf. Bde. and moved to BUS-LES-ARTOIS.	
"	20.		Casualties - Lt. G.STUBLEY, 2nd Bn. Coldstream Guards and 14 O.R. wounded, 1 O.R. killed. 1st Guards Brigade was relieved in the line by 6th Inf. Bde. and moved into the BOIS-de-WARNIMONT. 3rd Guards Brigade move to VAUCHELLES and SARTON.	
"	21.		Casualties - wounded 5 O.R., killed 1 O.R. Division was relieved by 2nd Division. D.H.Q. moved to Chateau, BUS-les-ARTOIS. 2nd Guards Brigade was relieved by 99th Inf. Bde. and moved to BUS-les-ARTOIS.	
"	22.		Casualties - Wounded 3 O.R. (accidentally, due to explosion of bomb store). 3rd Guards Brigade moved to GEZAINCOURT Area.	
"	23.		Casualties - Lt. KELLET, 74th Bde., R.F.A. accidentally killed. 1 O.R. wounded. D.H.Q. moved to BEAUVAL. 1st Guards Brigade moved to BEAUVAL. 2nd Guards Brigade moved to AMPLIER.	
"	24.		D.H.Q. moved to VIGNACOURT. 1st Guards Brigade moved to FLESSELLES. 2nd Guards Brigade moved to NAOURS. 3rd Guards Brigade moved to VIGNACOURT. Guards Division leaves V Corps and joins X Corps.	

Original Removed to
W/b 154/17

Army Form C. 2118

WAR DIARY
or
INTELLIGENCE SUMMARY

(Erase heading not required.)

Instructions regarding War Diaries and Intelligence Summaries are contained in F. S. Regs., Part II. and the Staff Manual respectively. Title Pages will be prepared in manuscript.

Place	Date	Hour	Summary of Events and Information	Remarks and references to Appendices
August	25.		Guards Division rejoins XIV Corps.	
"	26		D.H.Q. moved by road to TREUX.	
"	27		1st Guards Brigade entrained at CANAPLES and detrained at MERICOURT and marched to MEAULTE.	
"	28		2nd Guards Brigade " " " " and marched to MORLANCOURT.	
"	29		3rd Guards Brigade " VIGNACOURT " " and billeted there.	
			Transport moved by Brigade Groups by road.	
			Pioneer Bn. go into the line to dig under 20th Division.	
"	30		Casualties - wounded 2 O.R.	
			" - " 4 O.R.	
"	31		Casualties - wounded 4 O.R.	

W. Jack B.M.
Major-General,
Commanding GUARDS DIVISION.

Diaries
SEPT 1916
↓
March 1918

Army Form C. 2118.

WAR DIARY
INTELLIGENCE SUMMARY

(Erase heading not required.)

Administrative Staff
Headquarters
Guards Division.

September 1916

Vol 14

Date	Hour	Summary of Events and Information	Remarks and references to Appendices
Septr. 1.	—	Guards Divisional Artillery rejoined the division and billet in SAILLY-le-SEC and VAUX. General court martial reassembled at D.H.Q. and closed at 9 p.m. Casualties wounded 6 O.R.	
" 2.	—	Casualties wounded 6 O.R.	
" 3.	—	Casualties wounded 4 O.R. killed 1 O.R. Guards Divisional Artillery moved to BOIS des TAILLES to take over a portion of the line.	
" 4.	—		
" 5.	—		
" 6.	—		
" 7.	—	Casualties wounded 6 O.R.	
" 8.	—	Casualties killed 3 O.R. wounded 12 O.R. Division receives orders to relieve 16th Division in the line.	
" 9.	—	3rd Guards brigade moved into the line in relief of the 16th Division. 2nd Guards brigade moved to HAPPY VALLEY. Casualties killed 4 O.R. wounded 12 O.R.	
" 10.	—	Divisional Headquarters opens at MINDEN POST at 10 a.m. and relieves 16th Division. 4th Bn. Grenadier Guards and 1st Bn. Welsh Guards are in the line. 1 Bn. of 3rd Brigade at CARNOY and 1 Bn. " " BERNAFAY WOOD. 2nd Guards Brigade at HAPPY VALLEY. 1st Guards Brigade moves up to CARNOY. Lt. HAMBRO completes his attachment to "A" and "Q" Branch and is transferred to "G" Branch under instruction.	

Army Form C. 2118.

WAR DIARY
or
INTELLIGENCE SUMMARY
(Erase heading not required.)

Instructions regarding War Diaries and Intelligence Summaries are contained in F. S. Regs., Part II. and the Staff Manual respectively. Title Pages will be prepared in manuscript.

Place	Date	Hour	Summary of Events and Information	Remarks and references to Appendices
Septr.	11	—	2 Companies Pioneer Bn. move up from HAPPY VALLEY to MINDEN POST. Company for burying and salvage formed by drawing 100 men and 2 Officers from the 1st and 2nd Brigades – This together with the salvage section of 1 officer and 13 men, making a total of 5 Officers and 213 O.R. Orders regarding burial party cancelled. Brigades undertake to carry out this duty if men are not taken from them. Salvage section to be used on salvage work, working eastwards from MINDEN POST. Reserve of ammunition and bombs is moved up to the W. edge of BERNAFAY WOOD. Pipe line from MONTAUBAN to N. edge of BERNAFAY WOOD, carrying water to tanks, taken into use. Over 1000 petrol tins for water issued yesterday and today to units to carry water to the front lines.	
	12	—	On night of 12/13, 1st and 2nd brigades relieve 3rd brigade in the line. 3rd Brigade moves back to HAPPY VALLEY. Water supply fails at midday at CARNOY and MINDEN POST, water layed on again later. Pipe supply bursts about 8 p.m. at the main above MINDEN POST. Water supply reported by the Corps as critical, all horses not urgently required to be sent West.	
	13	—	Dumps of bombs, ammunition supplies and water are completed at BERNAFAY WOOD. Conference held at BERNAFAY WOOD to decide best method of carrying supplies forward. Water pipe supply at CARNOY and MINDEN POST opened again about midday. Lt. PENFOLD, 3rd Bn. Grenadier Guards, is transferred from MORLANCOURT to CARNOY as Camp Cmmdt. 2000 petrol tins of water have already been issued to troops. 2000 tins are being filled and kept in reserve at D.H.Q., MINDEN POST. For casualties during latter half of September, see schedule attached............	APP. 1.
	14.	—	Conference of Transport Officers to arrange for movements of supplies &c., during an advance. More petrol tins issued to units. General staff moves to BERNAFAY WOOD. Attack fixed for 6.20 a.m. tomorrow. Ammunition portions of 1st Line transport move to the vicinity of TRONES WOOD.	

Army Form C. 2118.

WAR DIARY
or
INTELLIGENCE SUMMARY

(Erase heading not required.)

Instructions regarding War Diaries and Intelligence Summaries are contained in F. S. Regs., Part II. and the Staff Manual respectively. Title Pages will be prepared in manuscript.

Place	Date	Hour	Summary of Events and Information	Remarks and references to Appendices
Septr	15th	-	1st and 2nd Guards Brigades carry out attack in conjunction with heavy machine gun batteries. 2nd Echelon of "A" and "Q" Branch moves to MINDEN POST. B.A.A.section returns to D.A.C. and ceases to be under dirsct command of the Division.	
-	16th	-	Attack continued. 61st Infantry Brigade came under instructions of Guards Division and attack with the Division. Division is relieved on the night of 16th/17th by the 20th Division.	
-	17th	-	3rd Guards Brigade moves back to CARNOY. 1st and 2nd Guards Brigades move to CITADEL. D.H.Q. to Forked Tree Camp. Pioneer Bn. and R.E. Companies move back to their old billets near MINDEN POST. Pioneer Bn. ordered to find 200 men to undertake burial duties and to commence tomorrow.	
-	18th	-	No movement. Col. S. GUISE MOORES, C.B., A.M.S., takes over duties from Lt.Col. GILL as A.D.M.S. vice Col. G.G.MCLOUGHLIN, C.M.G., D.S.O. Division commences to reorganize.	
-	19th	-	Reorganization continued. Several drafts arrive.	
-	20th	-	Night of 20th/21st - relief of 20th Division by Guards Division carried out. 1st and 3rd Guards Brigades go into the line with the 2nd Brigade in reserve. The weather having been bad for the last few days, the roads have become very difficult for transport.	
-	21st	-	D.H.Q. opens at MINDEN POST at 8 a.m. Rear Echelon remains at CITADEL.	
-	22nd	-	Weather greatly improved. Capt. Hon. E. M. PAKENHAM, 4th Bn. Coldstream Guards, taken over duties of Town Major, CARNOY.	

Army Form C. 2118.

WAR DIARY
or
INTELLIGENCE SUMMARY

(Erase heading not required.)

Instructions regarding War Diaries and Intelligence Summaries are contained in F. S. Regs., Part II. and the Staff Manual respectively. Title Pages will be prepared in manuscript.

Place	Date	Hour	Summary of Events and Information	Remarks and references to Appendices
Sept:	23rd	—	Drafts that have not joined up with units are detailed to assist in salvage work under Major BADEN POWELL. Owing to shortness of Officers and N.C.O.'s, units found that they are not able to absorb all their drafts at once. Drafts were absorbed on receipt of instructions that they would be used for salvage work.	
"	24th	—	Divisional Commander consults with Corps Commander as to hutting &c. for the coming winter.	
"	25th	—	G.S. and D.A.Q.M.G. move to advanced H.Qrs. in BERNAFAY WOOD. The 1st and 3rd Brigades make a successful attack on 3 objectives, all of which are taken. LES BOEUFS was captured and held. Attack commenced at 12.35 p.m.	
"	26th	—	2nd Guards Brigade relieves 1st and 3rd Guards Brigades in the line. Welsh Guards and 2nd Bn. Scots Guards to TRONES WOOD. 2nd and 3rd Bn. Coldstream Guards. } 1st and 4th Bn. Grenadier Guards. } to CARNOY. 1st Bn. Irish Guards. } 2nd Bn. Grenadier Guards. } TO CITADEL.	
"	27th	—	2nd Bn. Grenadier Guards and 1st Bn. Irish Guards move to the Camp of No. 7 (Guards) Entrenching Bn. near FRICOURT. 2nd and 3rd Bn. Coldstream Guards move to camp near MEAULTE, accompanied by Brigade H.Qrs. A German aeroplane dropped bombs near MINDEN POST during the night, killing 3 men, wounding others and killing and wounding 105 horses of the B.A.C. and other horses of various units of the Division.	
"	28th	—		
"	29th	—	B.H.Qrs. and 2 Bns., 1st Guards Brigade move from F.13 near MEAULTE to SANDPIT CAMPS. H.Qrs. and 2 Bns. of 3rd Guards Brigade move from TRONES WOOD and BERNAFAY WOOD to F.17.D. Camp near MINDEN POST.	

WAR DIARY
or
INTELLIGENCE SUMMARY

(Erase heading not required.)

Army Form C. 2118.

Place	Date	Hour	Summary of Events and Information	Remarks and references to Appendices
	Septr. 30th		1st Guards Brigade move to MORLANCOURT. 3rd Guards Brigade move H.Q. and 2 Bns. to Camp near MEAULTE. and 2 Bns. to Sandpits Camp. 2nd Guards Brigade are relieved by the 50th Division and come out to Camp near MINDEN POST in F17.b. Transport of H.Qrs. and 1st and 3rd Guards Brigade Groups moves to DAOURS and continues its journey to rest area on the 1st October.	

Major-General,
Commdg. GUARDS DIVISION.

Army Form C. 2118.

WAR DIARY
or
INTELLIGENCE SUMMARY

(Erase heading not required.)

Administrative Branch, Guards Division.

OCTOBER, 1916.

Place	Date	Hour	Summary of Events and Information	Remarks and references to Appendices
Belloy	Oct:	1.	1st and 3rd Guards Brigade Groups moved by busses arranged by the French to No.4 Area X Corps. Divisional Headquarters moved to Belloy-St.Leonard. Transport of 2nd Guards Brigade and Pioneer Bn. moved to DAOURS. do. of 1st and 3rd Gds. Bdes. arrived at the new area billets.	
"	"	2.	2nd Gds. Bde. Group and Pioneers moved by train to No. 4 Area. Transport of 2nd Gds. Bde. Group and Pioneer Bn. moved to AILLY. and PICQUIGNY.	
"	"	3.	2nd Gds. Bde. and Pioneer Transport arrived in New Area. The Brigadiers and Commanding Officers of Grenadier and Coldstream Guards met at D.H.Q. to discuss the redistribution of Officers.	
"	"	4.	—	
"	"	5.	The Major General presented medals to men of the 1st Guards Brigade. The Army Commander visited Divisional Headquarters.	
"	"	6.	The Major General presented medals to the men of the 2nd Guards Brigade. The Pioneer Bn. moved to MAMETZ Camp F.17.b. by Bus. The Transport of the Bn. moved by road.	
"	"	7.	The Major General presents medals to the men of the 3rd Guards Brigade.	
"	"	8.	—	
"	"	9.	The Major General presented medals to the men of the R.E., R.A.M.C., and Train.	
"	"	10.	—	
"	"	11.	Major General inspects the Field Ambulances.	
"	"	12.	List of Recommendations for half yearly Honours and Rewards submitted to XIV Corps. Major General inspects the 2nd Gds. Bde. Machine Gun Company.	

Army Form C. 2118.

WAR DIARY
or
INTELLIGENCE SUMMARY

(Erase heading not required.)

Instructions regarding War Diaries and Intelligence Summaries are contained in F. S. Regs., Part II and the Staff Manual respectively. Title Pages will be prepared in manuscript.

Place	Date	Hour	Summary of Events and Information	Remarks and references to Appendices
Belloy.	Oct:	13.	Lieut. HAMBRO who had been working in "A" Office since the 2nd instant, returns to "G" Office. First list of Retrospective Awards of Military Medal received. Gazette of 11/10/16.	
"	"	14.	Owing to number of Honours and Rewards allowed to A.G's and Q.M.G's Branches, amendments and additions to Honours list are forwarded by Special D.R. to XIV Corps.	
"	"	15.	Corps/Commander visits the Division.	
"	"	16.	Captain E. Sheppard, Grenadier Guards, joins Headquarters of the Division for instruction in Staff duties. Corps Commander Xth Corps visits the Division.	
"	"	17.	Major General proceeds on leave to England. Brigadier General C.E.PEREIRA assumes command of the Division. Transport of 75th and 55th Field Companies, R.E. commences its march to CARNOY.	
"	"	18.	75th and 55th Field Companies, R.E., moved by bus to huts between CARNOY and MONTAUBAN.	
"	"	19.	-	
"	"	20.	3rd Gds. Bde. carry out a Field Day. Major General SUTTON visited the Division. Lt.Col. HEYWOOD is ordered to XVthe Corps to take over the duties of Brig.Gen. G.S., as a temporary measure, to replace Brig.Gen.Anderson who went sick. Lt.Col.HEYWOOD left in the afternoon for H.Q., XVth Corps.	
"	"	21.	Mobile Veterinary Section moves to CARNOY to arrive there my march route on 24th.	
"	"	22.	-	
"	"	23.	-	
"	"	24.	-	
"	"	25.	-	

Army Form C. 2118.

WAR DIARY
or
INTELLIGENCE SUMMARY

(Erase heading not required.)

Place	Date	Hour	Summary of Events and Information	Remarks and references to Appendices
Belloy.	Oct:	26.	Major General returns from Leave. Lt.Col. HEYWOOD returns from XV Corps, where he had been doing the duties of Brig.Gen., G.S.	
"	"	27.		
"	"	28.		
"	"	29.		
"	"	30.		
"	"	31.	Rehearsal for the Duke of Connaught's Review tomorrow. The Corps Commander came over to see the Major General this afternoon.	

8/11/16.

[signature]
Major-General,
Commdg. GUARDS DIVISION.

Army Form C. 2118.

WAR DIARY
or
INTELLIGENCE SUMMARY

(Erase heading not required.)

ADMINISTRATIVE STAFF,
GUARDS DIVISION.
****
30th Nov: 1916.

Vol 16

Place	Date	Hour	Summary of Events and Information	Remarks and references to Appendices
Nov:	1st	-	H.R.H. The Duke of CONNAUGHT inspects the Division.	
"	2nd – 7th	-	Division remains in Rest Area – Nothing of Importance to report.	
"	8th	-	The Transport of the 1st Guards Brigade left DROMESNIL Area this morning, starting from HALLIVILLERS at 10 a.m. and marching via HALLIVILLERS – CAMPS-en-AMIENOIS – MOLLIENS-VIDAME – FOURDRINOY to AILLY-sur-SOMME where they halt for the night. The 4th Field Ambulance, less dismounted personnel, leaves VILLERS-CAMPSART and marches with Transport of the 1st Guards Brigade. The Transport of the 3rd Guards Brigade left AVESNE Area this morning, starting from HETIGNY at 10 a.m., marching via AIRAINES – SOUES – PICQUIGNY to AILLY-sur-SOMME where they halt for the night. The 76th Field Coy., R.E., leaves LALEU and 3rd Field Ambulance leaves VERGIES and both march with Transport of 3rd Guards Brigade. G.S.O.I and A.A.& Q.M.G. visit H.Qrs., 17th Division at BERNAFAY WOOD and H.Q., XIV Corps to arrange about relief.	
"	9th	-	Transport of 2nd Guards Brigade Group and Divisional Headquarters march by the same route as those of previous Brigade Groups. New car arrives for the Major General. Transport, 1st Guards Brigade and 3rd Guards Brigade move to DAOURS.	
"	10th	-	D.H.Q. moved to TREUX. 1st Guards Brigade Group moved by Bus to Citadel Camp. 3rd " " " " " to Sandpits " Transport of 1st and 3rd Guards Brigade Groups move to CITADEL and SANDPITS Areas. Transport of 2nd Guards Brigade Group moves to DAOURS.	
"	11th	-	2nd Guards Brigade move by Bus to MEAULTE. Conference held at D.H.Q. at 6 p.m. to discuss administrative questions relating to the line about to be taken over. Transport of Pioneer Battalion moves to AILLY-sur-SOMME. Movements of Battalions for relief of 17th Division commence.	

Army Form C. 2118.

WAR DIARY
or
INTELLIGENCE SUMMARY

(Erase heading not required.)

Instructions regarding War Diaries and Intelligence Summaries are contained in F. S. Regs., Part II. and the Staff Manual respectively. Title Pages will be prepared in manuscript.

Place	Date	Hour	Summary of Events and Information	Remarks and references to Appendices
Nov:	12th	–	Conference held at SANDPITS, 3rd Guards Brigade H.Qrs. Pioneer Transport moves to DAOURS.	
"	13th	–	Pioneer Bn. moves by Bus to CITADEL. Transport moves to CITADEL Camp.	
"	14th	–	D.H.Q. moves to BERNAFAY WOOD Opening at 10 a.m. Relief of 17th Division now complete. Roads in Forward Area are in very bad order. Huts in course of construction – Accommodation for the Division is inadequate at present.	
"	15th	–	The Major General inspects Camps "H" and "F" and Transport Lines of 1st Guards Brigade with a view to making improvements. Three companies, Pioneer Bn., move to WATERLOT FARM – Remaining Company to "F" Camp. H.Qrs. and half of the 93rd Field Company, R.E. and whole of the 78th Field Company, R.E. come under the orders of the C.R.E. to assist in improvement of Camps, etc. Sharp frost on night of 15th/16th.	
"	16th	–	Corps Commander holds a conference at D.H.Q. to discuss the use of roads and the laying of Decauville Railways. Orders received that the Division will be relieved by the 5th ANZAC Division, movement to be completed by the night of the 21st/22nd. Frost continues.	
"	17th	–	Lorries stopped running E. of a line GROVETOWN – POZIERES from Midnight 17th/18th. Frost continues.	
"	18th	–	Weather breaks – snow and sleet during the night of 17th/18th and rain on 18th. Meeting held to discuss Transport question, attended by G.O.C., A.A.& Q.M.G., D.A.A.& Q.M.G., C.R.E., O.C., Train, S.S.O.; and D.A.D.O.S. Accident to a Divisional Car occurred between CORBIE and MINDEN POST in which the Driver, Pte. GODBOLD, A.S.C., was killed.	

Army Form C. 2118.

WAR DIARY
or
INTELLIGENCE SUMMARY

(Erase heading not required.)

Instructions regarding War Diaries and Intelligence Summaries are contained in F. S. Regs., Part II. and the Staff Manual respectively. Title Pages will be prepared in manuscript.

Place	Date	Hour	Summary of Events and Information	Remarks and references to Appendices
Nov:	19th	—	Rain continues. Question on lighting new H.Qrs. at ARROW HEAD COPSE raised.	
"	20th	—	Weather fine. A meeting was held at Corps H.Qrs. to discuss the question of Transport, attended by A.A.& Q.M.G. Nothing was settled definitely as to how the question should be dealt with; suggestions were made which will be submitted at the Corps Conference. Relief of the Division by 5th Australian Division commences.	
"	21st	—	Thick fog all day. D.A.Q.M.G., 5th Australian Division arrives to take over. Relief continues.	
"	22nd	—	Relief completed. D.H.Q. move to TREUX and open at 10 a.m. Division is camped at "H" Camps, SANDPITS, MEAULTE and CITADEL. Application put forward for the return of the B.A.A. Section of the D.A.C.	
"	23rd	—	—	
"	24th	—	—	
"	25th	—	Conference held at D.H.Q., 6 p.m., to discuss administrative questions on the new line about to be taken over from the French. Present – G.O.C., G.S.O.I, A.A.& Q.M.G., D.A.Q.M.G., C.R.E. and A.D.M.S.	
"	26th	—	A.A.& Q.M.G. visited 9th French Corps and 152nd French Division to arrange administrative details. Also visited the French Ambulance and Dressing Station at COMBLES. Conference at Corps H.Qrs. attended by Staffs of 4 Divisions (Guards, 17th, 20th and 29th) to discuss the area about to be taken over.	

Army Form C. 2118.

WAR DIARY
or
INTELLIGENCE SUMMARY

(Erase heading not required.)

Instructions regarding War Diaries and Intelligence Summaries are contained in F. S. Regs., Part II. and the Staff Manual respectively. Title Pages will be prepared in manuscript.

Place	Date	Hour	Summary of Events and Information	Remarks and references to Appendices
Nov:	27th	-	French hutments at FORKED TREE CAMP at L.2.a. and L.2.b. taken over by the Division. 3rd Bn. Coldstream Guards, 1st Bn. Irish Guards, 3rd Bn. Grenadier Guards and 2nd Bn. Scots Guards move into these Camps which consist of 64 wooden ends each capable of holding 100 men.	
"	28th	-	Orders received to take over French Camp No.15 at BILLON FARM. French, however, had not vacated and have no intention of so doing before Dec:4th. Arrangements made to take over 181 French tents at MALZHORN FARM.	
"	29th	-	Ordered to take over Camp 108 from the French. Major BADEN-POWELL and advanced parties detailed to proceed there tomorrow morning. Conference of Heads of Administrative Depts. of Division to discuss the formation of a Labour Battalion.	
"	30th	-	Major BADEN POWELL reports that Camp 108 is not vacated and that the French have no instructions to leave before Dec:11th. D.D.S.& T., Fourth Army, decides that new H.Qrs. at ARROW HEAD COPSE should be lit with lamps. Orders issued to dismantle the Cinema set and put the plant up at the new Headquarters. 40 G.S.Wagons from 17th Divisional Train join Guards Divisional Train for duty under O.C.Train and C.R.E.	

[signature]
Major-General,
Commanding GUARDS DIVISION.

WAR DIARY
INTELLIGENCE SUMMARY
(Erase heading not required.)

Administrative Staff, Guards Division.
****

Army Form C. 2118

31/12/16.

Vol 17

Place	Date	Hour	Summary of Events and Information	Remarks and references to Appendices
Dec:	1st	—	Relief of 152nd French Division begins. 2nd Bn. Scots Guards and 3rd Bn. Grenadier Guards move to MALTZHORN Camp.	
"	2nd	—	Corps Commander visits Divisional Laundry. Relief continues.	
"	3rd	—	—	
"	4th	—	Line taken over from 152nd French Division. Headquarters open at Arrow Head Copse. Captain PAIN, O.C., Signal Company, goes to Hospital.	
"	5th	—	Captain PHILLIPS, Worcester Regt. takes over Command of Divisional Signal Company.	
"	6th	—	Brig:General BURNETT-HITCHCOCK visits D.H.Q. to discuss new arrangements in the area.	
"	7th	—	G.O.C. and A.A.& Q.M.G. visit ground near BOIS FAVIERE with a view to forming a Camp at this spot instead of MALZHORN. Instructions issued for improvement of existing Camps.	
"	8th	—	1000 Trench Boards drawn and laid down in Malzhorn Camp. Repair of Train line from Camp to road near TRONES WOOD Siding commenced. Material collected to build a Train line from the Road to Divisional Headquarters.	
"	9th	—	Instructions received that arrangements might now be made to carry rations to COMBLES on the 30 centimetre railway.	
"	10th	—	Meeting held at the H.Qrs. of the Train to discuss the transport of rations by Decauville from the Bateau to COMBLES. French authorities approached to provide Decauville trains for the above purpose commencing 13th.	
"	11th	—	Instructions received from Corps to move all details into the Divisional area as soon as possible.	

Army Form C. 2118.

WAR DIARY
or
INTELLIGENCE SUMMARY
(Erase heading not required.)

Instructions regarding War Diaries and Intelligence Summaries are contained in F. S. Regs., Part II. and the Staff Manual respectively. Title Pages will be prepared in manuscript.

Place	Date	Hour	Summary of Events and Information	Remarks and references to Appendices
Dec:	12th	-	Major General Sir. Francis LLOYD, G.O.C., London District, and Captain DOUGLAS, Brigade Major, Brigade of Guards, arrived at Divisional Headquarters. The G.O.C. inspected the new Transport Lines of the 3 Brigades and also visited BRONFAY CAMP.	
"	13th	-	Conference at Corps Headquarters. Attended by Major-General Sir Francis LLOYD, Major General, G.S.O.I and A.A.& Q.M.G. Trains were allotted to the Division on the Decauville line to convey rations from PLATEAU to COMBLES - Notice was too short to make arrangements.	
"	14th	-	First trainload of rations went up on the Decauville line from PLATEAU to COMBLES. Captain WITTS is placed in charge of Camp improvements at Camps 15 and 108. A.A.& Q.M.G. visited these Camps with C.R.E., 17th Division, who is now responsible for provision of material for all Camps. Camp 108 was said to be available for the Division, a Battalion arrived but found the camp occupied by the 8th Division Artillery details. The XIV Corps and XVth Corps both state that the camp was allotted to them by the Fourth Army. No decision received on 14th.	
"	15th	-	A.A.& Q.M.G. visited BRONFAY Camps with D.A.& Q.M.G., XIV Corps, also Transport Lines of 1st and 2nd Brigades. Fourth Army decide at 4 p.m. that the huts at Camp 108 belong to XIV Corps and instruct XVth Corps to move their troops.	
"	16th	-	Conference held at H.Qrs., 3rd Guards Brigade, 10.45 a.m., attended by Major General, G.S.O.I., A.A.& Q.M.G., Brigadiers, Brigade Majors and C.R.E. Camp 108 is not yet evacuated by XV Corps troops. Electric lighting broke down at D.H.Q. about 4 p.m.	
"	17th	-	Major General visits Camps 108 and 15, troops of XVth Corps are still in these camps but are said to be moving today. A soup kitchen is opened at TRONES WOOD Siding to give soup to men returning to BRONFAY FARM Camps 108 and 15 on the train leaving 3 a.m.	

Army Form C. 2118.

WAR DIARY
or
INTELLIGENCE SUMMARY

(Erase heading not required.)

Instructions regarding War Diaries and Intelligence Summaries are contained in F. S. Regs., Part II. and the Staff Manual respectively. Title Pages will be prepared in manuscript.

Place	Date	Hour	Summary of Events and Information	Remarks and references to Appendices
Dec:	18th	—	Conference held at the proposed new Railhead at MARICOURT to discuss the best arrangement for Decauville Sidings, etc. Attended by A.A.& Q.M.G., 20th Division and his S.S.O., A.A.& Q.M.G., O.C., Train, S.S.O., O.C., Supply Column of Guards Division. Camp 108 is now clear since 10.30 a.m. of XVth Corps Troops.	
"	19th	—	Conference held at 10 a.m. at Camp 15, BRONFAY FARM. Attended by A.A.& Q.M.G., Transport Officers, Quartermasters, O.C., Train, S.S.O., D.A.D.O.S., O.C., Sanitary Section.	
"	20th	—	A.A.& Q.M.G. met D.A.& Q.M.G., XIV Corps at BRONFAY Camp. Captain C.M.C.DOWLING takes over as Camp Commandant No. 15 from Lt. Hon A.E.F.YORKE. Corps Commander presented Montenegrian Order, Order of Danelo, 5th Class, to Capt. E.C.WARNER, etc., and medals to Capt. HEATH, 55th Coy., R.E., and C.S.M. GROOMBRIDGE, 2nd Bn. Coldstream Guards respectively at Divisional Headquarters.	
"	21st	—		
"	22nd	—	A.A.& Q.M.G., conducts A.A.& Q.M.G., 20th Division, round the Camps at BRONFAY FARM and the Transport Lines N. of MARICOURT.	
"	23rd.	—	A.A.& Q.M.G. conducts A.A.& Q.M.G., 20th Division, to COMBLES and BOIS DORE. Lt.Col. W.H.V.DARELL, A.A.& Q.M.G., appointed D.A.& Q.M.G., Fourth Corps with Temporary Rank of Brigadier-General.	
"	24th	—	Brig:General W.H.V.Darell leaves for IVth Corps H.Qrs. Capt. H.B.DYKES, Scots Guards, Staff Captain, 3rd Guards Brigade, joined Divisional Staff pending appointment as D.A.A.& Q.M.G.	
"	25th	—	Xmas day. Capt. W.M.GRIGG reassumed duties of B.Major, 2nd Guards Brigade on return from Staff Duties course at G.H.Q.	
"	26th	—	Brig:General C.E.PEREIRA commanding 1st Guards Brigade appointed to command 2nd Division and to be Temporary Major-General. Capt. AUBREY-FLETCHER, Grenadier Guards, G.S.O.3 proceeded to a Course of Staff Duties at G.H.Q.	

Army Form C. 2118.

WAR DIARY
or
INTELLIGENCE SUMMARY

(Erase heading not required.)

Instructions regarding War Diaries and Intelligence Summaries are contained in F. S. Regs., Part II. and the Staff Manual respectively. Title Pages will be prepared in manuscript.

Place	Date	Hour	Summary of Events and Information	Remarks and references to Appendices
Dec:	27th	—	D.A.A.& Q.M.G. and S.S.O. met D.A.A.& Q.M.G. and D.A.Q.M.G. of Corps and Officers of the 17th and 20th Divisions at 10.15 a.m. to discuss arrangements for new Supply Railhead at MARICOURT.	
"	28th	—	Lieut. VANNECK, Camp Commdt MALZHORN, was relieved by an Officer of the 29th Division at Malzhorn.	
"	29th	—		
"	30th	—	Brig:General Jeffreys reported arrival and assumed command of 1st Guards Brigade.	
"	31st	—	G.O.C., O.C., 4th Bn. Coldstream Guards, and D.A.A.& Q.M.G. met D.A.A.& Q.M.G., XIV Corps and C.E., XIV Corps at BRIQUETERIE to select Camp for the Pioneers.	

[signature]
Major-General,
Cmmdg. GUARDS DIVISION.

Instructions regarding War Diaries and Intelligence Summaries are contained in F.S. Regs., Part II and the Staff Manual respectively. Title Pages will be prepared in manuscript.

WAR DIARY
or
INTELLIGENCE SUMMARY
(Erase heading not required.)

Administrative Staff,
Guards Division.—
JANUARY, 1917.
****

Army Form C. 2118

Vol 18

Place	Date	Hour	Summary of Events and Information	Remarks and references to Appendices
January	1.	—	Pioneer Camp was begun at the BRIQUETERIE on MARICOURT–BERNAFAY WOOD Road. Relief by 20th Division begun.	
"	2.	—	Relief by 20th Division in progress. G.O.C., 2nd Guards Brigade, moved to CORBIE. Instructions received from Corps cancelling moves to back area on 10th inst., and to take over portion of line on right of Corps by 10th/11th.	
"	3.	—	Relief of 1st Guards Brigade completed, who moved to MEAULTE.	
"	4.	—	Divisional Headquarters moved to CORBIE on relief by 20th Division. G.O.C. held an Administrative Conference at 5 p.m. at D.H.Q. to discuss matters re. taking over the new line on Jan:11th.	
"	5.	—	G.O.C. accompanied by A.A.& Q.M.G. and G.S.O.II attended a Conference at Corps H.Qrs. The Band and Bugles of the 77th Regiment of the Line played in the Market Square at CORBIE today and were afterwards entertained by the Band of the Welsh Guards. The Officers of the Regiment were entertained at Divisional Headquarters "A" and "B" Messes and at H.Qrs., 2nd Guards Brigade. The Army Commander visited Divisional Headquarters this afternoon.	
"	6.	—	G.O.C. held a conference at 3rd Guards Brigade H.qrs. at 11 a.m. this morning. G.O.C. and A.A.& Q.M.G. attended at HAMEL when the Band of the Welsh Guards and Pipers of the 1st Bn. Scots Guards played for the 77th Regiment of the Line. Captain E. SEYMOUR, D.S.O., G.S.O.II went sick.	
"	7.	—	A.A.& Q.M.G., D.A.Q.M.G., and C.R.E. went up to Advanced 8th Division H.Qrs. at MAUREPAS; also met D.A.& Q.M.G., XIV Corps, at BRONFAY, regarding improvements in Farm buildings there. Captain E. SEYMOUR, G.S.O.II was admitted to hospital in AMIENS.	
"	8.	—	G.O.C. presented medal ribbons to 2nd Guards Brigade at CORBIE.	
"	9.	—	.... 3rd Guards Brigade at VILLE. 2nd Guards Brigade moved forward to BILLON FARM and MAUREPAS.	
"	10.	—	A.A.& Q.M.G. accompanied by Camp Commandant Major BAGOT–CHESTER went round BILLON FARM Camps 16 and 107. A.A.& Q.M.G. and A.D.M.S. met D.A.& Q.M.G. of Corps at MARICOURT, reference	

1875 Wt. W593/826 1,000,000 4/15 J.B.C. & A. A.D.S.S./Forms/C. 2118.

Army Form C. 2118

WAR DIARY
or
INTELLIGENCE SUMMARY

(Erase heading not required.)

Instructions regarding War Diaries and Intelligence Summaries are contained in F. S. Regs., Part II. and the Staff Manual respectively. Title Pages will be prepared in manuscript.

Place	Date	Hour	Summary of Events and Information	Remarks and references to Appendices
Jan:	10 (Contd.)		reference billets for "B" and "Q" Echelon of H.Qrs. 2nd Guards Brigade took over the line from the 8th Division, 2 Battalions in the line, one Battalion at MAUREPAS, one Battalion at Le PRIEZ Farm.	
"	11.	-	Divisional Headquarters moved from CORBIE - "Q" and C.R.E. to MAUREPAS, "A" and "Q", A.D.M.S., A.D.V.S., etc., to BRAY, A.P.M. to MARICOURT. A.A.& Q.M.G. visited MAUREPAS Camp.	
"	12.	-	A.A.& Q.M.G. and D.A.A.& Q.M.G. visited MARICOURT Area and BILLON FARM Camps. Arrangements made for A.D.M.S. and A.D.V.S. to move to MARICOURT.	
"	13.	-	D.A.Q.M.G. visited MARICOURT to meet XXX.A.Q.M.G., XIV Corps with reference to the allotment of areas.	
"	14.	-	D.A.A.& Q.M.G. visited MAUREPAS Camps with reference to accommodation.	
"	15.	-	D.A.A.& Q.M.G. visited back areas.	
"	16.	***	D.A.Q.M.G. went to COMBLES and MAUREPAS ※ Arrangements made to increase accommodation at MAUREPAS by removing huts at present at ※※BRIQUETERIE.	
"	17.	-	Brigadier General CORKRAN took over Command of Division during absence on leave of G.O.C. D.A.A.& Q.M.G. visited BILLON Farm Camp and MAUREPAS Ravine Camps - Work commenced on new hutments.	
"	18.	-	D.A.A.& Q.M.G. visited BROMFAY FARM and MAUREPAS. D.A.Q.M.G. visited new Railhead at MARICOURT BOIS and met A.Q.M.G., XIV Corps, in consultation on work in progress.	
"	19.	-	D.A.A.& Q.M.G. visited MAUREPAS.	
"	20.	-	Work commenced in removing 19 Nissen Huts from present site to MAUREPAS Ravine. D.A.Q.M.G. visited new Railhead.	

1875 Wt. W593/826 1,000,000 4/15 J.B.C. & A. A.D.S.S./Forms/C. 2118.

Army Form C. 2118

WAR DIARY
or
INTELLIGENCE SUMMARY
(*Erase heading not required.*)

Instructions regarding War Diaries and Intelligence Summaries are contained in F.S. Regs., Part II. and the Staff Manual respectively. Title Pages will be prepared in manuscript.

Place	Date	Hour	Summary of Events and Information	Remarks and references to Appendices
Jan:	21.	—	D.A.A.& Q.M.G. visited VILLE-sur-ANCRE and MERICOURT with reference to re-arrangement of Billeting area to be effected during next Brigade relief on 25th/26th inst. - Work in progress on Rest Billets, etc., inspected.	
"	22.	—	D.A.A.& Q.M.G. visited Camps in MAUREPAS and new Brigade Headquarters in BOIS DOUAGE. Work on Bath-house at MAUREPAS progressing well. Nine Nissen Huts are on hand and will be shortly erected.	
"	23.	—		
"	24.	—	D.A.A.& Q.M.G. accompanied G.O.C. round Camps at MAUREPAS RAVINE and inspected the proposed new Brigade Headquarters at BOIS DOUAGE. Brigade relief commenced.	
"	25.	—	"A & Q" Branch Staff moved from BRAY to Divisional Headquarters at MAUREPAS.	
"	26.	—	D.A.A.& Q.M.G. with Adjutant to C.R.E. visited BILLON FARM Camp 107 and 16 and discussed the proposed tramway to Camp 107. This work will be put in hand as soon as the frost permits. "B" Echelon quarters at MARICOURT were visited and various improvements decided on. Relief completed.	
"	27.	—	D.A.A.& Q.M.G. visited MAUREPAS Camps. Work considerably held up by frost and difficulty of getting lorry transport.	
"	28.	—	Capt. R.G.C.YERBURGH, 1st Bn. Irish Guards, and Capt. F.H.WITTS, 2nd Bn. Irish Guards, commenced their attachment to 20th Divisional Artillery under O.B.1329 dated 28/11/16, training for junior staff officers. Capt. O. LYTTELTON, D.S.O., 3rd Bn. Grenadier Guards joined 2nd Guards Brigade H.Qrs., and Capt. C.S.JACKSON, 3rd Bn. Coldstream Guards, joined 1st Guards Brigade Headquarters for preliminary month's instruction in Staff Duties. Capt. GIOVANNI FERRANDO of the Italian Army was attached to 3rd Guards Brigade till 8th Feb:	
"	29.	—	The D.A.A.& Q.M.G. and D.A.Q.M.G. visited MARICOURT to view improvements of billets.	

[signed] Major-General,
Commdg. Guards Division.

Army Form C. 2118

WAR DIARY
or
INTELLIGENCE SUMMARY

ADMINISTRATIVE STAFF, GUARDS DIVISION.

Month of February 1917.

(Erase heading not required.)

Instructions regarding War Diaries and Intelligence Summaries are contained in F.S. Regs., Part II. and the Staff Manual respectively. Title Pages will be prepared in manuscript.

Vol 19

Place	Date	Hour	Summary of Events and Information	Remarks and references to Appendices
	Feby. 1st.		The Major-General returned from leave.	
	Feby. 2nd.			
	Feby. 3rd.			
	Feby. 4th.			
	Feby. 5th.			
	Feby. 6th.		The D.A.& Q.M.G. of the Corps visited Divisional Headquarters. Recommendations for Italian Models forwarded to the Corps.	
	Feby. 7th.		G.O.C. went to see a Practice Attack of the 2nd Bn. Irish Guards at TREUX; several French Generals present. Reserve Thaw Rations moved from R. Pt., BILLON FARM, to 3rd Guards Brigade Headquarters, at BOIS DOUAGE.	
	Feby. 8th.		A Lecture on Court Martial Procedure was given at MERICOURT to the 2nd Guards Brigade, by Captain BAKER, Fourth Army Court Martial Officer. The Lecture, which was to have taken place at MAUREPAS RAVINE, for the 1st and 3rd Guards Brigades and Guards Divisional Artillery, was not held owing to breakdown of motor car of Captain J. HILLS, D.A.A.G., Fourth Army.	
	Feby. 9th.		The Corps Commander visited Divisional Headquarters this afternoon. Captain H.L. AUBREY FLETCHER, M.V.O., Grenadier Guards, lately G.S.O. III, Guards Division, assumed the appointment of Brigade Major, 3rd Guards Brigade on 8/2/17, on return from G.H.Q. Course in Staff Duties, vice Captain E.C.T. WARNER, Scots Guards, appointed as Brigade Major, attached Infantry Brigade, PORTUGUESE Division, dated 27/12/16. Lieutenant, (Temp. Capt.) J.J.P. EVANS, 1st Bn. Welsh Guards, performed the duties of Brigade Major, 3rd Guards Brigade in the absence of Captain H.L. AUBREY FLETCHER, Grenadier Guards. Lieutenant W.G. ORRISS, 3rd Bn. Grenadier Guards, wounded by Bomb Accident.	

Army Form C. 2118

WAR DIARY
or
INTELLIGENCE SUMMARY
(Erase heading not required.)

Administrative Diary James Wilson

Instructions regarding War Diaries and Intelligence Summaries are contained in F.S. Regs., Part II. and the Staff Manual respectively. Title Pages will be prepared in manuscript.

Place	Date	Hour	Summary of Events and Information	Remarks and references to Appendices
	Feby. 10th.			
	Feby. 11th.		G.O.C. accompanied by A.A. & Q.M.G., attended Church Service at 11 a.m. at Camp 16., BILLON.	
			Orders received appointing Lieutenant (Temp. Capt.) E.W.M. GRIGG, M.C. Grenadier Guards, Brigade Major, 2nd Guards Brigade, to be G.S.O. II., XIX Corps. XIV Corps asked that Captain H.C. LOYD, M.C., Coldstream Guards, Brigade Major, 51st Infantry Brigade, may be appointed to succeed Lieutenant (Temp. Captain) E.W.M. GRIGG.	
	Feby. 12th.			
	Feby. 13th.		A.A. & Q.M.G., and D.A.Q.M.G., held a Meeting of representatives of Brigades and Units, to discuss arrangements to be carried out for the new Railhead at MARICOURT BOIS.	
	Feby. 14th.		G.S.O. I. proceeded to 5th French Army to visit Schools of Instruction.	
	Feby. 15th.		Captain WITTS, 2nd Irish Guards, arrived to be attached to "G", after finishing a period of attachment to the Divisional Train.	
	Feby. 16th.		The XIV Corps Ammunition Dump was blown up at the PLATEAU today, caused by the fall of bombs from hostile aircraft. Time about 5 a.m. Explosions lasted all day.	
	Feby. 17th.			
	Feby. 18th.		Colonel LORD LOVAT arrived to stay at Divisional Headquarters for a few nights.	
	Feby. 19th.		Captain H.C. LOYD, Coldstream Guards, Brigade Major, 51st Infantry Brigade, is appointed Brigade Major, 2nd Guards Brigade, vice Captain E.W.M. GRIGG, Grenadier Guards, but does not join until 24th.	
	Feby. 20th.			

Army Form C. 2118

WAR DIARY
or
INTELLIGENCE SUMMARY

(Erase heading not required.)

Instructions regarding War Diaries and Intelligence Summaries are contained in F. S. Regs., Part II. and the Staff Manual respectively. Title Pages will be prepared in manuscript.

Place	Date	Hour	Summary of Events and Information	Remarks and references to Appendices
	Feby. 21st.		Lieutenant Q.S. GREENE, 3rd Bn. Coldstream Guards, wounded.	
	Feby. 22nd.		Lieutenants R. TERRELL, and A. Mc W. LAWSON JOHNSTON, 2nd Bn. Grenadier Guards and Lieutenant R.T. FOSTER, 3rd Bn. Coldstream Guards, wounded.	
	Feby. 23rd.		General LYAUTEY, French Minister of War, accompanied by Lieutenant-General Sir W.P. PULTENEY, Commanding the Fourth Army, inspected the 3rd Guards Brigade on parade at VILLE this morning. The Major-General met General LYAUTEY at 9-20 a.m. and accompanied him to the Parade Ground. The Brigade afterwards marched past in fours on the VILLE Road.	
	Feby. 24th.		Colonel Lord LOVATT left for G.H.Q.	
	Feby. 25th.		News received of a German Retirement at PYS-MIRAUMONT SERRE in front of 5th Army.	
	Feby. 26th.		2 Officers of H.M.S. "COURAGEOUS" arrived to be attached to the Division for one day and were sent to a Battalion in the Line for the night.	
	Feby. 27th.		The 2nd Guards Brigade relieved the 1st Guards Brigade at the BOIS DOUAGE Headquarters.	
	Feby. 28th.			

Major-General,
Commanding Guards Division.

Army Form C. 2118

WAR DIARY
or
INTELLIGENCE SUMMARY
(Erase heading not required.)

GUARDS DIVISION.
ADMINISTRATIVE BRANCH,
Month of March, 1917.

Instructions regarding War Diaries and Intelligence Summaries are contained in F. S. Regs., Part II. and the Staff Manual respectively. Title Pages will be prepared in manuscript.

Vol 30 2

Place	Date	Hour	Summary of Events and Information	Remarks and references to Appendices
	March	1st.		
	"	2nd.		
	"	3rd.	A.A. & Q.M.G. and D.A.Q.M.G. made final arrangements for the new Railhead at MARICOURT BOIS tomorrow. Lieut-Colonel R.C.A. McCALMONT, D.S.O., 1st Battalion Irish Guards, appointed to Temporary Command of 3rd Infantry Brigade, 1st Division.	
	"	4th.	MARICOURT BOIS Railhead opened this morning, and Decauville train load for Units of 1st Guards Brigade sent by rail to BRONFAY.	
	"	5th.	A.A. & Q.M.G., and D.A.Q.M.G., went to MARICOURT BOIS with reference to transport of rations.	
	"	6th.	A.A. & Q.M.G. went to a three days tour of French Area, (Group of Armies of the North), to visit the Administrative Services.	
	"	7th.		
	"	8th.	Lecture on Court Martial Procedure by D.A.A.G., Fourth Army to officers of 1st Guards Brigade in BILLON Camp.	
	"	9th.	A.A. & Q.M.G. returned from a visit to the French Army.	
	"	10th.		
	"	11th.		
	"	12th.		
	"	13th.	G.O.C., accompanied by G.S.O.I. and A.A. & Q.M.G. attended a Conference at Corps Headquarters at 10-30 a.m. The 1st Guards Brigade completed relief of 3rd Guards Brigade in SAILLISEL Sector.	

Army Form C. 2118.

WAR DIARY
or
INTELLIGENCE SUMMARY.

(Erase heading not required.)

Instructions regarding War Diaries and Intelligence
Summaries are contained in F. S. Regs., Part II.
and the Staff Manual respectively. Title pages
will be prepared in manuscript.

Place	Date	Hour	Summary of Events and Information	Remarks and references to Appendices
	March	14th.	Information received that the enemy is retiring on our Divisional Front. 1st Battalion Grenadier Guards moved from BILLON to tents at COMBLES.	
	"	15th.	Early this morning Division occupied German Front Line Trenches. 1st Battalion Welsh Guards moved from BILLON to Tents at COMBLES.	
	"	16th.	The Major-General awarded the "Commander" of the Order of St. MAURICE and ST LAZARUS by His Majesty the King of Italy. Works Battalion moved from MAUREPAS to TRONES WOOD.	
	"	17th.	Fall of BAPAUME reported.	
	"	18th.	Captain WITTS, 2nd Bn. Irish Guards lately attached to "G" office, was relieved by Lieutenant J.J.P. EVANS, 1st Bn. Welsh Guards, Captain WITTS going to "A and Q" office. Lieutenant Hon. A.A. VANNECK, lately attached to "A and Q" office became attached to Headquarters, 3rd Guards Brigade. (2nd Bn Scots Guards)	
	"	19th.		
	"	20th.	Orders received for the 20th Division to relieve the Left Brigade in the Line, and for the Guards Division to work on Roads and Railways.	
	"	21st.	Brigadier-General J. PONSONBY, C.M.G., D.S.O., from 21st Infantry Brigade took over the Command of the 2nd Guards Brigade. Brigadier-General Lord H.C. SEYMOUR, D.S.O. was transferred from Command of 2nd Guards Brigade to the Command of the 3rd Guards Brigade. Brigadier-General C.E. CORKRAN, C.M.G., from Command of 3rd Guards Brigade, proceeded home to England. Lieut-Colonel R.C.A. McCALMONT, on Parliamentary leave in England, ordered to take up appointment of Command of 3rd Infantry Brigade.	

Army Form C. 2118.

WAR DIARY
or
INTELLIGENCE SUMMARY.
(Erase heading not required.)

Instructions regarding War Diaries and Intelligence Summaries are contained in F. S. Regs., Part II. and the Staff Manual respectively. Title pages will be prepared in manuscript.

Place	Date	Hour	Summary of Events and Information	Remarks and references to Appendices
	March			
	22nd.		Orders received for 8th Division to relieve 3rd Guards Brigade in Right Sector. Rear	
	23rd.		G.O.C., accompanied by A.A. & Q.M.G. and A.D.C. inspected 20th Divisional Headquarters at BRIQUETERIE with a view to changing Headquarters there. G.O.C. decided owing to its position and bad state of repair not to move there.	
	24th.		The 4th Guards Machine Gun Company arrived at PLATEAU this morning under the Command of Captain BIRKBECK, Coldstream Guards and were quartered at BRONFAY CAMP.	
	25th.		The 1st Battalion Scots Guards proceeded to CLERY to work on the reconstruction of Railways. The 3rd Guards Brigade moved three Battalions to work on Railways near CLERY, the fourth Battalion (1st Bn. Welsh Guards), moving close to PERONNE for similar duties. Orders received for 4 Machine Gun Companies, 5 Trench Mortar Batteries and one Field Company R.E. to move to LE TRANSLOY to work on the Roads.	
	26th.		Machine Gun Companies and Trench Mortar Batteries and 76th Field Coy. R.E. marched to LE TRANSLOY.	
	27th.			
	28th.		The Corps Commander presented the CROIX de GUERRE to Lieut. J.A.D. PERRINS, Welsh Guards at Divisional Headquarters this morning.	
	29th.			
	30th.		Lieut-Colonel J.C.L. BLACK, C.M.G., Commanding Guards Divisional Train appointed as A.D. of S. & T., MALTA, and ordered to report at the War Office immediately.	
	31st.		The Commander-in-Chief called at Divisional Headquarters at 2-10 p.m. and in the absence of the Major-General, saw the A.A. & Q.M.G.	

Francis Norton
Colonel A.A.C.
for Major-General,
Comdg. Guards Division.

Army Form C. 2118.

WAR DIARY
or
INTELLIGENCE SUMMARY.
(Erase heading not required.)

ADMINISTRATIVE STAFF,
GUARDS DIVISION,
April, 1917.

Vol 21

Place	Date	Hour	Summary of Events and Information	Remarks and references to Appendices
	April 1st.			
	" 2nd.		Lieut-Colonel G.C. HAMILTON, D.S.O., Commanding 4th Battalion Grenadier Guards left today to take up appointment as Instructor at the Commanding Officer's School at ALDERSHOT.	
	" 3rd.		Lieut-Colonel H. DAVIES, C.M.G., Commanding 6th Divisional Train, appointed to Command Guards Divisional Train.	
	" 4th.		The Major-General met the Commander-in-Chief at 10-30 a.m. today at PERONNE.	
	" 5th.			
	" 6th.		3rd Bn. Coldstream Guards and 1st Bn. Irish Guards moved from MONTAUBAN and COMBLES respectively to the neighbourhood of LE TRANSLOY.	
	" 7th.			
	" 8th.		General SMUTS visited Divisional Headquarters this afternoon.	
	" 9th.		Brigadier-General PONSONBY took over Command of the Division on the Major-General proceeding on leave. 1st Bn. Coldstream Guards and 2nd Bn. Irish Guards went into Camp at LE TRANSLOY.	
	" 10th.			
	" 11th.			
	" 12th.		2nd Bn. Scots Guards and 4th Bn. Grenadier Guards moved Camp to CARTIGNY to continue work on Railway. Major Viscount GORT from G.S.O.II., G.H.Q., took over Command of 4th Bn. Grenadier Guards vice Lieut-Colonel G.C. HAMILTON, to ALDERSHOT as Instructor.	

P.T.O.

Army Form C. 2118.

WAR DIARY
or
INTELLIGENCE SUMMARY.
(Erase heading not required.)

Instructions regarding War Diaries and Intelligence Summaries are contained in F. S. Regs., Part II. and the Staff Manual respectively. Title pages will be prepared in manuscript.

Place	Date	Hour	Summary of Events and Information	Remarks and references to Appendices
	April 13th.		Orders issued for move of 1st Guards Brigade to BRONFAY CAMPS for training. Move to commence 15th instant.	
"	14th.			
"	15th.		2nd Bn. Coldstream Guards, 1st Bn. Irish Guards, 1st Guards Brigade Machine Gun Company and Trench Mortar Battery, moved from LE TRANSLOY to BRONFAY CAMPS.	
"	16th.		1st Guards Brigade Machine Gun Company and Trench Mortar Battery and 4th Guards Machine Gun Company moved from LE TRANSLOY to BRONFAY FARM CAMPS. 3rd Guards Brigade M.G. Company moved from LE TRANSLOY to CLERY to Camp.	
"	17th		2nd Bn. Grenadier Guards and 3rd Bn. Coldstream Guards moved from LE TRANSLOY to BRONFAY FARM CAMPS.	
"	18th		Divisional Headquarters moved from MAUREPAS to near CURLU, A.29.d. (Albert Sheet Combined). 3rd Bn. Grenadier Guards moved from MAUREPAS to CLERY.	
"	19th.			
"	20th.		G.O.C. attended Sports held by Guards Divisional Artillery.	
"	21st.		Major-General G.P.T. FEILDING returned from leave today.	
"	22nd.		1st Bn. Grenadier Guards moved from CLERY to TINCOURT.	
"	23rd.		1st Bn. Welsh Guards moved from HALLE to TINCOURT.	
"	24th.		G.O.C. went to see A.M.S. Fourth Army, at Army Headquarters.	

P.T.O.

Army Form C. 2118

WAR DIARY
or
INTELLIGENCE SUMMARY

(Erase heading not required.)

Instructions regarding War Diaries and Intelligence Summaries are contained in F. S. Regs., Part II. and the Staff Manual respectively. Title Pages will be prepared in manuscript.

Place	Date	Hour	Summary of Events and Information	Remarks and references to Appendices
	April 25th.		1st Bn. Scots Guards moved to ROCQUIGNY from CLERY. 2nd Bn. Irish Guards moved to CLERY from ROCQUIGNY. G.O.C. held a Conference of the Divisional Staff at Divisional Headquarters.	
	" 26th.			
	" 27th.			
	" 28th.			
	" 29th.		1st Bn. Coldstream Guards moved to LE TRANSLOY from CLERY. 2nd Bn. Irish Guards moved to LES BOEUFS from CLERY. 76th Field Company R.E. moved to LES BOEUFS from BRONFAY. 1 Company 4th Bn. Coldstream Guards moved to BRONFAY from CORBIE.	
	" 30th.		Divisional Staff Conference was held at 4-45 p.m. today.	

[signature]
Major-General,
Commanding GUARDS DIVISION.

WAR DIARY
or
INTELLIGENCE SUMMARY

Administrative Staff, Army Form C. 2118
Headquarters, Guards Division.
May, 1917.

(Erase heading not required.)

Place	Date	Hour	Summary of Events and Information	Remarks and references to Appendices
	May 1st.			
	" 2nd.		Captain C.V. FISHER-ROWE, M.C., 1st Battalion Grenadier Guards appointed Brigade Major, 51st Infantry Brigade. G.O.C. attended a Platoon Competition of the 1st Guards Brigade.	
	" 3rd.		2nd Battalion Scots Guards moved from CARTIGNY to NURLU to construct an Aerodrome for the R.F.C.	
	" 4th.			
	" 5th.			
	" 6th.		2nd Battalion Scots Guards returned from NURLU to CARTIGNY.	
	" 7th.			
	" 8th.		Guards Divisional Artillery warned to be ready to move to 2nd Army on 11th.	
	" 9th.		A.A. & Q.M.G. proceeded to AMIENS to arrange for entrainment of G.D.A. to Second Army. Entraining Stations, EDGEHILL and HEILLY, Detraining Stations ARQUES and ST. OMER. First train to leave EDGEHILL 11-15 a.m. on 11th.	
	" 10th.		The Army Commander and Corps Commander visited Divisional Headquarters today.	
	" 11th.		The Divisional Artillery begin entraining at EDGEHILL and HEILLY.	
	" 12th		The Divisional Artillery completed entraining for Second Army. Orders received for one Company (Pioneers) at ETRICOURT to rejoin Battalion at CORBIE. Train to leave ROCQUIGNY at 15-00 hours on 13th. 4th Battalion Coldstream Guards (Pioneers) to be prepared to move by train on or after 14th. Instructions received that His Majesty The King of the Belgians will inspect a Brigade of Guards on Tuesday, May 15th. 2nd Guards Brigade selected for inspection.	

P.T.O.

Army Form C. 2118

WAR DIARY
or
INTELLIGENCE SUMMARY
(Erase heading not required.)

Instructions regarding War Diaries and Intelligence Summaries are contained in F. S. Regs., Part II. and the Staff Manual respectively. Title Pages will be prepared in manuscript.

Place	Date	Hour	Summary of Events and Information	Remarks and references to Appendices
	May 13th.		The Major-General attended the Sports of the 2nd Battalion Scots Guards at CARTIGNY today.	
	May 14th.		A Rehearsal of tomorrow's Review was held at 4-30 p.m. in a very heavy thunderstorm.	
	" 15th.		His Majesty The King of the BELGIANS, K.G., accompanied by the Army Commander, the Corps Commander, and H.S.H. Prince Alexandre of TECK, inspected the 2nd Guards Brigade near CURLU today. The Brigade afterwards marched past in fours.	
	" 16th.			
	" 17th.		The 2nd Guards Brigade, 4th Guards M.G. Coy., 1st Guards Bde. M.G. Coy. and T.M. Battery moved from CURLU to BILLON. The 75th and 76th Field Companies R.E. moved from CLERY to BILLON. 1st Battalion Grenadier Guards moved from TINCOURT to CLERY.	
	" 18th.		The 2nd Guards Brigade, 4th Guards M.G. Company, 1st Guards Bde. M.G. Coy. and T.M. Battery moved from BILLON to VILLE-MERICOURT area. BONNAY and MORLANCOURT, respectively. The 75th and 76th Field Companies R.E. Moved from BILLON to SAILLY le SEC and BONNAY respectively. The 4th Battalion Grenadier Guards and 2nd Battalion Scots Guards moved from CARTIGNY to BILLON. The 1st Battalion Grenadier Guards moved from CLERY to BILLON. S.A.A. Section of D.A.C. moved from MINDEN POST to HEILLY.	
	" 19th.		The Divisional Headquarters moved from CURLU to HEILLY. The 3rd Guards Brigade less 1st Bn. Welsh Guards moved from BILLON to CORBIE.	
	" 20th.		1st Bn. Welsh Guards moved by rail from TINCOURT to CORBIE. 1st Guards Brigade moved from ETRICOURT-LE MESNIL Area to BILLON and CURLU today.	
	" 21st.		1st Guards Brigade moved from BILLON and CURLU to MORLANCOURT - SAILLY LE SEC Area, Headquarters at SAILLY-LAURETTE.	

P.T.O.

Army Form C. 2118.

WAR DIARY
or
INTELLIGENCE SUMMARY.

(Erase heading not required.)

Instructions regarding War Diaries and Intelligence Summaries are contained in F.S. Regs., Part II. and the Staff Manual respectively. Title pages will be prepared in manuscript.

Place	Date	Hour	Summary of Events and Information	Remarks and references to Appendices
	May	22nd.	Lieutenant-General Sir F.I. MAXSE, K.C.B., K.C.V.O. etc. delivered a Lecture to Brigadier-Generals and Officers Commanding Battalions in the morning. The G.O.C. inspected the Transport of the 2nd Guards Brigade at 4 p.m. The Band of the Grenadier Guards left for PARIS to join the Massed Bands of the Guards Regiments.	
	"	23rd.	G.O.C. visited the Battlefield of ARRAS.	
	"	24th.	No. 3 Field Ambulance moved from GROVETOWN to HEILLY.	
	"	25th.		
	"	26th.	2nd Guards Brigade held their Brigade Sports at MERICOURT-L'ABBE.	
	"	27th.		
	"	28th.	The D.A.A.G. accompanied by Staff Captains, proceeded north to Second Army Area to arrange billets.	
	"	29th.		
	"	(30-(31st.	The Division began entraining this morning for Second Army Area, 1st Guards Brigade Group and B.A.A.Section of D.A.G. from EDGEHILL to CASSEL, 2nd Guards Brigade Group, Divisional Headquarters from HEILLY to ARQUES and 3rd Guards Brigade Group from CORBIE to ST. OMER. Divisional Headquarters closed at 5 p.m. on 30th at HEILLY and re-opened at RENESCURE at 12 noon on 31st.	

[signature] Colonel
for Major-General,
Commanding GUARDS DIVISION.

Army Form C. 2118.

WAR DIARY
or
INTELLIGENCE SUMMARY.
(Erase heading not required.)

ADMINISTRATIVE STAFF,
GUARDS DIVISION.

Month of JUNE, 1917.

Instructions regarding War Diaries and Intelligence Summaries are contained in F.S. Regs. Part II. and the Staff Manual respectively. Title pages will be prepared in manuscript.

Place	Date	Hour	Summary of Events and Information	Remarks and references to Appendices
	June 1st.		Position of Division as follows :-	
			Divisional Headquarters at RENESCURE.	
			1st Guards Brigade at RENESCURE and along ARQUES - CASSEL ROAD.	
			2nd Guards Brigade at WARDRECQUES.	
			3rd Guards Brigade at CAMPAGNE, ECQUES-LE BIBEROU.	
			S.A.A. Section D.A.C., at RENESCURE, to move to ARQUES.	
			4th Guards Machine Gun Company at ARQUES.	
	" 2nd.		The Army Commander and D.A. & Q.M.G., Second Army, visited Divisional Headquarters today. The G.O.C. held a Divisional Conference at 6 p.m.	
	" 3rd.		S.A.A. Section of D.A.C. moved from RENESCURE to Billets in ARQUES. The Major-General visited the Pioneer Battalion at LOCRE.	
	" 4th.		The Major-General visited the Machine Gun Depot at CAMIERS.	
	" 5th.			
	" 6th.		4th Bn. Coldstream Guards rejoined the Division and were billetted in ARQUES. 2 Battalions 2nd Guards Brigade marched to TILQUES Area for Musketry.	
	" 7th.		G.O.C. attended a Conference at Corps Headquarters(in the morning and 1st Battalion Scots Guards Water Sports in the afternoon.	
	" 8th.		2 Battalions 2nd Guards Brigade returned from TILQUES Area from Musketry. 2 Battalions 2nd Guards Brigade proceeded to TILQUES Area for Musketry.	
	" 9th.			
	" 10th.		2 Battalions 2nd Guards Brigade returned from TILQUES Area from Musketry. 2 Battalions 1st Guards Brigade proceeded to TILQUES Area for Musketry.	

P.T.O.

WAR DIARY
or
INTELLIGENCE SUMMARY.

(Erase heading not required.)

Army Form C. 2118.

Place	Date	Hour	Summary of Events and Information	Remarks and references to Appendices
Guards	June 11th.		Divisional Artillery move into CAESTRE Area, rejoining Guards Division. The Divisional Competitions were held at RENESCURE this afternoon, with the following results :-	
			BAYONET FIGHTING :- 1st. 1st Bn. Grenadier Guards.	
			2nd. 2nd Bn. Grenadier Guards.	
			BAYONET FIGHTING INSTRUCTOR,-	
			1st. N.C.O., 3rd Bn. Grenadier Guards.	
			2nd. N.C.O., 2nd Bn. Grenadier Guards.	
			BEST TURNED OUT LIMBER:-	
			1st. Divisional Signal Company R.E.	
			2nd. 3rd Guards Brigade Machine Gun Company.	
			3rd. 2nd Guards Brigade Machine Gun Company.	
			BEST TURNED OUT COOKER :-	
			1st. 2nd Bn. Scots Guards.	
			2nd. 1st Bn. Grenadier Guards.	
			3rd. 3rd Bn. Grenadier Guards.	
			BEST TURNED OUT WATER CART :-	
			1st. 2nd Bn. Grenadier Guards.	
			2nd. 2nd Bn. Scots Guards.	
			3rd. No. 9 Field Ambulance.	
			BEST TURNED OUT G.S. WAGON:-	
			1st. 124 Coy. A.S.C.	
			2nd. H.Q. (456) Coy. A.S.C.	
			3rd. S.A.A. Section, D.A.C.	
			BEST TURNED OUT HORSE AMBULANCE:-	
			1st. No. 9 Field Ambulance.	
			2nd. No. 3 Field Ambulance.	
			BEST TURNED OUT 6 MULES & G.S. WAGONS:-	
			1st. "A" Sub Section of D.A.C.	
			BOXING.	
			HEAVY. 1st. Pte. HARRIS, 2nd Bn. Coldstream Guards.	
			2nd. L/Sergt. SHARPE, 4th Bn. Coldstream Guards.	

P.T.O.

Army Form C. 2118.

WAR DIARY
or
INTELLIGENCE SUMMARY
(Erase heading not required.)

Instructions regarding War Diaries and Intelligence Summaries are contained in F. S. Regs., Part II. and the Staff Manual respectively. Title pages will be prepared in manuscript.

Place	Date	Hour	Summary of Events and Information	Remarks and references to Appendices
	June 11th.		BOXING. (Contd).	
			LIGHT HEAVY:- 1st. L/Corpl. F. VAUGHAN, 3rd Bn. Coldstream Guards.	
			2nd. Pte. A. JONES, 3rd Bn. Grenadier Guards.	
			MIDDLE WEIGHT:- 1st. Pte. CHAMBERLAIN, 3rd Guards Bde. M.G. Company.	
			2nd. L/Cpl. McDERMOTT, 4th Bn. Coldstream Guards.	
			LIGHT WEIGHT:- 1st. Pte. WILLIAMS, 3rd Guards Bde. M.G. Company.	
			2nd. Pte. A. WALE, 2nd Bn. Coldstream Guards.	
			BANTAM:- 1st. Driver E. GOULD, No. 1 Coy. Guards Divl. Train.	
			2nd. Driver A. BIRT, R.F.A.	
			FEATHER WEIGHT:- 1st. Driver MORGAN, R.F.A. (S.A.A. Section).	
			2nd. Pte. COONEY, 1st Bn. Coldstream Guards.	
	June 12th.		G.O.C. visited Headquarters, Guards Divisional Artillery at BORRE. Brigadier-General F.I.M. WILSON, Brigadier-General, R.A., vice Brigadier-General W. EVANS, D.S.O., reported on arrival at Divisional Headquarters. 2nd Guards Brigade Group moved to WORMHOUDT Area.	
	" 13th.		The D.A.A.G. proceeded to Corps Headquarters and remained there to take over new area. 2nd Guards Brigade Group moved to L.M.Y.Z. Camps near POPERINGHE.	
	" 14th.		G.O.C., G.S.O.I., and A.A. & Q.M.G. attended a Conference at the Corps at 10-30 a.m. 2nd Guards Brigade moved 2 Battalions into the Line near BOESINGHE under the orders of the 38th Division.	
	" 15th.			
	" 16th.		The 1st Guards Brigade Group, 4th Guards M.G. Company and S.A.A. Section D.A.C., moved from RENESCURE Area to WINNEZEELE and OUDEZEELE Area. Grenadier Guards joined "A. & Q" staff under instruction. Captain R.S. LAMBERT M.C.,	

P.T.O.

Army Form C. 2118.

WAR DIARY
or
INTELLIGENCE SUMMARY.
(Erase heading not required.)

Instructions regarding War Diaries and Intelligence Summaries are contained in F. S. Regs., Part II. and the Staff Manual respectively. Title pages will be prepared in manuscript.

Place	Date	Hour	Summary of Events and Information	Remarks and references to Appendices
	June	17th.	The 1st Guards Brigade Group, less 1 Battalion, 4 Machine Gun Companies, and S.A.A. Section, D.A.C., moved to the PROVEN Area. 2 Battalions 3rd Guards Brigade and Brigade Headquarters moved to WINNEZEELE Area.	
	"	18th.	Divisional Headquarters moved from REMESCURE to J. Camp. 2 Battalions 3rd Guards Brigade and Brigade Headquarters moved to HERZEELE Area.	
	"	19th.	2 Battalions 3rd Guards Brigade passed from TILQUES Area to HERZEELE.	
	"	20th.	G.O.C., accompanied by A.A. & Q.M.G. attended Allied Parade at HERZEELE on the occasion of the Presentation by General ANTOINE, G.O.C., 1st French Army of French Decorations to British officers. The 2nd Bn. Grenadier Guards and 2nd Bn. Coldstream Guards and Band of Coldstream Guards formed the British Contingent, while 2 Battalions of French Infantry represented the French Army. G.O.C., Fifth Army and G.O.C., XIV Corps were present.	
	"	21st.	Captain Sir J. DYER, Bart., M.C., Scots Guards, Staff Captain 2nd Guards Brigade, appointed D.A.Q.M.G., vice Major R.H. HERMON-HODGE, M.V.O., D.S.O., Grenadier Guards, R. of O., to England.	
	"	22nd.	Lieut. C.E.M. ELLISON, M.C., Grenadier Guards, 3rd Guards Brigade M.G. Company joined the "A & Q" Staff under instruction. Captain R.S. LAMBERT, M.C., Grenadier Guards was transferred to "G" Office.	
	"	23rd.		
	"	24th.	Major R.H. HERMON-HODGE, M.V.O., D.S.O., Grenadier Guards, R. of O., proceeded to England. Captain Sir J. DYER, Bart., M.C., Scots Guards, Staff Captain, 2nd Guards Brigade, assumed the duties of D.A.Q.M.G., Guards Division. Captain O. LYTTELTON, D.S.O., Grenadier Guards assumed the duties of Staff Captain, 2nd Guards Brigade.	

P.T.O.

Army Form C. 2118.

WAR DIARY
or
INTELLIGENCE SUMMARY.
(Erase heading not required.)

Instructions regarding War Diaries and Intelligence Summaries are contained in F. S. Regs., Part II. and the Staff Manual respectively. Title pages will be prepared in manuscript.

Place	Date	Hour	Summary of Events and Information	Remarks and references to Appendices
	June 25th.			
	" 26th.		The Band played at Corps Headquarters on the occasion of the visit of Their Majesty's The King and Queen of the BELGIANS.	
	" 27th.		The Band proceeded to HERZEELE.	
	" 28th.			
	" 29th.		Relief of 2nd Guards Brigade in the line by the 1st Guards Brigade.	
	" 30th.			

Major-General,
Commanding GUARDS DIVISION.

Army Form C. 2118.

WAR DIARY
INTELLIGENCE SUMMARY.
(Erase heading not required.)

GUARDS DIVISION.
ADMINISTRATIVE STAFF.
JULY - 1917.

Place	Date	Hour	Summary of Events and Information	Remarks and references to Appendices
	July 1st.		4th Bn. Grenadier Guards and 2nd Bn. Scots Guards move from HERZEELE to B. Division Area. 1st Bn. Coldstream Guards and 3rd Bn. Grenadier Guards moving from B.Division Area to HERZEELE. Casualties - Killed 2 O.R. Wounded 13 O.R.	
"	2nd.		2nd Guards Brigade Headquarters move from A.4.d.8.2./Sheet 28, to HERZEELE. 3rd Guards Brigade Headquarters move from HERZEELE to A.4.d.8.2./Sheet 28 1st Bn. Grenadier Guards and 1st Bn. Welsh Guards moved from HERZEELE to B. Division Area. 1st Bn. Scots Guards and 2nd Bn. Irish Guards moved from B. Division Area to HERZEELE. Casualties - Wounded - 1 Offr. 4 O.R.	
"	3rd.		Casualties - Killed 1. O.R. Wounded - 16 O.R.	
"	4th.		G.O.C. and G.S.O.I. attended a Gas demonstration at HELFAUT today. Casualties - Killed - Officers 2. O.R. 15. Wounded- Officers 1. O.R. 17. Missing - Officers 2.	
"	5th.		Casualties - Killed - 10 O.R. Wounded 1 Offr. 22 O.R. Missing 1 O.R.	
"	6th.		G.O.C., accompanied by A.A. & Q.M.G. went to HERZEELE on the occasion of His Majesty The King witnessing Training Operations there by the 2nd Guards Brigade. Divisional Headquarters was bombed during the night. Casualties - Killed - 2 O.R. Wounded 2 Officers, 23 O.R.	
"	7th.		Divisional Headquarters was shelled about 1 p.m. by a long range gun. Casualties - Killed - 1 Officer, 5 O.R. Wounded 26 O.R.	
"	8th.		Casualties - Killed - 7 O.R. Wounded 8 O.R.	
"	9th.		Water from the YSER RIVER at HARINGHE was turned on to the Front areas. Casualties - Killed 7 O.R. Wounded 1 Offr., 27 O.R.	
"	10th.		Casualties - Killed - 1 Officer, 3 O.R. Wounded 12 O.R.	

Army Form C. 2118.

WAR DIARY
or
INTELLIGENCE SUMMARY.
(Erase heading not required.)

Instructions regarding War Diaries and Intelligence Summaries are contained in F. S. Regs. Part II and the Staff Manual respectively. Title pages will be prepared in manuscript.

Place	Date	Hour	Summary of Events and Information	Remarks and references to Appendices
	July 11th.		The Major-General held a Conference at 3.30 p.m. today. Casualties - Killed - 4 O.R. Wounded 21 O.R.	
"	12th.		Casualties - Killed - 1 O.R. Wounded 2 Officers, 20 O.R.	
"	13th.		G.O.C., Fifth Army lunched here and proceeded afterwards to a Demonstration by 4th Bn. Coldstream Guards and 1st Bn. Welsh Guards of practising crossing a Canal with Mats and Petrol Tin Bridges. G.O.C., 1st French Division and a number of French Officers were also present. Casualties - Killed - 7 O.R. Wounded 1 Officer, 33 O.R.	
"	14th.		Lieutenant H.J.B. EYRE, 1st Bn. Irish Guards reported missing. 1st Guards Brigade in the line relieved by 1 Battalion from each of the 2nd and 3rd Guards Brigades, G.O.C., 3rd Guards Brigade, Headquarters at ZOMMERBLOOM CABARET, in Command of Divisional Front. Casualties - Killed 4 O.R. Wounded 1 Officer, 35 O.R. Missing 1 Officer, 1 O.R.	
"	15th.		French Liaison Officer joined the Division. Casualties - Killed - 8 O.R. Wounded 55 O.R.	
"	16th.		Casualties - Killed 6 O.R. Wounded 37 O.R.	
"	17th.		A.A. & Q.M.G. and D.A.Q.M.G. visited Headquarters 1st French Division (1er. Bureau) at CROMBEKE. Casualties - Killed 3 O.R. Wounded 20 O.R.	
"	18th.		7 French Liaison officers reported for duty. Casualties - Killed 2 Other Ranks. Wounded 2 officers 8 O.R. Missing 2 O.R.	
"	19th.		Casualties - Killed 2 Officers, 3 O.R. Wounded 1 Officer, 69 O.R.	

WAR DIARY
or
INTELLIGENCE SUMMARY.

(Erase heading not required.)

Army Form C. 2118.

Place	Date	Hour	Summary of Events and Information	Remarks and references to Appendices
	July 20th.		Lieut-Colonel E.B.G. GREGGE-HOPWOOD, D.S.O. and Major S.J. BURTON, 1st Battalion Coldstream Guards both killed this afternoon. Casualties - Killed 2 Officers, 4 O.R. Wounded 36 O.R.	
	" 21st.		The Major-General proceeded at 2 p.m. to meet the Commander-in-Chief at Corps Headquarters. Casualties - Killed 6 O.R. Wounded 2 Officers, 14 O.R. 2nd Guards Brigade Headquarters relieve 3rd Guards Brigade Headquarters at ZOMMERBLOOM CABARET.	
	" 22nd.		Casualties - Killed 1 Officer (2/Lieut. J.F. SMYTH, 1st Bn. Scots Guards), 14 O.R. Wounded 2 Officers, 52 Other Ranks. Missing 1 O.R.	
	" 23rd.		Casualties - Killed 1 Officer (Lieut. E.G.L. KING, 1st Bn. Grenadier Gds.) 13 O.R. Wounded 63 O.R. Missing 1 O.R.	
	" 24th.		3rd Bn. Coldstream Guards and 1st Bn. Irish Guards moved from HERZEELE to FOREST Area. Casualties - Killed 19 O.R. Wounded 7 Officers, 182 O.R., including 4 officers and 53 O.R. previously gassed now diagnosed.	
	" 25th.		1st Bn. Grenadier Guards and 1st Bn. Coldstream Guards moved from FOREST AREA to ST. SIXTE, exchanging Camps with 1st Essex Regiment and 2nd Hants Regiment. Casualties - Killed - 14 O.R. Wounded 9 Officers, 114 O.R. Missing 1 O.R.	
	" 26th.		1st Guards Brigade Headquarters from HERZEELE relieved the 2nd Guards Brigade Headquarters at ZOMMERBLOOM CABARET. 3rd Bn. Coldstream Guards relieved the 2nd and 3rd Guards Brigades Battalions in front line. Casualties - Killed 19 O.R. Wounded 2 officers, 49 O.R. Missing 1 O.R.	
	" 27th.		Casualties - Killed 14 O.R. Wounded 57 O.R.	
	" 28th.		1st Bn. Grenadier Guards moved from Wood near ST. SIXTE to FOREST AREA. Casualties - Killed 23 O.R. Wounded 5 Officers, 89 O.R.	

P.T.O.

Army Form C. 2118.

WAR DIARY
or
INTELLIGENCE SUMMARY.
(Erase heading not required.)

Instructions regarding War Diaries and Intelligence Summaries are contained in F. S. Regs., Part II. and the Staff Manual respectively. Title pages will be prepared in manuscript.

Place	Date	Hour	Summary of Events and Information	Remarks and references to Appendices
	July 29th		2nd Bn. Coldstream Guards move from HERZEELE to FOREST AREA, completing concentration of Division in Forward Area. Casualties - Killed 13 O.R. Wounded 3 officers, 104 O.R. Missing 4 O.R.	
	" 30th		"G" Branch and A.A. & Q.M.G. moved to advanced Headquarters, ZOMMERBLOOM CABARET. Casualties - Killed 2 officers, 27 O.R. Wounded 7 officers, 141 O.R. Missing 9 O.R.	
	" 31st		Third Battle of YPRES Begins, the Division attacking at 3.50 a.m. Casualties reported - Killed 13 officers, 2 O.R. Wounded 33 officers, 13 O.R. 1st Bn. Welsh Guards and 1st Bn. Scots Guards were withdrawn to bivouacs West of ELVERDINGHE. Captain Sir JOHN DYER, Bart., M.C., Scots Guards, D.A.Q.M.G., Guards Division was killed this afternoon at the Divisional Bomb Store, ONDANK. Lieutenant Hon. A.N.A. VANNECK, M.C., Scots Guards, attached Headquarters, 3rd Guards Brigade was withdrawn to act temporarily as D.A.Q.M.G.	

[signature] A.A. & Q.M.G.

[signature]
for Major-General,
Commanding GUARDS DIVISION.

Army Form C. 2118.

WAR DIARY
or
INTELLIGENCE SUMMARY.

(Erase heading not required.)

GUARDS DIVISION.
ADMINISTRATIVE BRANCH,
AUGUST, 1917.

Instructions regarding War Diaries and Intelligence Summaries are contained in F.S. Regs., Part II. and the Staff Manual respectively. Title pages will be prepared in manuscript.

Place	Date	Hour	Summary of Events and Information	Remarks and references to Appendices
A	Aug. 1st.		The 2nd Bn. Irish Guards and 2nd Bn. Scots Guards were withdrawn from the battle to bivouacs West of ELVERDINGHE. Reported casualties :- Killed 2 officers, 61 O.R. Wounded 13 officers, 297 O.R. Advanced "Q" closed.	
"	2nd.		"G" returned to "J" Camp. 2nd Bn. Irish Guards and 1st Bn. Scots Guards relieved 2nd Bn. Grenadier Guards and 2nd Bn. Coldstream Guards, in the line. Reported casualties :- Killed 4 officers, O.R. 78. Wounded 5 officers, 382 O.R. Missing 27 O.R.	
"	3rd.		2nd Guards Brigade H.Qrs. relieved 1st Guards Brigade Headquarters in the line. Reported casualties :- Killed 4 O.R. Wounded 15 O.R. Missing 1 O.R.	
"	4th.		Relief of Division in the line by the 29th Division begins. Casualties :- Killed 1 officer. 51 O.R. Wounded 1 officer 22 O.R. Missing 10 O.R.	
"	5th.		Casualties :- Killed 2 officers, 2 O.R. Wounded 1 officer, 16 O.R.	
"	6th.		Captain TROUSDELL, A.S.C., Senior Requisitioning Officer was killed and Capt. ESTALL, A.S.C. was wounded at Refilling Point today by a bomb, there being cloudy weather at the time. Casualties :- Killed 1 Officer, 40 O.R. Wounded 4 officers, 215 O.R. Missing 17 O.R.	
"	7th.		Relief of Division completed tonight. Casualties 1 officer 101 O.R. Killed. 2 officers, 477 O.R. Wounded. 45 O.R. Missing.	
"	8th.		Divisional Headquarters moved from "J" Camp, INTERNATIONAL CORNER, to PROVEN. G.O.C. attended the Funeral of Lieut. Hon. EDMUND ELLIOT, 2nd Bn. Scots Guards.	
"	9th.		G.O.C. held a Conference at Divisional Headquarters to discuss future operations and any suggestions emanating from the experience of the recent fighting.	
"	10th. 11th.		G.O.C. attended the Court of Inquiry at MERRIS Headquarters, 30th Division. " " " " " " " " " " " "	

P.T.O.

Army Form C. 2118.

WAR DIARY
or
INTELLIGENCE SUMMARY.
(Erase heading not required.)

Instructions regarding War Diaries and Intelligence Summaries are contained in F. S. Regs., Part II. and the Staff Manual respectively. Title pages will be prepared in manuscript.

Place	Date	Hour	Summary of Events and Information	Remarks and references to Appendices
	Aug. 12th.			
"	13th.			
"	14th.			
"	15th.		The 2nd Guards Brigade moved forward to Camps - DE WIPPE CABARET, DUBLIN Camp, BEDFORD Camp, BURKE Camp, in support of the 29th Division. Working parties proceeded in MOTOR buses and remainder entrained at 12 midnight at PROVEN for ELVERDINGHE. G.O.C. attended Court of Inquiry at Headquarters, 30th Division.	
"	16th.			
"	17th.			
"	18th.		1st Bn. Scots Guards moved to BLEUET FARM.	
"	19th.		2nd Guards Brigade Headquarters, McCoy. T.M. Battery and 1st Bn. Coldstream Guards moved to HERZEELE.	
"	20th.		2nd Bn. Irish Guards moved to BLEUET FARM. G.O.C. held a Conference at Divisional Headquarters at 5 p.m.	
"	21st.		Visit of Commander-in-Chief to Brigades cancelled. G.O.C. accompanied by A&A. & Q.M.G., visited the Guards Reinforcement Battalion at HERZEELE. 1st Bn. Scots Guards and 2nd Bn. Irish Guards relieved by 2nd Bn. Grenadier Guards and 2nd Bn. Coldstream Guards at BLEUET FARM, the former Battalions moved to PICCADILLY and PADDINGTON Camps.	
"	22nd.		Brigadier-General B.N. SERGISON-BROOKE, D.S.O., Grenadier Guards arrived to take over Command of 2nd Guards Brigade, vice Brigadier-General J. PONSONBY, C.M.G., D.S.O., appointed to Command the 40th Division.	
"	23rd.			
"	24th.			

P.T.O.

Army Form C. 2118.

WAR DIARY
or
INTELLIGENCE SUMMARY.
(Erase heading not required.)

Instructions regarding War Diaries and Intelligence Summaries are contained in F. S. Regs., Part II. and the Staff Manual respectively. Title pages will be prepared in manuscript.

Place	Date	Hour	Summary of Events and Information	Remarks and references to Appendices
	Aug.	25th.	General ANTOINE, G.O.C., 1st French Army inspected 3rd Guards Brigade and presented CROIX de GUERRE to officers and men of the Division. Captain E. SEYMOUR, M.V.O., D.S.O., Grenadier Guards, G.S.O.II., Guards Division, appointed G.S.O.II., XIVth Corps. Captain M.B. BECKWITH-SMITH, D.S.O., M.C., was appointed G.S.O.II. to Guards Division.	
	"	26th.	4th Bn. Coldstream Guards less 1 Company moved from PIGEON Camps near PROVEN to BLEUET FARM Area. 55th Field Coy. R.E. from PORTSDOWN Farm to LUNAVILLE FARM. 76th Field Company, PROVEN to ELVERDINGHE. 3rd Gds. Bde. M.G. Coy. and 4th Guards M.G. Coy. from PROVEN to DE WIPPE CABARET Area. Captain E. SEYMOUR, M.V.O., D.S.O., G.S.O.II., took up duties of G.S.O.II., XIVth Corps.	
	"	27th.	2nd Bn. Scots Guards moved from PROVEN and took over left sector of line POELCHAPELLE. 1st Bn. Welsh Guards, PROVEN to WELLINGTON Camp near BLEUET FARM. Headquarters 2nd Guards Brigade, 3rd Br. Grenadier Guards, 1st Bn. Coldstream Guards, moved from HERZEELE to DE WIPPE CABARET Area. Casualties, 2 officers wounded. 1 O.R. Killed, 1 O.R. wounded.	
	"	28th.	Headquarters 3rd Guards Brigade, 1st Bn. Grenadier Guards, 4th Bn. Grenadier Guards, moved from PROVEN Area to WHITE HOPE CORNER Area. 4th Bn. Grenadier Guards taking over right sector of the line. Headquarters, 1st Guards Brigade, 2nd Bn. Grenadier Guards and 2nd Bn. Coldstream Guards, moved to ZOMMERBLOOM CABARET and BLEUET FARM Area. 2nd Gds. Bde. M.G. Coy. and T.M. Battery to DE WIPPE CABARET Area. Casualties, 1 officer wounded, 5 O.R. Killed, 11 O.R. wounded.	
	"	29th.	3rd Bn. Coldstream Guards and 1st Bn. Irish Guards moved from PROVEN Area to BLEUET Farm. 1st Gds. Bde. M.G. Coy. and T.M. Battery, PROVEN Area to "J" Camp near INTERNATIONAL CORNER. Capt. J.J.P. EVANS, M.C., Welsh Guards appointed Brigade Major, 1st Guards Brigade vice Capt. M.B. BECKWITH-SMITH, D.S.O., M.C., Lieut. Hon. A.N.A. VANNECK M.C. appointed Staff Captain 1st Guards Brigade vice Capt. J.J.P. EVANS, M.C. Casualties, 5 O.R. Killed, 14 O.R. wounded.	
	"	30th. 31st.	Casualties, 2 offrs. wounded. 1 officer missing. 8 O.R. killed, 27 O.R. wounded. 2nd Bn. Grenadier Guards and 2nd Bn. Coldstream Guards moved Camp to West side of ELVERDINGHE -WOESTEN Rd. on account of heavy shelling. Orders received for G.S.O.I. to proceed to England. Casualties, 7 O.R. Killed, 11 O.R. wounded.	

H.W.Seay
Brigadier-General,
Commanding GUARDS DIVISION.

WAR DIARY or INTELLIGENCE SUMMARY.

Army Form C. 2118.

Place: ADMINISTRATIVE STAFF, GUARDS DIVISION.
Month: SEPTEMBER, - 1917.

Date	Hour	Summary of Events and Information	Remarks and references to Appendices
Sept. 1st.		G.O.C., Guards Division proceeded on leave. Temporary Command of Division taken over by Brigadier-General G.D. JEFFREYS, C.M.G., Commanding 1st Guards Brigade. Lecture by D.A.D.V.S. on "Stable Management", at 2 p.m. Bt.Lt.Colonel R.S. TEMPEST, D.S.O., 1st Bn. Scots Guards proceeded to take over temporary Command of 43rd Infantry Brigade. Major M. ROMER took over Command of Battalion. Casualties - 5 O.R. Killed, 20 O.R. Wounded.	
" 2nd.		Casualties - 3 O.R. Killed, 22 O.R. Wounded, 1 O.R. Missing.	
" 3rd.		Casualties - 2/Lieut. G.C.S. TENNANT, 1st Bn. Welsh Guards and 8 O.R. killed. Lieut. R.H. CARSON, 1st Bn. Grenadier Guards and 24 O.R. wounded.	
" 4th.		Casualties - 2/Lieut. G.P. BOYD, 1st Bn. Irish Guards and 25 O.R. killed. 63 O.R. Wounded. Relief 1st Bn. Welsh Guards from line to De WIPPE Camp. 2nd Bn. Coldstream Guards from ETON Camp to line. 3rd Bn. Grenadier Guards from De WIPPE Camp to ETON Camp. 2nd Bn. Scots Guards from WELLINGTON Camp to 28/A.4.d.8.4. Half 1st Guards M.G. Company from FOREST AREA to line. Half 3rd Guards Bde. M.G. Company from line to FOREST Area. 2nd Guards Bde. M.G. Company from FOREST AREA to B.8.d.5.8. and T.M. Bty.,	
" 5th.		Lieut.Colonel C.P. HEYWOOD, D.S.O., G.S.O.I., Coldstream Guards, proceeded to England as Instructor at Staff Course, CAMBRIDGE. Lieut.Colonel Hon. A.G.A. HORE-RUTHVEN, V.C., D.S.O., Welsh Guards, G.S.O.I., 62nd Division assumed duties as G.S.O.I., Guards Division. Casualties - 19 O.R. Killed, 3 Officers, 32 O.R. Wounded.	
" 6th.		Casualties - 10 O.R. Killed, 4 Officers, 67 O.R. wounded.	
" 7th.		Casualties - 8 O.R. Killed, 4 Officers, 47 O.R. wounded. Band of Scots Guards, under Lieut. J.C.I. McCONNEL, arrived from HAVRE.	
" 8th.		Casualties - 2 Officers, 13 O.R. Killed, 6 Officer, 73 O.R. Wounded.	

P.T.O.

Army Form C. 2118.

WAR DIARY
or
INTELLIGENCE SUMMARY.
(Erase heading not required.)

Instructions regarding War Diaries and Intelligence Summaries are contained in F.S. Regs., Part II and the Staff Manual respectively. Title pages will be prepared in manuscript.

Place	Date	Hour	Summary of Events and Information	Remarks and references to Appendices
	Sept.	9th.	Casualties - 4 O.R. Killed, 38 O.R. Wounded.	
	"	10th.	Casualties - 5 O.R. Killed, 39 O.R. Wounded.	
	"	11th.	Casualties - 10 O.R. Killed, 1 Officer, 46 O.R. Wounded, 6 O.R. Missing.	
	"	12th.	2 Battalions, 1st Guards Brigade relieved by 2 Battalions, 2nd Guards Brigade. Casualties - 5 O.R. Killed, 3 Officers, 53 O.R. Wounded.	
	"	13th.	1st Guards Brigade relieved by 2 Battalions 2nd Guards Brigade and relief complete. 2nd Guards Brigade in the line, 3rd Guards Brigade at ZOMMERBLOOM and 1st Guards Brigade in FOREST AREA. Casualties - 8 O.R. Killed, 68 O.R. Wounded.	
	"	14th.	Casualties - 11 O.R. Killed, 3 Officers, 46 O.R. Wounded, 1 Officer, 81 O.R. Missing.	
	"	15th.	Casualties - 5 O.R. Killed, 27 O.R. Wounded, 2 O.R. Missing.	
	"	16th.	Casualties - 9 O.R. Killed, 1 Officer, 42 O.R. Wounded,	
	"	17th.	Casualties - 1 Officer, 3 O.R. Killed, 27 O.R. Wounded. (Major M. BARNE, 1st Bn. Scots Guards killed).	
	"	18th.	Casualties - 1 Officer, 10 O.R. Killed, 1 Officer, 17 O.R. Wounded, 4 O.R. Missing.	
	"	19th.	Casualties - 2 O.R. Killed, 2 Officers, 12 O.R. Wounded. Relief of R.E. and Pioneers by 29th Divisional R.E. and Pioneers.	
	"	20th.	Casualties - 6 O.R. Killed, 21 O.R. Wounded, 3 O.R. Missing. The 1st Guards Brigade moved to PROVEN today. Headquarters, 3rd Guards Brigade, 4th Bn. Grenadier Guards and 2nd Bn. Scots Guards moved to PROVEN Area.	

P.T.O.

Army Form C. 2118.

WAR DIARY
or
INTELLIGENCE SUMMARY.

(Erase heading not required.)

Instructions regarding War Diaries and Intelligence Summaries are contained in F.S. Regs., Part II and the Staff Manual respectively. Title pages will be prepared in manuscript.

Place	Date	Hour	Summary of Events and Information	Remarks and references to Appendices
	Sept. 21st.		1st Bn. Grenadier Guards and 1st Bn. Welsh Guards moved to PROVEN. Casualties - 5 O.R. Killed, 26 O.R. Wounded.	
	" 22nd.		Relief of Division complete. 2nd Guards Brigade to P.2. Area PROVEN. D.H.Q. to PROVEN. Casualties, 4 O.R. Killed, 1 Officer 13 O.R. Wounded. *[handwritten note]*	
	" 23rd.		Guards Divisional Artillery were relieved today. Cinema Tent at Headquarters 2nd Bn. Coldstream Guards opened. Casualties, NIL.	
	" 24th.		Casualties - 11 O.R. Killed, 2 Officers 11 O.R. Wounded.	
	" 25th.		Casualties - 1 O.R. Wounded.	
	" 26th.			
	" 27th.		Corps Commander saw all officers who have been decorated during the War.	
	" 28th.		Casualties, 1 O.R. Wounded.	
	" 29th.		2nd Guards Brigade relieved 3rd Guards Brigade at HERZEELE, the latter moving to P.2. Camps.	
	" 30th.		Casualties - 1 O.R. Killed, 7 O.R. Wounded.	

[signature]
Major-General,
Commanding GUARDS DIVISION.

WAR DIARY
~~INTELLIGENCE~~ **SUMMARY**

(Erase heading not required.)

Army Form C. 2118.

"A" & "Q" Branch,
Headquarters,
GUARDS DIVISION.

Instructions regarding War Diaries and Intelligence Summaries are contained in F. S. Regs., Part II and the Staff Manual respectively. Title Pages will be prepared in manuscript.

October, 1917.

Place	Date	Hour	Summary of Events and Information	Remarks and references to Appendices
	Oct. 1.		Major Sir V.A.F.MACKENZIE, Bt., M.V.O., D.S.O.; 1st Bn. Scots Guards, and Major Hon. H.R.L.G. ALEXANDER, M.C.; 2nd Bn. Irish Guards, reported arrival as 2nd in command, and Commanding Officer respectively. Casualties - Nil.	
	2.		Casualties, Killed 1 O.R.	
	3.		Casualties, Killed 2 O.R., wounded 1 Officer, 5 O.R.	
	4.		The Concert party of the 1st French Army gave a performance at the Cinema Hut, Plurenden Camp at 3 p.m. to-day. G.O.C. was present. The Matinee was a huge success.	
	5.		3rd Guards Brigade took over the Divisional front line. 2nd Guards Brigade moved from HERZEELE to PROVEN area. Guards Reinforcement Battalion under the command of Major Sir V.A.F.MACKENZIE, Bt., M.V.O., D.S.O., was formed at HERZEELE.	
	6.		D.H.Q. moved from PROVEN to "J" Camp, International Corner.	
	7.		1st Guards Brigade moved to ZOMMERBLOOM, 2nd Guards Brigade to Forest Area, Belgian H.Q.	
	8.		Advanced D.H.Q. moved to ZOMMERBLOOM Cabaret.	
	9.		The 1st and 2nd Guards Brigades attacked with the 29th Division on the right, and the 2nd French Division on the left, and obtained all their objectives.	
	10.		Major-General NIGETT, and Lt. Col. CRAIG, U.S.Army, arrived for 2 days visit to the Division, 3rd Guards Brigade relieved 1st and 2nd Guards Brigades in the line.	
	11.			
	12.		3rd Guards Brigade attacked this morning, and obtained all their objectives.	

Army Form C. 2118.

"A" & "Q" Branch.
Headquarters,
GUARDS DIVISION.

WAR DIARY
& INTELLIGENCE SUMMARY
(Erase heading not required.)

October (Contd.)

Instructions regarding War Diaries and Intelligence Summaries are contained in F. S. Regs., Part II and the Staff Manual respectively. Title pages will be prepared in manuscript.

Place	Date	Hour	Summary of Events and Information	Remarks and references to Appendices
	Oct. 13		Casualties, Killed 2 offs., 24 O.R. Wounded 4 off., 125 O.R. Missing 3 O.R.	
	14.		1st Guards Brigade relieve 3rd Guards Brigade in the line.	
	15.		A.A. & Q.M.G. went to EPERLECQUES to arrange new billets.	
	16.		Total Casualties from 9th October, 1917, to 15th same month. Killed. Off. 24 O.R. 399 Wounded. 56 1621 Missing. Nil. 164 TOTAL. Off. 80 O.R. 2184 GRAND TOTAL. 2264	
	17.		Division moved from "J" Camp to PROVEN.	
	18.		Division moved from PROVEN to EPERLECQUES. 2nd Guards Brigade entrained for EPERLECQUES in tactical train.	
	20.		3rd Guards Brigade moved from PROVEN to SERQUES Area by tactical train.	
	21.		H.R.H. The Duke of Connaught visited the Division, visiting Battalion billets; afterwards lunching at Divisional H.Q. Notification received that Division would be inspected by C. in C. on 25th instant.	
	24.		Final preparations for Commander-in-Chief's inspection.	
	25.		Division was inspected by C. in C.	
	27.		Divisional Conference. New formation of Machine Gun Companies suggested. English leave extended to 14 days.	
	28.		D.A.A.G. visited 2nd and 3rd Guards Brigades reference improvements in billets.	
	29.		A.A. & Q.M.G. and D.A.A.G. visited refilling points. Division leave XIX Corps and join II. Corps.	

October, 1917. (Contd.)

"A" & "Q" Branch.
Headquarters,
GUARDS DIVISION.

Army Form C. 2118.

WAR DIARY
or
INTELLIGENCE SUMMARY.
(Erase heading not required.)

Instructions regarding War Diaries and Intelligence Summaries are contained in F. S. Regs., Part II. and the Staff Manual respectively. Title pages will be prepared in manuscript.

Place	Date	Hour	Summary of Events and Information	Remarks and references to Appendices
	Oct. 30.		A.A. & Q.M.G. VISITED XIVth Corps re Immediate Awards and Honours.	

Ivan MacLeod
for Major-General,
Commanding GUARDS DIVISION.

Army Form C. 2118.

WAR DIARY
— of —
INTELLIGENCE SUMMARY.
(Erase heading not required.)

GUARDS DIVISION.
ADMINISTRATIVE STAFF.
November, 1917.

Instructions regarding War Diaries and Intelligence Summaries are contained in F.S. Regs., Part II. and the Staff Manual respectively. Title pages will be prepared in manuscript.

Place	Date	Hour	Summary of Events and Information	Remarks and references to Appendices
Novr.	5th		A.A. & Q.M.G. marked out Ground for Review of Division by General ANTHOINE, Commanding 1st. French Army, near EPERLECQUES.	
"	6th		Review of Division by General ANTHOINE, G.O.C. 1st. French Army. Owing to bad weather the troops were dismissed. 1st. Battalion Scots Guards formed a hollow square for the presentation of the Croix de Guerre, which was conducted in a downpour of rain.	
"	7th		A.A. & Q.M.G. motored to H.Q. First Army. (RANCHICOURT) re move of the Division South.	
"	8th		D.A.A.G. motored to new area. (ST.POL) billeting.	
"	9th		D.A.A.G. motored to new area. (ST.POL) billeting. The Divn. on commence moving south by march route in three stages. 3rd. Guards Brigade move from EPERLECQUES Area to CLARQUES Area. (1st. Stage).	
"	10th		Divisional H.Q. and Divl. troops move from EPERLECQUES Area by motor lorry to ST.POL Area. Divisional Headquarters, ROELLECOURT. 2nd. Guards Brigade move from EPERLECQUES Area to CLARQUES Area. 3rd. Guards Brigade move from CLARQUES Area to FONTAINE-LES-HERNANS Area (2nd. Stage).	
"	11th		1st. Guards Brigade move from EPERLECQUES Area to CLARQUES Area. 2nd. Guards Brigade move from CLARQUES Area to FONTAINE-LES-HERNANS Area. 3rd. Guards Brigade move from FONTAINE-LES-HERNANS Area to AUBIGNY Area. (3rd. Stage).	
"	12th		1st. Guards Brigade move from CLARQUES Area to FONTAINE-LES-HERNANS Area. 2nd. Guards Brigade move from FONTAINE-LES-HERNANS Area to AUBIGNY Area. A.A. & Q.M.G. visited 3rd. Guards Brigade Billeting Area re accommodation. D.A.Q.M.G. visited refilling point.	
"	13th		1st. Guards Brigade move from FONTAINE-LES-HERNANS Area to AUBIGNY Area. D.A.Q.M.G. visited refilling points. A.A. & Q.M.G. visited Brigade billets. Conference of Guards Brigadiers and C.O's with G.O.C.	
"	14th		D.A.A.G. visited BUS-LES-ARTOIS Area. re billeting of Reinforcement Battalion.	

"A" & "Q" Branch.
Headquarters,
GUARDS DIVISION.

Army Form C. 2118.

October, 1917. (Contd.)

WAR DIARY
of
INTELLIGENCE SUMMARY.

(Erase heading not required.)

Instructions regarding War Diaries and Intelligence Summaries are contained in F. S. Regs., Part II. and the Staff Manual respectively. Title pages will be prepared in manuscript.

Place	Date	Hour	Summary of Events and Information	Remarks and references to Appendices
	Oct. 30.		A.A. & Q.M.G. VISITED XIVth Corps re immediate Awards and Honours.	

for Major-General,
Commanding GUARDS DIVISION.

Army Form C. 2118.

WAR DIARY
or
INTELLIGENCE SUMMARY.
(Erase heading not required.)

GUARDS DIVISION.
ADMINISTRATIVE STAFF.
November, 1917.

Instructions regarding War Diaries and Intelligence Summaries are contained in F.S. Regs., Part II. and the Staff Manual respectively. Title pages will be prepared in manuscript.

Place	Date	Hour	Summary of Events and Information	Remarks and references to Appendices
	Novr. 5th		A.A. & Q.M.G. marked out ground for Review of Division by General ANTHOINE, Commanding 1st. French Army, near EPERLECQUES.	
	" 6th		Review of Division by General ANTHOINE, G.O.C. 1st. French Army. Owing to bad weather the troops were dismissed. 1st. Battalion Scots Guards formed a hollow square for the presentation of the Croix de Guerre, which was conducted in a downpour of rain.	
	" 7th		A.A. & Q.M.G. motored to H.Q., First Army, (RANCHICOURT) re move of the Division South.	
	" 8th		D.A.A.G. motored to new area (ST.POL) billeting.	
	" 9th		D.A.A.G. motored to new area (ST.POL) billeting. The Divn. on commence moving South by march route in three stages. 3rd. Guards Brigade move from EPERLECQUES Area to CLARQUES Area. (1st. Stage).	
	" 10th		Divisional H.Q. and Divl. troops move from EPERLECQUES Area, by motor lorry to ST.POL Area. Divisional Headquarters, ROELLECOURT. 2nd. Guards Brigade move from EPERLECQUES Area to CLARQUES Area. 3rd. Guards Brigade move from CLARQUES Area to FONTAINE-LES-HERNANS Area. (2nd. Stage).	
	" 11th		1st. Guards Brigade move from EPERLECQUES Area to CLARQUES Area. 2nd. Guards Brigade move from CLARQUES Area to FONTAINE-LES-HERNANS Area. 3rd. Guards Brigade move from FONTAINE-LES-HERNANS Area to AUBIGNY Area. (3rd. Stage).	
	" 12th		1st. Guards Brigade move from CLARQUES Area to FONTAINE-LES-HERNANS Area. 2nd. Guards Brigade move from FONTAINE-LES-HERNANS Area to AUBIGNY Area. A.A. & Q.M.G. visited 3rd. Guards Brigade Billeting Area re accommodation. D.A.Q.M.G. visited refilling point.	
	" 13th		1st. Guards Brigade move from FONTAINE-LES-HERNANS Area. to AUBIGNY Area. D.A.Q.M.G. visited refilling points. A.A. & Q.M.G. visited Brigade billets. Conference of Guards Brigadiers and C.O's with G.O.C.	
	" 14th		D.A.A.G. visited BUS-LES-ARTOIS Area, re billeting of Reinforcement Battalion.	

Army Form C. 2118.

WAR DIARY
or
INTELLIGENCE SUMMARY.
(Erase heading not required.)

GUARDS DIVISION
ADMINISTRATIVE STAFF.
November, 1917.

Instructions regarding War Diaries and Intelligence Summaries are contained in F.S. Regs., Part II. and the Staff Manual respectively. Title pages will be prepared in manuscript.

Place	Date	Hour	Summary of Events and Information	Remarks and references to Appendices
	Novr. 15th		A.A. & Q.M.G. visited Vth. Corps.	
	" 16th		D.A.A.G. visited BUS-LES-ARTOIS re billeting. A.A. & Q.M.G. visited Vth. Corps.	
	" 17th		Continuing move South, Division move from ST.POL Area to LE CAUROY Area by march route.	
	" 18th		Division move from LE CAUROY Area to BASSEUX Area by march route.	
	" 19th		Division move from BASSEUX Area to ACHIET-LE-GRAND Area by march route. The Division came under Vth. Corps.	
	" 20th		Division hold themselves in readiness to support 51st. Division.	
	" 21st		Division move from ACHIET-LE-GRAND to HAPLINCOURT by bus.	
	" 24th		Division move from HAPLINCOURT to rLESQUIERES Area. 1st. Guards Brigade relieve 51st. Division in front line South of BOURLON WOOD. The Division comes under IVth. Corps.	
	" 26th		2nd. Guards Brigade relieve 1st. Guards Brigade in order to attack FONTAINE.	
	" 27th		2nd. Guards Brigade attack rONTAINE village. 62nd. Divn. on left flank and 6th. Divn. on right. Objective taken but could not be held owing to heavy losses. Relieved by 3rd. Guards Brigade.	
	" 28th		3rd. Guards Brigade relieved by 59th. Division.	
	" 29th		Division relieved by 59th. Division, and move to NEUVILLE in Corps support. The Division comes under IIIrd. Corps.	
	" 30th		Enemy attack British front in GOUZEAUCOURT Area. 1st. and 3rd. Guards Brigades move from METZ and TRESCAULT Area and counter-attack. 2nd. Guards Brigade move up in support from BERTINCOURT Area. Counter-attack successful and enemy driven from GOUZEAUCOURT.	

Major-General,
Commanding Guards Division.

Army Form C. 2118.

WAR DIARY
or
INTELLIGENCE SUMMARY.
(Erase heading not required.)

"A" & "Q" BRANCH,
GUARDS DIVISION. December, 1917.

Instructions regarding War Diaries and Intelligence Summaries are contained in F. S. Regs., Part II and the Staff Manual respectively. Title pages will be prepared in manuscript.

Place	Date	Hour	Summary of Events and Information	Remarks and references to Appendices
December	1st		1st. & 3rd. Guards Brigades successfully attacked enemy trenches east of GOUZEAUCOURT, capturing several guns and about 200 prisoners.	
"	2nd.		Divisional Train move from YTRES to DESSART WOOD, near FINS.	
"	3rd.		A.A. & Q.M.G. and D.A.A.G. visited all three Brigades H.Qrs. in the line. 1st. Guards Brigade relieve 3rd. Guards Brigade in the left sector of Divisional Front.	
"	4th		D.A.A.G. visited new area re billeting.	
"	5th		3rd. Guards Brigade entrain at ETRICOURT for BARLY Area. A.A. & Q.M.G. visited ETRICOURT re entrainment. D.A.A.G. visited new area.	
"	6th		Divisional H.Qrs. move from NEUVILLE to FOSSEUX by train. 1st. & 2nd. Guards Brigades move from NEUVILLE Area to FOSSEUX Area by tactical train. A.A. & Q.M.G. & D.A.A.G. entrained the troops at ETRICOURT. Administered by XVIIth. Corps.	
"	8th		G.S.O.III visited Third Army.	
"	9th		Irish Guards Band join Division from England. G.O.C. 29th. Division visited the Division.	
"	10th		4th. Bn. Coldstream Guards move by train from YTRES to FOSSEUX Area.	
"	11th		3rd. Guards Brigade moved from BARLY to ARRAS.	
"	12th		Divisional H.Qrs. moved from FOSSEUX to ARRAS.	
"	14th		Guards Divl. Artillery moved from line to BEAULENCOURT.	
"	15th		Reinforcement Battalion moved by train from BUS-LES-ARTOIS, detraining at ARRAS, and marched to camp in AGNEZ-LES-DUISANS.	

Army Form C. 2118.

WAR DIARY
or
INTELLIGENCE SUMMARY.

"A" & "Q" BRANCH, GUARDS DIVISION. December, 1917.

(Erase heading not required.)

Instructions regarding War Diaries and Intelligence Summaries are contained in F.S. Regs., Part II. and the Staff Manual respectively. Title pages will be prepared in manuscript.

Place	Date	Hour	Summary of Events and Information	Remarks and references to Appendices
December	20th		Major G.M. DARELL, M.C., returned from Staff Course, Cambridge, and resumed duties of D.A.Q.M.G.	
"	21st		D.A.A.G. inspected proposed site of farm, but owing to ground being covered with snow and there being a thick mist, nothing definite was settled.	
"	22nd		Capt. M. BECKWITH-SMITH, D.S.O., M.C., ordered to proceed to G.H.Q., as G.S.O. Training. Capt. H. AUBREY FLETCHER arrives as G.S.O.II.	
"	24th		Lieut.-Colonel HORE-RUTHVEN, V.C., D.S.O., left the Division to take up duties as Brigadier-General, General Staff, VIIth. Corps. Lieut.-Colonel MAC CLINTOCK, R.E., assumed duties as G.S.O.I.	
"	29th		Divisional Train took over their permanent horse standings at BAUDIMONT.	

Captain,
for
D.A.A.G.,
A.A. & Q.M.G., GUARDS DIVISION.

Army Form C. 2118.

WAR DIARY
—or—
INTELLIGENCE SUMMARY.
(Erase heading not required.)

"A" & "Q" BRANCH,
GUARDS DIVISION.

JANUARY, 1918.

Place	Date	Hour	Summary of Events and Information	Remarks and references to Appendices
January	1st		3rd. Guards Brigade relieve Infantry Brigade in the line North of the SCARPE.	
"	2nd		3rd. Guards Brigade relieve Infantry Brigade in the line South of the SCARPE. 1st. Guards Brigade move from BERNEVILLE to ARRAS. Means of communication in the Sector are excellent. There being a well organised system of Decauville Rly. and barges for feeding the Support Line.	
"	10th		The Brigadier-General Commanding, visited the Barracks and COLLEGE COMMUNAL and discussed the improvement of billets.	
"	16th		The Brigadier-General Commanding presented ribbon of the V.C. to Sgt. McAULAY, 1st. Bn. Scots Guards, at the PRISON, ARRAS, at 2-30 p.m.	
"	26th		The Brigadier-General Commanding motored to G.H.Q. with the A.A. & Q.M.G.	
"	27th		The following Officers appointed (temporarily) to the staff of the 4th. Guards Brigade on formation :- G.O.C., Colonel Lord R. le N. ARDEE, C.B., Irish Guards. Brigade Major, Lieut. (T/Capt.) O. LYTTELTON, D.S.O., Grenadier Guards. Staff Captain. Captain E.D. MACKENZIE, D.S.O., Scots Guards.	
"	30th		Capt. W.H. WYNNE-FINCH, M.C., 2nd. Bn. Scots Guards, appointed staff Captain, 2nd. Guards Brigade, vice Lieut. (T/Capt.) LYTTELTON, D.S.O., 3rd. Bn. Grenadier Guards.	

_____
Brigadier-General,
Commanding GUARDS DIVISION.

Army Form C. 2118.

WAR DIARY
or
INTELLIGENCE SUMMARY.

"A & Q" BRANCH,
GUARDS DIVISION.
Month of February, 1918.

(Erase heading not required.)

Instructions regarding War Diaries and Intelligence Summaries are contained in F.S. Regs., Part II. and the Staff Manual respectively. Title pages will be prepared in manuscript.

Vol 31

Place	Date	Hour	Summary of Events and Information	Remarks and references to Appendices
ARRAS.	1/2/18.		Lieutenant T.S.C. STEPHENSON, R.F.A., appointed staff officer for Reconnaissance, Guards Divisional Artillery, vice Lieutenant R. CARPENTIER. Assumed duties, 22/1/18.	
"	4/2/18.		Captain F.F. GRAHAM, Irish Guards, joined the Division as A.D.C. to the G.O.C.	
"	8/2/18.		General ROQUES, Inspector of Defences, French Ministry of War, visited the Division today. 3rd Battalion Coldstream Guards left the Division for 31st Division, XIIIth Corps (4th Guards Brigade.) (Came under orders of G.O.C., 4th Guards Brigade on 8/2/18).	
"	12/2/18.		Major-General G.P.T. FEILDING, C.B., C.M.G., D.S.O., rejoined the Division from leave. 4th Battalion Grenadier Guards and 2nd Bn. Irish Guards left the Division for 31st Division, XIIIth Corps (4th Guards Brigade.) (Came under orders of G.O.C., 4th Guards Brigade on 8/2/18).	
"	17/2/18.		Band of the Irish Guards proceeded to PARIS to join Massed Bands en route for ROME.	
"	19/2/18.		General ORTH (Belgian Army), had Lunch at D.H.Q., and presented the Major-General with the Belgian Croix de GUERRE.	
"	22/2/18.		Field Marshal Commanding-in-Chief visited D.H.Q.	
"	23/2/18.		Orders received to form the Battalion of Machine Gun Guards.	
"	25/2/18.		M. CLEMENCEAU visited ARRAS for a short time, about 4.45 p.m.	
"	27/2/18.		Capt. (T/Major) R.C. BINGHAM, D.S.O., 3rd Bn. Coldstream Guards, appointed to Command the Battalion of Machine Gun Guards. Capt. (T/Major) R.M. WRIGHT, M.C., 1st Bn. Coldstream Guards appointed 2nd-in-Command of the Battalion of Machine Gun Guards.	

[signature]
Major-General,
Commanding Guards Division.

Army Form C. 2118.

WAR DIARY
or
INTELLIGENCE SUMMARY.

(Erase heading not required.)

"A" & "Q" BRANCH,
GUARDS DIVISION.

MARCH 1918.

Place	Date	Hour	Summary of Events and Information	Remarks and references to Appendices
ARRAS	1st.	3 p.m	The Major-General & Lt.H.S.MCKAIG motored to Army H.Qrs., returning about 6 p.m.	
"	4th.	2-30pm	A.A. & Q.M.G., & D.A.Q.M.G. motored to Corps H.Qrs.	
"	6/7th	12 mdnt	"Estimated casualties" phase begins (first in 1918).	
"	9th.		Capt. R.S.LAMBERT,M.C., Grenadier Guards, appointed Staff Captain 2nd.Guards Brigade vice Capt. W.H.WYNNE-FINCH,M.C., Scots Guards.	
"	9th.		Capt. W.H.WYNNE-FINCH,M.C., Scots Guards, appointed Brigade Major 2nd. Guards Brigade vice Capt. H.C.LOYD,D.S.O.,M.C., Coldstream Guards.	
"	9th.		Capt. H.C.LOYD,D.S.O.,M.C., Coldstream Guards, appointed G.S.O.II, 42nd. Division.	
"	11th.	p.m.	Moves in connection with expected enemy offensive. Viz :- 1st.Bn.Irish Gds. from PRISON to STIRLING CAMP (less 2 Coys. forward to 3rd. System). 1st.Bn.Coldstream Gds.from GORDON CAMP to ST.LAURENT BLANGY(less 1 Coy. forward to 3rd. System). Reserve Battn. of 3rd.Brigade (1st.Bn.Welsh Gds.) to GORDON CAMP on relief, instead of to BAUDIMONT BARRACKS. 76th. Field Coy. R.E. from STIRLING CAMP to ST. LAURENT BLANGY. 55th. " " " " " " ARRAS. 75th. " " " remains in " TRIANGLE CAMP taken over for parties attached to 55th. & 76th. Field Coys. R.E. Balance of Working parties from LEWIS BARRACKS to GORDON CAMP. (LEWIS BARRACKS, BAUDIMONT BARRACKS, and the PRISON now cleared for 4th. Division.	
"	17th.		Capt. F.H.BALLANTINE-DYKES, D.S.O., Scots Guards, D.A.A.G. Guards Division, appointed D.A.D.G.T., G.H.Q., and to be T/Major while so employed. Major G.M.DARELL, M.C., Coldstream Guards, D.A.Q.M.G., Guards Division, appointed D.A.A.G., Guards Division. Capt. C. BEWICKE,M.C., Scots Guards, Staff Captain 3rd. Guards Brigade, appointed D.A.Q.M.G., Guards Division, and to be T/Major while so employed. Lieut.(T/Capt.)F.P.ACLAND, HOOD, M.C., Coldstream Guards appointed Staff Capt. 3rd.Guards Bde. vice Capt.(T/Capt.)BEWICKE,M.C., Scots Guards.	
"	19/20th.		Relief of 2nd. & 3rd. Guards Brigades by 10th.& 12th. Infantry Brigades, 4th. Division.	

Army Form C. 2118.

WAR DIARY
or
INTELLIGENCE SUMMARY.
(Erase heading not required.)

MARCH, 1918.
"A" & "Q" BRANCH,
GUARDS DIVISION.

Instructions regarding War Diaries and Intelligence Summaries are contained in F.S. Regs., Part II. and the Staff Manual respectively. Title pages will be prepared in manuscript.

Place	Date	Hour	Summary of Events and Information	Remarks and references to Appendices
ARRAS.	20/21		Relief of 1st. Guards Brigade by 11th. Infantry Brigade, 4th. Division.	
"	19/20/21.		Relief of 4/Battn. M.G. Guards by 4th. Bn. M.G. Corps.	
"	21st.		Move of 2nd. Guards Brigade to MERCATEL. Shell pitched near D.H.Q. killing Capt.J.BALFOUR,M.C., Lieut. J.M.PATON, 2/Lieut.H.C.BOYCOTT, and wounding Lieut.A.H.WILLIAMS and 2/Lieut.C.H.BOVILL, also Lt.Col.H.B.FAWCUS,C.M.G.,D.S.O., Capt.W.F.MACLEAN,R.A.M.C. wounded at duty. 2/Lieut.C.H.BOVILL died of wounds 24/3/'18. ARRAS and vicinity were shelled throughout the day.	
BRETON-COURT.	22nd.		2nd. Guards Brigade moved into 3rd. system of trenches, and 3rd. Guards Brigade moved to MERCATEL, and afterwards into the 3rd. system. The 1st. Guards Brigade moved up behind in support. The Divisional Headquarters moved about 11 p.m. to BRETONCOURT, when the VIth. Corps vacated this village and moved to HUMBER CAMP.	
"	23rd.		Capt.F.G.BEAUMONT-NESBITT, Grenadier Guards, joined as Brigade Major 3rd. Guards Brigade.	
"	23/24. Mdnt.		Estimated Heavy Casualty phase commences.	
"	24th.		VIth. Corps moved from HUMBER CAMP to PAS.	
"	25th.		Transport Lines of Guards Brigades, M.G. battn., Field Coys. R.E. & Pioneer Battn. moved to BAILLEULMONT Area. Major (Bt.Lt.Col.) G.B.S.FOLLETT, D.S.O.,M.V.O., 2nd.Bn.Coldstream Guards appointed to Command 2nd. Guards Brigade, and to be Temp.Brig: General whilst so employed, vice Bt.Lt.Col. (T/Brig:Gen.) B.N.SERGISON BROOKE,D.S.O., Grenadier Guards.	
"	26th.		VIth. Corps moved from PAS to FINQUES.	
"	27th.		VIth. Corps moved from FINQUES to NOYELLE VION. Reinforcement Battn. moved from HALLOY to BERLES-AU-BOIS, and bivouacked in trenches west of RANSART.	
"	27/28. Mdnt.		97th. Infantry Brigade attached to Guards Division, and moved up to RANSART.	

Army Form C. 2118.

WAR DIARY
or
INTELLIGENCE SUMMARY
(Erase heading not required.)

MARCH, 1918.

"A" & "Q" BRANCH,
GUARDS DIVISION.

Place	Date	Hour	Summary of Events and Information	Remarks and references to Appendices
BRETON-COURT.	28th.		Major H.E.WHALEY, 4th.Bn.Coldstream Guards to Command Reinforcement Battn. (Strength 2200) as a fighting or working unit. Four cookers, two water carts & two G.S. wagons attached to them from surplus transport.	
"	29th.		H.Q. Reinforcement Battn. moved to BRETONCOURT. Major E.C. ELLICE, D.S.O. rejoined Reinforcement Battn. from leave and took over Command from Major H.E. WHALEY.	
"	30th.		Lieut. (T/Major) E.W.M.GRIGG, D.S.O., M.C., Grenadier Guards (S.R.) from G.S.O. 2nd. Grade, G.H.Q. joined the Division, and appointed G.S.O.I of the Division, to date 1/4/'18; vice Major (T/Lt.Col.) R.S. McCLINTOCK, D.S.O., R.E., who left the Division 1/4/'18 to take up duties as G.S.O.I, L. of C. Area.	
"	30th.		97th. Infantry Brigade no longer attached to Division.	
"	31st.		Casualties since midnight 23/24th. (all arms) :- Killed.　　　　　13 officers.　　230 O.R. Wounded.　　　　46　　"　　　　832 O.R. Missing.　　　　　-　　"　　　　　18 O.R. 　　TOTAL.　　　59 officers.　1080 O.R. Heaviest casualties occurred in :- 　1/Bn.Grenadier Gds.　6 officers.　110 O.R. 　2/Bn.　　"　　　　"　6　　"　　　130 O.R. 　3/Bn.　　"　　　　"　12　"　　　135 O.R. 　2/Bn. Scots Gds.　　4　　"　　　138 O.R. 　1/Bn. Irish Gds.　　8　　"　　　114 O.R.	

for Major-General,
Commanding GUARDS DIVISION.

APRIL 1918
V
APRIL 1919

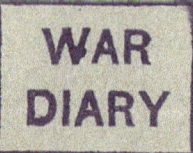

A. & Q.

GUARDS DIVISION

APRIL 1918

CASUALTY RETURN 20th March to 17th April

WAR DIARY / INTELLIGENCE SUMMARY

Army Form C. 2118.

"1" & "4" Brigade
GUARDS DIVISION.

APRIL 1916.

Place	Date	Hour	Summary of Events and Information	Remarks and references to Appendices
	2		Draft of 3 officers & 180 O.R. for 1st.. Battn. joined from Base.	
			Drafts of 3 officers & 323 O.R. from base for Battns. as under joined from Base.	
			1st. Bn. Gren. Gds. 1 off. 22 O.R.	
			2nd. Bn. Gren. Gds. 1 off. 83 "	
			3rd. Bn. Gren. Gds. 1 off. 38 "	
			1st. Bn. Grey. Gds. 1 off. 38 "	
			1st. Bn. Cold. Gds. - 28 "	
			2nd. Bn. Cold. Gds. 1 " 55 "	
			4th. Bn. Cold. Gds. 1 " 18 "	
	3		1st. Bn. Scots Gds. 1 off. 48 O.R.	
			2nd. Bn. Scots Gds. 1 off. 62 "	
			1st. Bn. Irish Gds. 1 " 74 "	
			1st. Bn. Welsh Gds. 1 " 21 "	
	4		265th. M.G. Coy. attached to the Division with H.Q. in Harponville.	
			Major (Bt. Lt. Col.) J.V. Ponsonby (Col.) Lord Henry Seymour D.S.O. relinquished command of 3rd. Guards Bde.	
			Lt. Col. (Temp. Bt. Col.) R.L. Cd-Still. D.S.O. Scots Guards assumed temporary command of 3rd. Guards Brigade.	
	5		Conference at G.H.Q. Montreuil. G.G.C., A.A. & Q.M.G., C.R.E. and G.S.O. 1st. & 4th. Guards Bdes. were present.	
	6		Draft of 31 officers and 1150 O.R. for Battns. as under joined from base.	
			1st. Bn. Gren. Gds. 3 off. 107 O.R.	
			2nd. Bn. Gren. Gds. 5 " 216 "	
			3rd. Bn. Gren. Gds. 6 " 224 "	
			1st. Bn. Cold. Gds. 3 " 166 "	
			2nd. Bn. Cold. Gds. - 54 "	
			4th. Bn. Cold. Gds. 3 " 85 O.R.	
			1st. Bn. Welsh Gds. 2 off. 100 "	
			1st. Bn. Scots Gds. 1 " 1 "	
			1st. Bn. Irish Gds. 2 " - "	
	7		265th. M.G. Coy. left this Division.	
	10		Draft of 20 officers & 427 O.R. for Battns. as under arrived from Base.	
			1st. Bn. Gren. Gds. 1 off. - O.R. 4th. Bn. Cold. Gds. 22 O.R.	
			2nd. Bn. Gren. Gds. 1 " 24 " 1st. Bn. Scots Gds. 2 off. 17 "	
			3rd. Bn. Gren. Gds. 1 " 120 " 2nd. Bn. Scots Gds. 1 " 143 "	
			1st. Bn. Cold. Gds. 1 " 35 " 1st. Bn. Irish Gds. 1 " 22 "	
			2nd. Bn. Cold. Gds. 3 " 93 " 1st. Bn. Welsh Gds. 3 " 40 "	
			Employment Coy. 69 O.R.	

Army Form C. 2118.

WAR DIARY of GUARDS DIVISION.

INTELLIGENCE SUMMARY.

APRIL, 1918.

(Erase heading not required.)

Instructions regarding War Diaries and Intelligence Summaries are contained in F.S. Regs., Part II. and the Staff Manual respectively. Title pages will be prepared in manuscript.

Place	Date	Hour	Summary of Events and Information	Remarks and references to Appendices
BRETONCOURT	11.		Draft of 50 O.R. 1st.Bn.Grenadier Guards, 50 O.R. 3rd.Bn.Grenadier Guards, arrived from Base.	
"	13.		Army Commander visited D.H.Q. and had tea with the Major-general.	
"	13.		A.A. & Q.M.G. motored to Details Camp of Reinforcement Batn. at MAISON-PONTHIEU.	
"	12/14/15.		Relief of Division by 2nd. Division.	
"	13/14.		1st. Guards Brigade moved from Line to BAVINCOURT Area.	
"	14.		D.H.Q. moved to BAVINCOURT.	
BAVINCOURT	14/15		2nd. Guards Brigade moved from Line to LARBRET Area.	
"	14/15		3rd. Guards Brigade moved from Line to SAULTY Area.	
"	14/15		Personnel of Reinforcement Batn. less Permanent Staff, rejoined Batns. Permanent staff of Reinforcement Batn. moved to LARBRET.	
"	14.		Draft of 50 O.R. M.G. Guards joined from Base.	
"	17.		Batn. H.Q. and 3 Companies of M.G. Batn. moved to BIENVILLERS.	
"	18.		General LEMAISTRE, Commanding Xth. French Army visited D.H.Q.	
"	20.		Total casualties from noon 20/3/'18 to noon 17/4/'18 :- Killed. 16 officers. 301 O.R. Wounded. 61.* " 1504 O.R. Missing. Nil. " 33 O.R. ——— ——— 77 " 1838 O.R. ===== =====	* Includes 5 since died of wounds. 11 at duty.
"	20.		Batn. H.Q. and 1 Coy. of M.G. Batn. moved back to SAULTY.	
"	21.		Draft of 2 officers & 226 O.R. joined 1st. Bn. Scots Guards. " 1 " & 177 O.R. " 2nd. Bn. Scots Guards.	
"	22.	2-30 pm.	The Commander-in-Chief visited D.H.Q.	

INTELLIGENCE SUMMARY.   APRIL, 1918.

(Erase heading not required.)

Place	Date	Hour	Summary of Events and Information	Remarks and references to Appendices
BAVINCOURT.	24.		1st. Guards Brigade moved to line (centre sub-sector) be relieve 14th. Inf. Bde. 32nd. Division. 3rd. Guards Brigade moved up to BIENVILLERS for the night.	
HUMBERCAMP.	25.		D.H.Q. moved to HUMBERCAMP relieving 32nd. Division. 2nd. Guards Brigade moved by bus into line (left sub-sector) relieving 97th. Infantry Brigade. 3rd. Guards Brigade moved into line (right sub-sector) relieving 96th. Infantry Brigade. Brig. Gen.B.N.SERGISON-BROOKE,D.S.O. arrived and took over command of 2nd. Guards Brigade. Brig. Gen.G.B.S.FOLLET,M.V.O.,D.S.O., took over command of 3rd. Guards Brigade.	
"	27.		Army Commander visited D.H.Q. and had tea with the Major-General.	
"	27.		Drafts as under left Base for Battns. 2nd.Bn.Grenadier Gds.. 1 O.R. 1st.Bn.Irish Gds.. 6 O.R. 3rd.Bn. -do- 2 " M.G. Battn. 18 "	
"	29.		The Major-General held a Conference at 1st. Guards Bde. H.Q. at 4 p.m. this afternoon. The following attended :- Brigadiers, G.S.O.I., A.A. & Q.M.G., C.R.A., C.R.E., O.C. M.G.Battn. and Brigade Majors. Drafts as under joined units from Base. 1st.Bn.Gren.Gds.. 28 O.R. 4th.Bn.Cold.Gds.. 7 O.R. 2nd.Bn.Gren.Gds.. 27 O.R. 1st.Bn.Scots Gds.. 12 O.R. 3rd.Bn.Gren.Gds.. 12 O.R. 2nd.Bn.Scots Gds.. 3 Offs..17 O.R. 1st.Bn.Cold.Gds.. 22 O.R. 1st.Bn.Irish Gds.. 120.R. 2nd.Bn.Cold.Gds.. 18 O.R. 1st.Bn.Welsh Gds.. 20 B.R. Employment Coy.. 3 O.R.	
"	29.		Captain L.M.GIBBS,A.C., Coldstream Guards, G.S.O.III, Guards Division, took over the duties of Brigade Major, 140th. Infantry Brigade. Lieut.(a/Capt.) J.A. BUCHANAN,M.C., Grenadier Guards, G.S.O took over the duties of G.S.O.III, Guards Division.	

[signature]
Major-General,
Commanding Guards Division.

Casualties

from 20 March to 17 April

1918

SECRET.

HEADQUARTERS,
GUARDS' DIVISION.
No. 673/229A
Date 21/4/18

The Brigade Major,
   Brigade of Guards,
      Carlton House Terrace,
         LONDON.S.W.

      Enclosed statement is forwarded for your information.

H.Q., Guards Division.
21/4/'18.

Jn Darell
Major,
D.A.A.G.,
GUARDS DIVISION.

NCO Casualties from Noon, 29th March, 1918 to Noon, 17th April, 1918.

UNIT.	Killed. Officers.	Killed. O.R.	Wounded. Officers.	Wounded. O.R.	Missg. Officers.	Missg. O.R.	Total Officers.	Total O.R.	Remarks.
1st. Guards Brigade.									
2/Grenadier Gds.	2	46	6	131	—	9	177		
3/Coldstream Gds.	1	26	3	105	—	3	133		
2/Irish Gds.	2	23	12	145	—	13	188		
"									
total.	5	95	20	381	—	25	477		
2nd. Guards Brigade.									
3/Gren.Gds.	3	38	10	131	—	15 (a)	179		(a) 2/Lieutenant
1/Cold.Gds.	1	22	5	124	—	6	155		E.K.Smithson
1/Scots Gds.	1	13	5	69	—	6	109		Brooks, C.S.O.
total.	5	77	21	324	1(a)	19	445		
3rd. Guards Brigade.									
1/Gren.Gds.	3	44	6	125	—	8	174		
2/Scots Gds.	1	32	4	154	—	7	7	200	
1/Welsh Gds.	1	16	2	102	—	5	130		
total.	4	102	11	349	—	16	10	503	
4th. m.Coldstream Gds.	1	5	—	12	—	1	19		(b) Includes :—
Div. Employment Coy.	—	—	—	1	—	—	1		11 at duty 5 sick/died of wounds.
4/Grenadier Guards.	1	10	9	147	—	4	10	170	
1st.Guards M.G.Btty.	—	3	—	5	—	—	8		(c) Includes:—
2nd. " " "	—	—	—	9	—	—	9		8 now reported kt.
3rd. " " "	—	4	—	9	—	—	13		5 " wd.
									3 " rejoined.
GRAND TOTAL.	16	301	61(b)	1204	33(c)	77(b)	1638.		

Oct 1915

a/c of Opuab. Br Gen. J. Ransomly p/c Gaska
dt - 9 Oct
a/c op Opun by Cmdy Gas du 17/10/15
a/c of Opuns by Col Corry (3 Swriska)

End

Army Form C. 2118.

WAR DIARY
or
~~INTELLIGENCE SUMMARY~~

"A & Q" BRANCH,
H.Q.,
GUARDS DIVISION.

MONTH OF MAY, 1918.

(Erase heading not required.)

Instructions regarding War Diaries and Intelligence Summaries are contained in F.S. Regs., Part II. and the Staff Manual respectively. Title pages will be prepared in manuscript.

Place	Date	Hour	Summary of Events and Information	Remarks and references to Appendices
HUMBER- CAMP.	May 1st.			
"	" 3rd.		Drafts as under joined Units from Base :-	

			Offrs. O.R. Offrs. O.R.
			1st Bn.G.G. 3 5 1st Bn. C.G. - 2
			2nd Bn.G.G. 1 3 2nd Bn. C.G. 1 4
			3rd Bn.G.G. 1 9 4th Bn. C.G. 1 3
			1st Bn.I.G. 1 4 76thFieldCo.R.E. - 2
			1st Bn.W.G. - 4 Field Ambces. - 2
			               1st Bn. S.G. 4 8
			               2nd Bn. S.G. 2 19
			
			There was a "Q" Conference at VIth Corps Headquarters at 2.30 p.m. The A.A. & Q.M.G. attended.	

"	" 4th.		The Band of the Welsh Guards came up from the Base, and went to WARLINCOURT, (3rd Guards Brigade Details).
			  Captain R.S. LAMBERT, M.C., Staff Captain, 2nd Guards Brigade, appointed Brigade Major, 4th Guards Brigade, vice Captain O. LYTTLETON, D.S.O., Wounded.
			  Lieut. C.E.M. ELLISON, M.C., Grenadier Guards, appointed Staff Captain, 2nd Guards Brigade, and to be Temp. Captain whilst so employed, vice Captain R.S. LAMBERT, M.C., appointed Brigade Major, 4th Guards Brigade.	

"	" 6th.		The Major-General held a Conference at 1st Guards Brigade Headquarters at 4 p.m. today. The following attended :- Brigadiers, C.R.A., C.R.E., G.S.O.I., A.A. & Q.M.G., O.C., 4th Bn. Guards M.G. Regt.	
"	" 7th.		Draft of 1 Officer and 53 Other Ranks joined the 4th Bn. Guards M.G. Regt. from Base.	

/contd.

Army Form C. 2118.

WAR DIARY
or
INTELLIGENCE SUMMARY.
(Erase heading not required.)

Instructions regarding War Diaries and Intelligence Summaries are contained in F. S. Regs., Part II. and the Staff Manual respectively. Title pages will be prepared in manuscript.

Place	Date	Hour	Summary of Events and Information	Remarks and references to Appendices
HUMBER-CAMP.	May. 7th.		Draft as under left Base for Units :-	
			Offrs. O.R. Offrs. O.R.	
			1st Bn. G.G. - 12 1st Bn. C.G. - 14 1st Bn. S.G. - 12	
			2nd Bn. G.G. - 12 2nd Bn. C.G. 2 10 2nd Bn. S.G. - 78	
			3rd Bn. G.G. - 190 4th Bn. C.G. 1 9	
			1st Bn. I.G. 1 7 D.H.Q. - 2 No. 3 Field	
			1st Bn. W.G. - 10 55th Field - 1 Ambulance. - 1	
			Co. R.E.	
"	9th.		Draft of 10 O.R. joined 2nd Bn. Scots Guards.	
			Band of Welsh Guards went to ST. AMAND to play and returned to WARLINCOURT in the evening.	
"	10th.		Draft of 13 signallers joined 1st Bn. Scots Guards.	
			" " 14 " 2nd Bn. "	
"	11th.		Drafts as under joined Battalions :-	
			Offrs. O.R. Offrs. O.R. Offrs. O.R.	
			1st Bn. G.G. 3 6 1st Bn. C.G. - 9 1st Bn. S.G. - 9 1st Bn. W.G. - 4	
			2nd Bn. G.G. 1 9 2nd Bn. C.G. - 10 2nd Bn. S.G. - 14 Div.Employ.Co. - 4	
			3rd Bn. G.G. - 10 4th Bn. C.G. - 5 1st Bn. I.G. - 6 4th.Gds.M.G.Bn. - 36	
"	13th.		Drafts as under joined Battalions :-	
			Offrs. O.R. Offrs. O.R.	
			1st Bn. C.G. 2 - 55th Field Coy. R.E. - 18	
			2nd Bn. S.G. 1 2 75th Field Coy. R.E. - 6	
			76th Field Coy. R.E. - 1	
			/Contd.	

Army Form C. 2118.

WAR DIARY
or
INTELLIGENCE SUMMARY.
(Erase heading not required.)

Place	Date	Hour	Summary of Events and Information	Remarks and references to Appendices
HUMBERCAMP.May.	16th.		Drafts as under joined Battalions :-	
			Offrs. O.R. Offrs. O.R.	
			1st Bn. G.G. - 10 1st Bn. S.G. - 10 1st Bn. W.G. - 4	
			2nd Bn. G.G. - 14 2nd Bn. S.G. - 14	
			3rd Bn. G.G. - 8 1st Bn. I.G. - 4 G.D.Arty. 49 9.	
"	17th.		Welsh Guards Band played to Americans at LA BAZEQUE FARM.	
			The Major-General held a Conference at the 1st Guards Brigade Headquarters at 5.30 p.m.	
			Following reinforcements left HAVRE for units :-	
			Offrs. O.R. Offrs. O.R.	
			1st Bn. G.G. 1 5 1st Bn. S.G. - 30 Div.Train. 1 1	
			2nd Bn. G.G. - 19 2nd Bn. S.G. - 18 Gds.D.A.C. - 8	
			3rd Bn. G.G. - 11 1st Bn. I.G. - 1 (Indians).	
			1st Bn. W.G. 1 10	
"	20th.		The 4th Guards Brigade arrived at MONDICOURT and came under orders of Guards Division for administration. Brigade H.Q. at GRENAS.	
			4th Bn. Grenadier Guards at SAULTY.	
			2nd Bn. Irish Guards at BARLY.	
			3rd Bn. Coldstream Guards under IVth Corps.(At THIEVRES).	
			Advanced Divisional Headquarters moved to Wood, V.27.a. Central.	
"	22nd.		Lieut.Colonel N.A. ORR-EWING, D.S.O., 2nd Bn. Scots Guards appointed to Command 45th Infantry Brigade, 15th Division and to be Temporary Brigadier-General whilst so employed.	
			Following drafts joined Battalions :-	
			Offrs. O.R. Offrs. O.R.	
			1st Bn. G.G. 1 4 1st Bn. S.G. - 11 1st Bn. I.G. - 7	
			2nd Bn. G.G. 2 5 2nd Bn. S.G. 1 10 1st Bn. W.G. - 8	
			4th Bn. C.G. 1 4	
			Field Cos. 1 8	
			Field Amb. - 2.	

/contd.

Army Form C. 2118.

WAR DIARY
or
INTELLIGENCE SUMMARY.
(Erase heading not required.)

Instructions regarding War Diaries and Intelligence Summaries are contained in F.S. Regs., Part II. and the Staff Manual respectively. Title pages will be prepared in manuscript.

Place	Date	Hour	Summary of Events and Information	Remarks and references to Appendices
HUMBERCAMP.	May. 24th		Following Reinforcements joined Battalions :-	
			Offrs. O.R. Offrs. O.R. Offrs. O.R.	
			1st Bn. G.G. 1 11 1st Bn. C.G. 1 17 1st Bn. S.G. - 7 1st Bn. W.G. - 9	
			2nd Bn. G.G. 1 14 2nd Bn. C.G. 1 12 2nd Bn. S.G. - 2 A.O.C. 1
			3rd Bn. G.G. 1 3 4th Bn. C.G. 1 2 1st Bn. I.G. 1 7 76th FieldCo.R.E. 1	
			Field Amb. 5	
			4th GUARDS BRIGADE.	
			Offrs. O.R.	
			4th Bn. G.G. 2v 1	
			3rd Bn. C.G. 2 2	
			2nd Bn. I.G. 1 1	
"	"	26th	Following Reinforcements joined units :-	
			Offrs. O.R. Offrs. O.R.	
			1st Bn. G.G. - 1 3rd.Bn. C.G. - 126	
			3rd Bn. G.G. 2 4 1st Bn. W.G. 2 2	
			4th Bn. G.G. - 28 1st Bn. I.G. 1 1	
"	"	28th.	3 Officers joined 4th Bn. Guards Machine Gun Regiment today.	
			"A & Q" Branch, Guards Division moved to Wood at V.27.c.7.7. (Sheet 51.C.S.E.).	
			TOTAL CASUALTIES FOR MONTH OF MAY:-	
			Officers. O.R.	
			Killed. 10 108	
			Wounded. 32 590	
			Gassed. 4 23	
			Missing. 2 11	
			TOTAL:- 48. 732. GRAND TOTAL. 780.	
	5th June, 1918.			

Signed for Major-General,
Commanding GUARDS DIVISION.

Army Form C. 2118.

WAR DIARY
or
INTELLIGENCE SUMMARY.
(Erase heading not required.)

"A" & "Q" BRANCH.
H.Q., GUARDS DIVISION.

JUNE. 1918.

Vol 35

Place	Date	Hour	Summary of Events and Information	Remarks and references to Appendices
V.27.c.7.7. (Sheet 51C. S.E.) LA BAZEQUE WOOD.	7th		Division relieved by 2nd. Division. Div. H.Qrs. moved to BAVINCOURT. The following drafts joined their units :—	
			O. O.R. O. O.R.	
			1/Bn.Grenadier Gds. — 4 1/Bn.Coldstream Gds. 0. 7	
			2/Bn. -do- — 3 2/Bn. -do- — 4	
			3/Bn. -do- — 1 3/Bn. -do- — 6	
			4/Bn. -do- — 2	
			1/Bn.Scots Gds. 4 5 1/Bn.Irish Gds. — 20	
			2/Bn. -do- 1 9 2/Bn.Irish Gds. — 7	
			1/Bn.Welsh Gds. 6 7 Field Coys.R.E. — 10	
			Div.Employment Coy. — 15	
			A.O.D. 1 —	
BAVINCOURT	10th		The following drafts joined their units :—	
			1/Bn.Grenadier Gds. — 4 1/Bn.Coldstream Gds. 2 4	
			2/Bn. -do- — 5 2/Bn. -do- — 4	
			3/Bn. -do- — 4 3/Bn. -do- — 5	
			4/Bn. -do- 1 4 4/Bn. -do- — 2	
			1/Bn.Scots Gds. — 5 1/Bn.Irish Gds. 1 4	
			2/Bn. -do- — 5 2/Bn.Irish Gds. — 5	
			1/Bn.Welsh Gds. — 2	
"	11th		The 4th. Guards Brigade less H.Qrs. & 3rd. Bn. Coldstream Guards moved nearer the line to dig a new switch. The 4th.Bn. Grenadier Guards & T.M. Battery went to LA CAUCHIE, and 2nd.Bn. Irish Guards to BAVINCOURT WOOD.	
"	12th		The 3rd. Bn. Coldstream Guards moved to a wood in V.22 & V.23.	

Army Form C. 2118.

WAR DIARY
INTELLIGENCE SUMMARY

"A" & "Q" BRANCH,
H.Q., GUARDS DIVISION.

JUNE, 1918.

(Erase heading not required.)

Place	Date	Hour	Summary of Events and Information	Remarks and references to Appendices
BAVINCOURT	12th.	(cont.)	The Divisional Commander held a Conference at which the Brigadier Generals Commanding the 1st., 2nd., 3rd. & 4th. Guards Brigades and all Commanding Officers were present. The Major-General laid down rules re Officers' Mess expenses.	
"	14th.		A draft of 4 O.R. joined the 4th. Bn. Guards M.G. Regt.	
"	15th.		The following drafts joined their units :-	
			O. O.R. O. O.R.
1/Bn.Grenadier Gds. 0. 17.   1/Bn.Coldstream Gds. 1 10
2/Bn. -do-   1 17.   2/Bn. -do-   1 10
3/Bn. -do-   1 14.   3/Bn. -do-   1 14
4/Bn. -do-   1 16.   4/Bn. -do-   1 6

1/Bn.Scots Gds.   3 10.   1/Bn.Welsh Gds.   - 5
2/Bn. -do-   1 21.   Emplyt.Coy.   - 15
                                              Field Amb.   - 1
1/Bn.Irish Gds.   - 5.
2/Bn. -do-   - 10. | |
"	15th.		The Band of the Grenadier Guards arrived from England.	
"	22nd.		Divisional Horse Show held at U.5.b.	
"	23rd.		The following Reinforcements arrived from the Base:-	
			O. O.R. O. O.R.
1/Bn.Grenadier Gds. 0. 2   1/Bn.Coldstream Gds. 1 1
2/Bn. -do-   2 1   4/Bn. -do-   1 1
3/Bn. -do-   1 1   1/Bn.Scots Gds.   1 1
4/Bn. -do-   2 1   2/Bn. -do-   1 2

1/Bn.Irish Gds.   - 1   Field Coys. R.E.   1 5
1/Bn.Welsh Gds.   1 -   R.A.M.C.   1 2 | |
| " | 24th. | | Captain C.J.M. RILEY, M.C., who had been acting A.D.C. to the Major-General, returned to his Battalion, and Lieut. J.R. SAUNDERS, 1st. Bn. Coldstream Guards, came as A.D.C. | |
| " | 28th. | | Defence Scheme rehearsed. | |

Army Form C. 2118.

WAR DIARY
— or —
INTELLIGENCE SUMMARY
(Erase heading not required.)

"A" & "Q" BRANCH,
H.Q., GUARDS DIVISION.

JUNE, 1918.

Instructions regarding War Diaries and Intelligence Summaries are contained in F. S. Regs., Part II. and the Staff Manual respectively. Title pages will be prepared in manuscript.

Place	Date	Hour	Summary of Events and Information	Remarks and references to Appendices
BAVINCOURT.	28th	(cont.)	11 O.R.'s joined the Field Coys. R.E.	
"	30th		H.R.H. The Duke of Connaught, K.G., K.T.,etc., came to Div'l Headquarters. He was received with a Guard of Honour from 1st. Bn. Irish Guards. Officers on Div.H.Qrs. were drawn up and each one introduced to His Royal Highness. Luncheon was served in the Chateau. After Lunch, Inspection of Prize Winners at the Divisional Horse Show. After inspection, Commanding Officers of all Units in the Division were presented to His Royal Highness. The Duke then motored to BARLY and witnessed a Mass Football Match between 1st.Bn.Grenadier Guards and 1st.Bn.Welsh Guards, and then proceeded to SOMBRIN to watch the 2nd.Bn.Scots Guards Sports.	

[signature]

for Major-General,
Commanding GUARDS DIVISION.

"A" & "Q" BRANCH, Army Form C. 2118.
H.Q., GUARDS DIVISION.
MONTH OF JULY, 1918.

WAR DIARY
or
INTELLIGENCE SUMMARY.
(Erase heading not required.)

Place	Date	Hour	Summary of Events and Information	Remarks and references to Appendices
BAVINCOURT.	2nd.		1st. Guards Brigade. held a Gymkhana at LA BAZEQUE. The Major-General rode his own horse in the last event of the afternoon (13 stone Hurdle Race) and won same.	
"	6th.		The Division relieved the 32nd. Division and went to a Camp at W.3.d.4.5. (Sheet 51C) just outside BAILLEULVAL. The Camp was in a state of construction. Casualties Nil.	
W.3.d.4.5.	7th.		The following drafts joined their units:- 4th. Bn. Guards M.G. Regt. 2 O.R. R.A.M.C. 2 O.R. Field Coys. R.E. 9 O.R. D.A.C. 2 O.R. The A.A. & Q.M.G., D.A.A.G. and D.A.Q.M.G visited the three Brigades in the line. Casualties - wounded 7 O.R.	
"	8th.		BAILLEULVAL was slightly shelled between 9 p.m. & 10 p.m. Casualties - Killed 1 O.R. Wounded 9 O.R.	

"	9th.		The Division was detailed by the Third Army to find a Battalion H.Qrs., a Coy. H.Qrs. and one Company to take part in a review to be held in PARIS on the 14th. July. This party was composed as follows:-
			 Lt.Col. Hon. H.R.L.G. ALEXANDER, D.S.O., M.C. 2nd.Bn. Irish Guards. Commanding.
			 Major C.F.A. WALKER, M.C. 4th.Bn.Grenadier Guards. 2nd-in-Command.
			 Capt. W.D. FAULKNER. 2nd.Bn.Irish Guards. Adjutant.
			 Hon.Capt. D. KINLAY, M.C. 1st.Bn.Scots Guards. Quartermaster.
			 2 platoon Commanders from the 4th. Bn. Grenadier Guards.
			 1 " " " 3rd. Bn. Coldstream Guards.
			 1 " " " 2nd. Bn. Irish Guards.
			                               4th. Bn. Grenadier Guards.
			       100 O.R. 3rd. Bn. Coldstream Guards.
			        50 O.R. 2nd. Bn. Irish Guards.
			        50 O.R.
			 The other ranks comprising Battalion and Company H.Qrs. were drawn from the three abovementioned Battalions. The Band of the Grenadier Guards, & the drums of the 2nd. Bn. Irish Guards also accompanied the party. They entrained at MONDICOURT on 9/7/'18.	

Army Form C. 2118.

(2).

WAR DIARY

"A" & "Q" BRANCH,
H.QRS., GUARDS DIVISION.

or

INTELLIGENCE SUMMARY.

MONTH OF JULY, 1918.

(Erase heading not required.)

Instructions regarding War Diaries and Intelligence Summaries are contained in F. S. Regs., Part II. and the Staff Manual respectively. Title pages will be prepared in manuscript.

Place	Date	Hour	Summary of Events and Information	Remarks and references to Appendices
W.3.d.4.5.	9th.	(tm.)	The 4th. Guards Brigade was transferred to the Fourth Army Area. The move was carried out by strategical train. The Units entrained at MONDICOURT & detrained at EU. Brigade Headquarters closed at GRENAS and reopened at CRIEL PLAGE. Lieut. M. DUQUENOY, 3rd. Bn. Grenadier Guards arrived to take up duties of Camp Commandant. Casualties - wounded 3 O.R.	
"	10th.		The Corps held a Horse Transport Show & Band Contest in a field on the SAULTY - COUTURELLE Road. The following units of the Division took part:— Infantry Transport. 2/Bn.Grenadier Guards (Winners of the Major-General's Cup at the Div'l Horse Show). Field Ambulances. No.4 Field Ambulance. Div'l Trains. No.1 Company. D.A.C. S.A.A. SECTION. Field Companies R.E. 75th. Field Coy. R.E. R.F.A. D/75th. Brigade. R.F.A. Nearly all the Drums and Pipes & Drums and Fifes took part in the Band Contest. The 3rd. Bn. Grenadier Guards were first, and the 1st. Bn. Grenadier Guards second. Heavy rain storms fell throughout the day, thus ending the long spell of fine weather. The following drafts joined their units:— B/75th. Bde. R.F.A.; 1 O.R. D.A.C.(Indians) 10 O.R., Div'l Train 1 O.R. R.A.M.C. 1 O.R. Casualties - Wounded 1 O.R.	
"	11th.		Casualties - Wounded 2 officers (R.F.A.) and 9 O.R.	
"	12th.		Casualties - Killed 4 O.R., wounded 8 O.R.	
"	13th.		The following drafts joined their units:— 1/Bn.Gren.Gds. 2 O.R. 3/Bn.Gren.Gds. 1 O.R. 1/Bn.Scots Gds. 1 O.R. 4/Bn.Guards M.G.Rgt. 1 O.R. Casualties - Wounded 2 O.R.; Missing 1 O.R.	
"	14th.		Casualties. - Wounded 2 O.R.	
"	15th.		Casualties. - Killed 1 O.R. Wounded 6 O.R. The following drafts joined arrived:— 1/C.G. 1 off. 1 O.R. 1/W.G. 1 off. 1 O.R. Div'l Train. 2 O.R. 2/C.G. 1 " 1 O.R. 4/Bn.Guards M.G. Rgt. 2 O.R. Div'l M.T. Coy. 1 O.R. 4/C.G. 1 " 1 O.R. Field Coys.R.E. 2 Offrs.	

Army Form C. 2118.

WAR DIARY
or
INTELLIGENCE SUMMARY

(Erase heading not required.)

"A" & "Q" BRANCH,
H.QRS., GUARDS DIVISION.
MONTH OF JULY, 1918.

Place	Date	Hour	Summary of Events and Information	Remarks and references to Appendices
W.3.d.4.5.	16th.		Casualties. - Killed 1 O.R. wounded 9 O.R.	
"	17th.		Casualties. - Wounded 4 O.R.	
"	18th.		Casualties. - Wounded 4 O.R. The following joined their units:- 1/G.G. 1 Off. 15 O.R. 1/C.G. 4 Off. 2/S.G. 13 O.R. 2/G.G. 6 O.R. 2/C.G. 13 O.R. 1/I.G. - 3/G.G. - 4/C.G. 1 Off. 12 O.R. 1/W.G. 19 O.R.	
"	19th.		Casualties. - Killed 2 O.R. wounded 20 O.R.	
"	20th.		Casualties.- " 2 O.R. " 1 Officer.(Bde.Major,1/Gds.Bde. Capt.J.J.P.EVANS,M.C. W.Gds.) 8 O.R.	
"	21st.		Casualties. - Killed 1 O.R. wounded 13 O.R.	
"	22nd.		During the afternoon about ten shells fell in the camp, but did no harm. The hostile battery then switched on to the village of BAILLEULVAL, and the shelling there for a short time was severe. Casualties. - Wounded (gas) 9 O.R..	
"	23rd.		The following drafts arrived from Base:- 1/G.G. 4 O.R. 1 Off. 1/G.G. 1 Off. 1 O.R. 2/G.G. 3 O.R. 1/W.G. 1 " 1 O.R. 3/G.G. 3 O.R. Casualties. - Killed 3 O.R. Wounded 1 Off. (2/Lt.R.B.JONES, Y/T.M.Bty.) & 41 O.R. The Band of the Grenadier Guards returned from PARIS.	
"	24th.		Casualties. - Killed 1 O.R. Wounded 12 O.R. 1 American Officer killed.(attd.3/G.G.). The area between BAILLEULMONT and BAILLEUVAL was intermittently shelled during the afternoon and evening with H.V. guns.	

Army Form C. 2118.

WAR DIARY
or
INTELLIGENCE SUMMARY.

"A" & "Q" BRANCH,
H.Qrs., GUARDS DIVISION.
MONTH OF JULY, 1918.

(Erase heading not required.)

Place	Date	Hour	Summary of Events and Information	Remarks and references to Appendices
W.3.d.4.5.	25th.		The following reinforcements arrived:- 4/Bn. Cold.Gds.(P). 1 officer. Div'l Train. 1 O.R. A Conference was held at D.H.Q. in the afternoon at which were present the following:- Major-General, C.R.A., G.Os.C. 1st, 2nd. & 3rd. Guards Brigades, C.R.E., O.C. 4/Bn.C.G.(P). O.C. 4/Bn. Guards M.G. Regt., A.D.M.S., O.C. Div. Train, "G" & "Q" representatives The plan of winter organisation in the Divisional Sector, required by VI Corps was discussed. The other subjects before the meeting were of a "G" nature. Casualties. - Killed 1 O.R.; Wounded 1 off.(at duty-Capt.ANDERSON, R.A.M.C. attd.3/G.G.) 5 O.R. 20.R	
"	26th.		Casualties - Wounded 2 O.R. (Americans).	
"	27th.		The following joined their units:- 1/Bn.Irish Gds. 50 O.R. Field Coy. R.E. 1 O.R. Casualties - Killed 1 O.R., Wounded 24 O.R. and 1 O.R. (American). Very heavy rain all day.	
"	28th.		Casualties - Wounded 3 O.R.	
"	29th.		3 officers, 162 O.R. arrived from Base. Casualties - Killed 2 O.R., Wounded 13 O.R., Missing 1 O.R. Wounded 2 O.R. (Americans).	
"	30th.		Casualties - Killed 1 O.R. Wounded 1 officer (2/Lt.J.A.CAMPBELL,1/G.G.) & 12 O.R. Americans,- killed 1 officer & 1 O.R., wounded 5 O.R.	
"	31st.		During the afternoon, BAILLEULMONT, BAILLEULVAL were shelled by high velocity guns. A draft of 1 officer & 16 O.R. Indians, arrived for D.A.C. Casualties. - Killed 4 O.R., wounded 7 O.R.	

Major-General,
Commanding GUARDS DIVISION.

Army Form C. 2118.

WAR DIARY
or
INTELLIGENCE SUMMARY.

"A & Q" OFFICE.
H.Qrs. GUARDS DIVISION. AUGUST, 1918.

(Erase heading not required.)

Place	Date	Hour	Summary of Events and Information	Remarks and references to Appendices
W.3.d.4.5.	1st.		Casualties. Killed 3 O.R. wounded 24 O.R. (American 1 O.R. wounded).	
"	2nd.		Casualties. Killed 1 O.R. (American) wounded 2 O.R. Very heavy rain all day.	
"	3rd.		Casualties. Killed 2 O.R. Wounded 7 O.R. missing 1 O.R. The following drafts joined their units:- R.A.M.C. 5 O.R., 75th Field Coy. R.E. 1 O.R., Div'l Train. 3 O.R. A pierrot troupe called "The Glad Eyes" came over from the M.T. Col. and gave a performance at D.H.Q.	
"	4th.		Casualties. Killed 1 O.R. Wounded 9 O.R.	
"	5th.		Casualties. Killed 1 officer (Lt.G.HUGHES, 1/G.G.) wounded 9 O.R. Killed 1 O.R. (American). A draft of 1 officer and 60 O.R. arrived. The 75th. Brigade R.F.A. held their mounted sports at BERLES-AU-BOIS. A good programme but spoilt by heavy rain.	
"	6th.		A draft of 2 officers and 5 O.R. joined the Division. Between 12 noon and 1 p.m. the camp was shelled. One shell falling within 20 yards of 'G' office, fortunately doing no damage. Casualties. Wounded 3 O.R.	
"	7th.		The Divisional Troupe gave a performance at D.H.Q. Considerable talent was shewn. Casualties. Killed 4 O.R. wounded 1 officer (75th.Field Coy.R.E., Lt.J.R.FEW) and 9 O.R. Killed 1 O.R. wounded 5 O.R. (Americans). 1 New Zealander attached, wounded.	
"	8th.		Casualties. Wounded 3 O.R.	
"	9th.		Casualties. Killed 1 officer. (2/Lt.G.CREED, 74th.Brigade R.F.A.) and 6 O.R. Killed 1 O.R. Wounded 3 O.R. (Americans).	
"	10th.		Following drafts joined their units :- 1/Bn.Gren.Gds. 56 O.R. 1/Bn.Cold.Gds. 21 O.R. 2/Bn.Scots Gds. 1 off. 2 O.R. 2/Bn.Gren.Gds. 3 O.R. 2/Bn.Cold.Gds. 6 O.R. 1/Bn.Irish Gds. 3 O.R. 3/Bn.Gren.Gds. 7 O.R. 1/Bn.Scots Gds. 5 O.R. 1/Bn.Welsh Gds. 1 off. 3 O.R. 76th. Field Coy. R.E. 1 officer. Casualties. Killed 1 O.R. Wounded 1 officer(2/Lt.T.MATHEW,1/W.G.) and 11 O.R. (1 gas) wounded 1 O.R. (American).	

Army Form C. 2118.

WAR DIARY
or
INTELLIGENCE SUMMARY.

(Erase heading not required.)

"A & Q" BRANCH.
H.Qrs. GUARDS DIVISION.

MONTH OF AUGUST. 1918.

Instructions regarding War Diaries and Intelligence Summaries are contained in F.S. Regs., Part II. and the Staff Manual respectively. Title pages will be prepared in manuscript.

Place	Date	Hour	Summary of Events and Information	Remarks and references to Appendices
W.3.d.4.5.	11th.		Casualties. Killed 2 O.R. Wounded 1 off.(at duty)Lt.E.N.de GEIJER,3/G.G. and 13 O.R. BERLES;AU-BOIS was bombed between 10 & 11 p.m. and the B.A.C., 155th.A.Bde.R.F.A. suffered very heavy casualties in animals. 81 being killed and wounded, also 2 O.R. were wounded. 1st.Bn.Welsh Guards relieved by 3rd.Bn.320th.Regt. A.E.F., and moved back to SAULTY.	
"	12th.		Casualties. Wounded 1 O.R. VI Corps H.Qrs. closed at NOYELLE VION & reopened at LUCHEUX at 12(noon).	
"	13th.		Casualties. Wounded 2 offrs.(2/Lt.W.JACKSON,2/C.G.(at duty) & 2/Lt.T.H.SWEENY,55/F.Coy.R.E.=2 O.R. killed 6 O.R., wounded 13 O.R. (Americans).	
"	14th.		Casualties. Killed 3 O.R. wounded 4 O.R. Killed 1 O.R. Wounded 11 O.R.(American)	
"	15th.		A draft of 3 offrs. & 22 O.R. arrived. Casualties Killed 1 O.R. wounded 3 O.R. (1 at duty) wounded 2 O.R. (gas). 1st.Bn.Scots Guards came out of the line and moved back to BAVINCOURT, their place in Brigade being taken by 2nd.Bn.320th.Regt.A.E.F. The 1st.Bn.Welsh Guards moved up into the line. A conference was held at VI Corps Headquarters, and was attended by G.Os.C. Guards, 2nd., 3rd. 5th. and 59th. Divisions.	
"	16th.		Sudden orders were issued for the 1st. Bn. Coldstream Guards and the 3rd.Bn.Grenadier Guards to move back to the SAULTY-BAVINCOURT area, and their places were taken by 2 Battns. of the 320th. Regt. A.E.F. No trains were available owing to all available rolling stock being required for ammunition. The Coldstream were brought back by lorries and the Grenadiers moved back by march route. Casualties,wounded 5 O.R.	
"	17th.		2 O.R. joined R.A.M.C. Casualties. Killed 2 O.R. wounded 10 O.R. At 12 noon, G.O.C. 1st. Guards Brigade took over the H.Qrs. of the 2nd. Guards Brigade and command of the Right Brigade Sector, the 1st. Brigade having side slipped. Colonel PEYTON, Commanding 320th. Regt. A.E.F. took over the centre Brigade at the same hour. The 2nd. Guards Brigade H.Qrs. moved back to SAULTY CHATEAU. The weather which had been very fine and dry for several days, turned cold and very windy, with a little rain.	
"	18th.		30 O.R. came up from the Base for 4th. Bn. Guards M.G. Regt. Casualties. Wounded 4 O.R. (gas). The 320th.Regt.A.E.F. were withdrawn from the line and the Divisional Front reorganised into two~~(2nd).~~ ~~Casualties killed 2 O.R. wounded 1 O.R. at duty~~	

Wt.W.25g/M1997 750,000. 1/17. D.D & L., Ltd. Forms/C2118/4.

Army Form C. 2118.

WAR DIARY
or
INTELLIGENCE SUMMARY

(Erase heading not required.)

"A & Q" BRANCH.
H.QRS., GUARDS DIVISION.
MONTH OF AUGUST. 1918.

Place	Date	Hour	Summary of Events and Information	Remarks and references to Appendices
W.3.d.4.5.	19th.		Casualties. Killed 1 O.R. Wounded 11 O.R. (1 at duty). Administrative Instructions No.10 re Supplies, R.E. material and Ordnance Stores placed at disposal of 2nd. Guards Brigade were issued to all concerned.	Appendix 1.
"	20th.		The Commander-in-Chief lunched with the Major-General. Forward D.H.Q. opened at X.13.d.5.5. at 6 p.m. The A.A. & Q.M.G., & D.A.Q.M.G. went to forward H.Qrs. The D.A.A.G. went to hospital and Captain FURZE took over his work. The 2nd. Guards Bde. and No.3 Coy. Guards M.G.Regt. moved up to their battle positions after dark by motor lorries. The day was overcast, ideal conditions for concentration of troops. Casualties Killed 2 O.R. Wounded 5 O.R.	
"	21st.		The battle opened at 4.55 a.m. The 2nd. Guards Brigade made the attack. Little opposition was encountered and the casualties were light. The night being wonderfully clear, the enemy were very active dropping bombs in the back area. In BAILLEULMONT 2 bombs were dropped, killing 4 men and wounding 16 belonging to the Division. In BERLES-AU-BOIS, 8 bombs were dropped but no casualties caused. The engine at the Div'l Cinema was injured and put out of action.	Casualties See Appendix 2.
"	22nd.		The Band of the Grenadier Guards proceeded by train from WARLINCOURT to PARIS to take part in a performance to be given by the Bands of the Allied Nations for the victims of Big Bertha, (The German long range gun firing on PARIS 70 miles away).	" -/.-
"	23rd.		Continuation of the battle. The weather very hot and dry. Captain E.D. MACKENZIE,D.S.O., Scots Guards, arrived from 4th. Guards Brigade to take over the duties of D.A.A.G.	Casualties See Appendix 2.
"	24th.		Lt.Col. A.H. ROYDS, O.C., Guards Division Base Depot arrived to see the Major-General and left in the evening.	" -/.-
"	25th.		Capt. E.D.MACKENZIE, D.S.O. assumed temporarily the duties of Brigade Major of 3rd. Guards Brigade as Capt. F.G. BEAUMONT-NESBITT went sick. The weather wet and cold, a great change after the heat and dust of the last week. The following drafts arrived :- Offrs. O.R. Offrs. O.R. 1/Bn.Gren.Gds. 1 1 1/Scots Gds. 1 3/Bn.Gren.Gds. 1 1 1/Irish Gds. 1 1/Bn.Cold.Gds. 1 76 Div'l Train. 2 The details and Q.M. stores in BAILLEULMONT & LA CAUCHIE moved to BERLES-AU-BOIS.	Casualties. See Appendix 2.

Army Form C. 2118.

WAR DIARY

or INTELLIGENCE SUMMARY

"A. & Q." BRANCH.
H.QRS., GUARDS DIVISION.
MONTH OF AUGUST, 1918.

(Erase heading not required)

Place	Date	Hour	Summary of Events and Information	Remarks and references to Appendices
W.3.d.4.5.	26th		Major G. DARELL, M.C. returned from hospital and resumed duties of D.A.A.G. The weather cool and windy. A draft of 3 officers & 107 O.R. joined the Division. Casualties as per attached list.	
"	27th.		The Band of the Grenadier Guards returned from PARIS. A draft of 200 O.R. from the 3rd. Bn. Coldstream Guards arrived as draft for the Division. Casualties. Killed,offrs. 7, 69 O.R.; wounded, 21 offrs. 414 O.R., missing, 1 offr. 66 O.R.D.	
"	28th.		The Division was relieved by the 3rd. Division, and were concentrated in the ADINFER WOOD area. Total casualties suffered by the Division during the battle were as per Appendix 2. Drafts, 1 Officer & 75 O.R.	
"	29th.		Advanced D.H.Q. returned to W.3.d.4.5. A draft of 90 O.R. arrived. The A.A. & Q.M.G. motored to G.H.Q. to obtain permission to have reinforcements sent up from the 4th. Guards Brigade. The permission having been granted, he proceeded on to CRIEL PLAGE and arranged matters with the Brigadier.	
"	30th.		A draft of 4 officers and 400 O.R. joined the Division. The cinema reopened at BERLES-AU-BOIS.	
"	31st.		A draft of 4 officers and 81 O.R. arrived.	

[signature]

Major-General,
Commanding GUARDS DIVISION.

S E C R E T.   G.D. No. 1089/78/A.

1st. Guards Brigade.
2nd. Guards Brigade.   S.S.O.
3rd. Guards Brigade.   Divisional Burial Officer.
4th.Bn. Coldstream Gds.   VIth. Corps "Q".
4th.Bn. Gds. M.G. Regt.   12th. Tank Battn., BAILLEULVAL.
G.D.A.   No. 3 Tank Supply Coy., LA BAZEQUE WOOD.
G.R.E.   "G".
A.D.M.S.   Camp Commandant.
D.A.D.V.S.   Div. Salvage Officer.
O.C., S.A.A. Section, D.A.C.   D.A.D.O.S.
A.P.M.   S.C.F., D.C.G., Branch.
Divisional Train.   "   P.C. Branch.

===

GUARDS DIVISION ADMINISTRATIVE INSTRUCTIONS, No. 10.

SUPPLIES, R.E. MATERIAL AND ORDNANCE STORES, PLACED AT DISPOSAL of 2nd. GUARDS BRIGADE.

1. TO BE CARRIED ON THE MAN.
   1 day's Rations   )
   1 day's Iron Rations)   per man.

   1800 Mills Bombs.
   1500 Smoke or Phosphorous Bombs.
    450 Picks.
   1350 Shovels.
    300 Ground flares (18 per Company).
    300 Wire cutters.
   5400 Sandbags (3 per man).
    100 S.O.S.

   The above is being delivered to Headquarters, 2nd. Guards Brigade, SAULTY CHATEAU, by 12 noon, tomorrow, August 20th.

2. ON FIGHTING TANKS (16) FOR USE OF INFANTRY.

   128 Lewis Gun Magazines, i.e., 8 per tank.
    64 carriers for Lewis Gun Magazines.
     4 boxes of S.A.A. (rifle).
     4 petrol tins filled with water.

   The above will be delivered to Tanks in BERLES-AU-BOIS and ADINFER WOOD, X.27.c., tonight, August 19th.

3. ON EACH SUPPLY TANK (3).
    15 Tracing tapes.
     8 lbs. 6" Nails.
    11 bundles F.W.E.
    70 coils Barbed wire.
   180 long Screw pickets.
   200 medium   "   "
    50 petrol tins of water.
     4 boxes of S.A.A. (rifle).
     6   "   "   "   (M.G.).
    10 boxes of No. 23 bombs.

   Of the above, R.E. Stores at RANSART and other stores in the Divisional Bomb Store, W.12.a.9.7., respectively, will be loaded up in wagons by zero hour, when the wagons will move up to the supply tanks in ADINFER WOOD, X.26.a., near Cross Roads. The stores will then be loaded on to Supply Tanks. As soon as ready they will move forward and dump in the front line.

/Contd.

(2).

G.O.C., 2nd. Guards Brigade will detail 3 N.C.O's and 9 men to report to O.C. Supply Tanks at zero hour at X.26.a., near Cross Roads.

1 N.C.O. and 3 men will accompany each Supply Tank in action. They will be rationed for 48 hours from zero hour.

4. 2nd. GUARDS BRIGADE FORWARD DUMPS.
(a) A Forward Dump will be formed at X.26.c.7.2., during zero day, and will consist of :-

```
100  boxes of S.A.A. (Rifle).
150    "    "  "    (M.G.).
200    "    "  No. 5 Bombs.
200    "    "  No. 23    "
 10    "    "  Very lights.
100  S.O.S. rockets.
1000 Flares.
500  Coils of Barbed wire.
3000 mixed screw pickets.
```

(b) 500 rounds Stokes Mortars (Always fuze) will be dumped at S.21.c.9.8., during Zero day.

GENERAL.

1. REPLACEMENT OF FIELD GUNS, MACHINE AND LEWIS GUNS.
During operations the above will be indented for by wire direct to D.A.D.O.S., repeated to "Q" Office.

2. PRISONERS OF WAR.
Divisional Prisoners of War Cage at RANSART, X.8.c.6.3., near Cross Roads.
Corps. Prisoners of War Cage at HUMBERCAMP.

Prisoners will be evacuated as quickly as possible to the Divl. Prisoners of War Cage under an escort of about 5% of the number of prisoners. The Escort, after obtaining a receipt from the officer in charge, will return to their units.
G.O.C., 3rd. Guards Brigade will detail 3 N.C.O's. and 16 O.R. to report to the A.P.M. at the Div. P. of W. Cage at 5 a.m. on Zero day. They will carry two days rations.

3. MEDICAL.
Separate instructions will be issued by the A.D.M.S.

4. STRAGGLERS POSTS.
The 2nd. Guards Brigade will make its own arrangements as regards the sites and organisation of Straggler Posts, EAST of RANSART and BLAIREVILLE.

5. S.A.A. Section, D.A.C.
O.C., S.A.A. Section D.A.C. will detail an orderly to report to "Q" Office, D.H.Q., W.3.d.4.5. at 5 a.m., on Zero day.
He will be rationed by the Camp Commandant.
All wagons will be at the disposal of "Q" Office during operations.

6. DETAILS, QUARTERMASTER's STORES, SURPLUS KITS AND TRANSPORT.
The above, belonging to the 2nd. Guards Brigade, will be accommodated in their old lines in BAILLEULMONT, and in the Camp near LA CAUCHIE. Move to be carried out on August 20th.

/7.

(3).

7. **SALVAGE.**
   The Divisional Salvage Officer will arrange to work up to the present front British Line.

8. **BURIALS.**
   Lieut. M.M. HENDERSON, 1st. Bn. Irish Guards will be responsible, as far as the situation allows, for the burial of men of the Guards Division. The Burial party will be concentrated in RANSART by the night of the 20th. AUGUST.

   The existing cemeteries EAST of the present line, will be used as much as possible.

   O.C., 4th.Bn. Coldstream Guards will detail 1 Sergeant and 6 O.R. to report to the Div. Burial Officer at RANSART at 5 a.m. on ZERO Day.

   The party, strength 1 Officer and 15 O.R. will be rationed by Headquarters, 1st. Guards Brigade.

   Strict attention will be paid to VIth. Corps A/2096/18, issued to the Divisional Burial Officer and Senior Chaplains.

   A C K N O W L E D G E.

H.Q. Guards Division.   Lieutenant-Colonel,
19th. August, 1918.   A.A. & Q.M.G., GUARDS DIVISION.

APPENDIX 2.

TOTAL CASUALTIES FROM NOON 20/8/18 to NOON 31/8/18.

U N I T.	Killed. Offrs.	O.R.	Wounded. Offrs.	O.R.	Missing. Offrs.	O.R.	TOTAL Offrs.	O.R.	REMARKS.
1st. Guards Brigade.									
2nd.Bn.Grenadier Guards.	7	60	6	203	-	24	13	287	(a) Includes 2 at duty.
2nd.Bn.Coldstream Guards.	3	39	7	195	-	73	10	307	(b) " 4 " "
1st.Bn.Irish Guards.	2	12	5	163	-	12	7	187	(c) " 11 " "
TOTAL.	12	111	18a	561b	-	109	30	781	(d) " 3 " "
2nd. GUARDS BRIGADE.									(e) " 1 " "
3rd.Bn.Grenadier Guards.	-	28	3	147	-	8	3	183	(f) " 2 " "
1st.Bn.Coldstream Guards.	3	26	3	165	-	34	6	225	(g) " 1 " "
1st.Bn.Scots Guards.	-	20	7	159	-	19	7	198	(h) " 7 " "
TOTAL.	3	74	13	471c	-	61	16	606	(i) " 1 " "
3rd. Guards Brigade.									
1st.Bn.Grenadier Guards.	4	31	8	177	1	48	13	256	
2nd.Bn.Scots Guards.	1	18	2	88	-	-	3	106	
1st.Bn.Welsh Guards.	1	19	2	120	-	13	3	152	
TOTAL.	6	68	12d	385	1	61	19	514	
4th.Bn.Coldstream Guards.	-	2	-	7e	-	-	-	9	
4th.Bn. Guards M.G. Regt.	2	6	7	103f	-	3	9	112	
Grenadier Guards Band.	-	-	-	2	-	-	-	2	
Div.Employment Coy.	-	-	-	2	-	-	-	2	
G.D.A. & attd.Artillery.	5	20	8g	149h	-	2	13	171	
R.E. and attd. R.E.	1	1	-	9	-	-	1	10	
R.A.M.C.	-	1i	-	51	-	-	-	6	
A.S.C.	-	-	-	1	-	-	-	1	
GRAND TOTAL.	29	283	58	1695	1	236	88	2214	

Names of officer casualties on separate list.

LIST OF OFFICER CASUALTIES IN THE DIVISION FROM
20th. to 29th. AUGUST. 1918.

UNIT.	Nature of Casualty.	Date.
1st. Guards Brigade.		
2nd. Bn. Grenadier Guards.		
Lieut. R.M. OLIVER.	Killed.	28/8/'18.
2/Lieut. F.J. LANGLEY.	-do-	27/8/'18.
Lieut. C. GWYER.	-do-	27/8/'18.
2/Lieut. H.A. FINCH.	-do-	28/8/'18.
2/Lieut. H. WHITE.	Died of wounds.	28/8/'18.
Lieut. M.H. PONSONBY.	-do-	27/8/'18.
Lieut. G.F. LAWRENCE.	Killed.	28/8/'18.
Lieut. N.Mc.K. JESPER.	Wounded.	27/8/'18.
Capt. O. MARTIN-SMITH.	-do-	27/8/'18.
2/Lieut. A.P.J.M.P. de LISLE.	-do-	27/8/'18
2/Lieut. J.A. PATON.	-do-	27/8/'18.
Lieut. C.C.T. GILES.	-do-	27/8/'18.
2nd. Bn. Coldstream Guards.		
2/Lieut. G.C. BRASSEY.	Killed.*	27/8/'18.
Lieut. G.F.B. HANDLEY, M.C.	-do-	27/8/'18.
Capt. E.J. WATSON-SMYTH.	-do-	28/8/'18.
Lieut. E.F. LUTYENS.	Wounded.	27/8/'18.
2/Lieut. W. JACKSON.	-do-	27/8/'18.
2/Lieut. G.C.L. ATKINSON. M.C.	-do-	27/8/'18.
Lieut. H.M.D. BARLOW.	-do-	27/8/'18.
Lieut. C.E. ESPIN.	-do-	27/8/'18.
Capt. L.W.G. ECCLES. M.C.	-do-	27/8/'18.
2/Lieut. E.F.S. GRAHAM.	-do-	27/8/'18.
1st. Bn. Irish Guards.		
Lieut. J.N. WARD.	Killed.	27/8/'18.
Lieut. H.R. BALDWIN.	-do-	27/8/'18.
2/Lieut. J.A.M. FARADAY.	Wounded.	22/8/'18.
2/Lieut. H. CONNOLLY.	-do-	27/8/'18.
Capt. W.J.P. JOYCE.	-do-	27/8/'18.
Lieut. P.S. MacMAHON.	-do-	27/8/'18.
2/Lieut. A.E. HUTCHINSON.	-do- (at duty).	27/8/'18.
Lieut. C.A.J. VERNON.	-do- (gas)	28/8/'18.
2nd. GUARDS BRIGADE.		
3rd. Bn. Grenadier Guards.		
Lieut. R.G. WEST.	Wounded.	23/8/'18.
2/Lieut. R. DELACOMBE.	-do-	23/8/'18.
2/Lieut. E.L.F. CLOUGH-TAYLOR.	-do- (at duty).	23/8/'18.
1st. Bn. Coldstream Guards.		
Capt. R.C.B. FELLOWES.	Killed.	21/8/'18.
Lieut. J.V.T. RODERICK.	-do-	21/8/'18.
Lieut. R.D. GAMBLE.	-do-	22/8/'18.
2/Lieut. A.J. MAXWELL-STUART.	Wounded.	22/8/'18.
2/Lieut. J. ROWLATT.	-do-	22/8/'18.
Capt. A.K. FORBES, R.A.M.C. attd.	-do- (gas)	22/8/'18.
1st. Bn. Scots Guards.		
Capt. W.A. BOYD. M.C.	Wounded.	21/8/'18.
Lieut. G.V. THOMSON.	-do-	21/8/'18.
Capt. T.B. TRAPPES-LOMAX.	-do-	22/8/'18.
2/Lieut. H.J. HOPE.	-do-	23/8/'18.
Lieut. C.H. MACKENZIE.	-do-	23/8/'18.
2/Lieut. W.H. STEWART.	-do-	23/8/'18.
Lieut. R.V. POWELL.	-do- (gas).	25/8/'18.

P.T.O. 3/Guards Bde.

UNIT.	Nature of Casualty.	Date.
3rd GUARDS BRIGADE.		
1st. Bn. Grenadier Guards.		
2/Lieut. C.O. ROCKE.	Killed.	23/8/'18.
2/Lieut. G.E. BARBER.	-do-	24/8/'18.
2/Lieut. A.A.J. WARNER.	-do-	23/8/'18.
Lieut. L.G. BYNG. M.C.	Died of wounds.	24/8/'18.
Major Hon. W.R. BAILEY. D.S.O.	Wounded. (at duty).	24/8/'18.
2/Lieut. R.J.E. CONANT.	-do-	23/8/'18.
Lieut. H.B. VERNON.	-do-	24/8/'18.
Lieut. E.G. HAWKESWORTH.	-do-	25/8/'18.
Capt. Hon. P.P. CARY.	-do-	23/8/'18.
Capt. A.S. CHAMBERS.	-do-	23/8/'18.
2/Lieut. R.L. WEBBER.	-do-	24/8/'18.
Capt. P. MALCOLM.	Missing.	25/8/'18.
2/Lieut. C. CRUTTENDEN.	-do-	25/8/'18.
2nd. Bn. Scots Guards.		
2/Lieut. E.M.M. BALFOUR. M.C.	Killed.	24/8/'18.
Lieut. W.A.A. LESLIE. M.C.	Wounded. (at duty).	24/8/'18.
2/Lieut. E.R. NEWBIGGING.	-do- -do-	25/8/'18.
1st. Bn. Welsh Guards.		
Lieut. W.M. UPJOHN.	Killed.	24/8/'18.
Lt.Col. H. DENE. D.S.O.	Wounded.	24/8/'18.
2/Lieut. J.E. GLOAG.	-do- (gas).	25/8/'18.
4th. Bn. Guards M.G. Regt.		
2/Lieut. H.W. BAILEY.	Wounded (gas)	24/8/'18.
2/Lieut. R.W. DANIELS.	-do-	25/8/'18.
2/Lieut. H.D.F. FRASER.	-do-	26/8/'18.
2/Lieut. H.W. STEWART.	Killed.	27/8/'18.
2/Lieut. H.A. CONNOLLY.	-do-	27/8/'18.
Major G.M. PERRY.	Wounded.	27/8/'18.
Major R.M. WRIGHT. M.C.	-do-	27/8/'18.
2/Lieut. O.S.A. JONES.	-do-	27/8/'18.
2/Lieut. F.F. FULWOOD.	-do-(gas)	25/8/'18.
Guards Div. Arty.		
74th. Brigade R.F.A.		
2/Lieut. J.M.H. GERRARD.	Died of wounds.	28/8/'18.
75th. Brigade R.F.A.		
Major H.B. DRESSER. D.S.O.	Wounded.	21/8/'18.
Major L. HOLT.	-do-	24/8/'18.
Capt. J.A. GASCOYNE-CECIL. M.C.	Killed.	27/8/'18.
Lieut. J. WILLIAMS.	Wounded.	27/8/'18.
Signal Coy. R.E.		
2/Lieut. F.A. FORD.	KILLED.	28/8/'18.
attached.		
14th. "A" Bde. R.F.A.		
Lieut. C. GOULD. M.C.	-do-	28/8/'18.
2/Lieut. C.V. HILL.	Wounded.	27/8/'18.
Lieut. A.F.M.C. CURE.	-do-	28/8/'18.
72nd. "A" Bde. R.F.A.		
Lieut. A.G. SHARP.	Killed.	24/8/'18.
2/Lieut. R.P. HILL.	Died of wounds.	25/8/'18.
Lieut. E.C. JONES.	Wounded.	27/8/'18.
2/Lieut. M.W.B. WARD.	-do- (at duty).	27/8/'18.
155th. "A" Bde. R.F.A.		
2/Lieut. P.O. WILSON.	-do-	22/8/'18.

Army Form C. 2118.

WAR DIARY
of
"A & Q" BRANCH.
HEADQUARTERS,
INTELLIGENCE SUMMARY. GUARDS DIVISION.
MONTH OF SEPTEMBER, 1918.

(Erase heading not required.)

Place	Date	Hour	Summary of Events and Information	Remarks and references to Appendices
W.3.d.4.5.	1st. Sept.		The following appointments were made on the Bde. and Divisional Staffs :- Lieut. (a/Capt.) J.N. BUCHANAN, M.C., Grenadier Gds., to be Brigade Major, 3rd. Guards Bde., vice Capt. F.G. BEAUMONT-NESBITT, Grenadier Guards (sick). Lieut. (a/Capt.) C.G. KEITH, M.C., Grenadier Guards to be Staff Capt., 3rd. Guards Bde., vice Captain F.P. ACLAND-HOOD, Coldstream Guards, to England, for 6 months duty. Lieut. N.R. HELY-HUTCHINSON, M.C., Irish Guards, to be G.S.O. III., vice Lieut. (a/Capt.) J.N. BUCHANAN, M.C. Captain E.D. MACKENZIE, D.S.O., Scots Guards, who had been temporarily acting as Brigade Major for 3rd. Guards Brigade returned to 4th. Guards Brigade to resume duties of Staff Captain. Major (a/Lt.Col.) A.F.A.N. THORNE, D.S.O., Commdg. 3rd. Bn. Grenadier Guards, left the Division to take up appointment of Commandant, IXth. Corps School. A draft of 17 officers and 600 O.R. arrived from 4th. Guards Brigade. The weather was fine but the wind was extraordinarily cold for the time of year. Casualties - NIL.	
"	2nd.		The battle was resumed and in the evening the 2nd. and 3rd. Guards Brigades took over the line from the 3rd. Division. An advanced D.H.Q. was opened at A.11.b.8.7. in a sunken road near HAMELINCOURT. The weather was very cold and squally. Major F. PENN, M.C., 2nd. Life Guards reported for duty as 2nd in-Command of the 4th. Bn. Guards M.G. Regt. Lieut. (a/Capt.) C.G. KEITH, M.C., arrived to take up duties of Staff Captain, 3rd. Guards Brigade. Casualties :- 2 killed & 6 O.R. wounded - caused by E.A. bombs dropped at ADINFER. Adv. D.H.Q. again moved forward and went into dug-outs at B.17.a.8.3., L'HOMME MORT. Rear "Q"	
"	3rd.		took over the dug-outs vacated at A.11.b.8.7. Several heavy showers of rain in the morning but later in the day turning warm and fine. Casualties :- NIL.	
A.11.b.8.7. HAMELINCOURT.	4th.		The weather fine and dry. Casualties :- 2/Lt. H. GORDON, 3/G.G., wounded (at duty). Capt. P.R. BORRETT, 2/S.G.; wounded. Lieut. H.G.B. DRUMOND, 1/S.G., killed. 2/Lt. J.A. HOWFIELD, 75th. Bde. R.F.A. killed. Major A. RHODES, 2/Lt. S.H. WELCH, M.C., } 155th. Bde. (Army). wounded. 2/Lt. G.R. TRAIN, O.R., Killed 10. Wounded 74. Missing 5.	

/5th.

Army Form C. 2118.

WAR DIARY
or
INTELLIGENCE SUMMARY.
(Erase heading not required)

Instructions regarding War Diaries and Intelligence Summaries are contained in F. S. Regs., Part II. and the Staff Manual respectively. Title Pages will be prepared in manuscript.

Place	Date	Hour	Summary of Events and Information	Remarks and references to Appendices
A.11.b.8.7. HEMELINCOURT.	5th.		Advanced D.H.Q. moved forward again into shelters in LAGNICOURT and Rear D.H.Q. took over the dug-outs at B.17.a.8.8. Captain J.J.F. EVANS, M.C., Welsh Guards arrived from England and resumed duties of Brigade Major, 1st. Guards Brigade. CASUALTIES:- 2/Lieut. H.B. TROTTER, M.M., 1/Welsh Gds., wounded. 2/Lieut. J.W. NAYLOR, 40th. Bde. R.F.A. (wounded at duty). --do-- Major J.M. LAIRD. O.R. Killed 2, Wounded 6. Administrative Instructions No. G.D. Adv.Q./95 were issued and are attached herewith Appendix I. A draft of 5 O.R. joined 4/C.G. (P). Lieut. G.V. WILLIAMS, M.C., Irish Guards joined Division as Educational officer. Weather fine and dry.	Append:I.
B.17.a.8.8. L'HOMME MORT.	6th.		Casualties:- Capt. C.R. JONES, 2/S.G. wounded. O.R. 5 killed, 47 wounded, 3 missing. Weather fine and dry.	
"	7th.		Lieut. (a/Capt.) B. HUSSEY, O.C., "S" Corps Signal Co., VIII Corps appointed O.C., Signals, Div. Signal Co., vice Capt. (a/Maj.) G. PHILLIPS, M.C., ordered to proceed to England for duty at the Signal Service Training Centre. Weather hot and sultry. Casualties :- O.R. 3 killed, 55 wounded.	
"	8th.		A draft of 1 officer and 65 O.R. joined the Division. The Band of the Coldstream Guards arrived under Major J. MACKENZIE-ROGAN, M.V.O., Director of Music. High wind and heavy showers of rain. CASUALTIES:- Officers. Capt. G.A.I. DURY, M.C. Lieut. A.G. ELLIOTT,) 3rd. Bn. Grenadier 2/Lt. S. CALVOCORESSI, 2/Lieut. R.K. HENDERSON,) Guards. 2/Lt. J.A. INGLIS-JONES. 2/Lieut. W.B.L. MANLEY,) Wounded (Gas). O. R. 4 killed, 113 wounded (including 87 gas).	
"	9th.		Very stormy all day with bright intervals. CASUALTIES:- Officers:- Lt. W.H. LOVELL, M.C., 1st. Bn. Gren. Gds. wounded. 2/Lieut. C.H.F. SAMUELSON, 4th.Bn.Gds.M.G.Regt. Wounded (gas). Capt. (a/Maj.) E.J.T. HOUSDEN, M.C., 75th. Bde. R.F.A., wounded. O. R. 3 killed, 32 wounded.	
"	10th.		Heavy rain showers during the day. CASUALTIES. Officers. 2/Lieut. H.G. PALMER, Coldstream Gds., 2nd.Gds.Bde.T.M. Bty. O. R. 4 killed, 50 wounded (35 gas) 5 missing.	

/11th.

Army Form C. 2118.

WAR DIARY
or
INTELLIGENCE SUMMARY.
(Erase heading not required.)

Place	Date	Hour	Summary of Events and Information	Remarks and references to Appendices
B.17.a.8.8.		11th.	The Band of the Grenadier Guards left for England on completion of their tour of duty.	
			CASUALTIES:- O.R., 7 wounded.	
			Major-General G.P.T. FEILDING, C.B., C.M.G., D.S.O., left for England to take command of the London District.	
"		12th.	Major-General T.G. MATHESON, C.B., arrived to take command of the Division.	
			Heavy rain and a gale blowing all day.	
			The following draft arrived :-	
			4th.Bn.Gds.M.G.Regt. 3 officers, 33 O.R. R.A.M.C. 2 O.R.	
			CASUALTIES:- Officers. 1st.Bn. Irish Gds. Lieut. C.A.J. VERNON, wounded (gas).	
			do. 2/Lt. G.T. HEATON, do.	
			1/Gren. Gds. Lieut. H.B. SHELLEY, Killed.	
			do. 2/Lt. A.F. PAYNE, Wounded.	
			do. Capt. J.H.C. SIMPSON, do. (at duty).	
			2/Scots Gds. 2/Lieut. L.B. MABY, Killed.	
			75th.Bde.R.F.A. Lieut. (a/Maj.) T.R.B. SEINNE, M.C. wounded (at duty).	
			do. Lieut. T.F.H. READ. do.	
			14th.A.Bde.R.H.A. 2/Lieut. H. McD. PATERSON, Wounded.	
			" 2/Lt. A.E. BALDWIN. "	
			11 killed, 64 wounded.	
			Weather very stormy.	
			Major-General MATHESON C.B. having brought Capt. J.D.P. ASTLEY-CORBETT, S.G. as his A.D.C.,	
			Lieut. I.R. SAUNDERS relinquished his appointment of A.D.C.	
"		13th.	CASUALTIES:- Officers. 75th. Bde. R.F.A. Lieut. A.K. WILLIAMSON-NAPIER, Missing.	
			O.R. 5 killed, 11 wounded.	
			High wind and low clouds but no rain.	
"		14th.	CASUALTIES:- O.R. 1 killed, 8 wounded.	
			Fine but overcast.	
"		15th.	CASUALTIES:- O.R. 1 killed, 17 wounded.	
		16th.	Rear Div. H.Qrs. closed at MORT HOMME and joined the rest of the Headquarters at LAGNICOURT.	
			CASUALTIES:- Officers. 4th.Bn. Guards M.G. Regt. 2/Lt. W.R. MILLER, killed.	
			G.F. attd. 1st.Bn.Gren.Gds. Rev. J.O. VENABLES, wounded (gas).	
LAGNICOURT.			O.R. 7 killed, 19 wounded.	
			It was very close and hot all day.	

Army Form C. 2118.

WAR DIARY
or
INTELLIGENCE SUMMARY.
(Erase heading not required.)

Instructions regarding War Diaries and Intelligence Summaries are contained in F. S. Regs., Part II. and the Staff Manual respectively. Title pages will be prepared in manuscript.

Place	Date	Hour	Summary of Events and Information	Remarks and references to Appendices
LAGNICOURT	17th.		A very severe thunderstorm in the early morning accompanied with torrential rain. A draft of 8 O.R. joined 1st. Bn. Irish Guards. CASUALTIES:- Officers. 1st. Bn. Coldstream Guards. Capt. O.G. BARCLAY, M.C. Wounded. O.R. 22 wounded.	
"	18th.		A draft of 22 O.R. joined the 1s. Bn. Welsh Guards. CASUALTIES:- Officers. 2/Lt. J. PATERSON, 2nd. Bn. Scots Guards. Wounded (at duty). " E.R. BOWRING, 74th. Bde. R.F.A. " " T.C. TUCKER, 36th. Bde. R.F.A. " O.R. 6 killed, 50 wounded.	
"	19th.		CASUALTIES:- Officers. Lt. C.A.J. VERNON, 1st. Bn. Irish Guards. Wounded (at duty). 2/Lt. V.E. FOOT, 1st. Bn. Welsh Guards. " Lt. K.W. MAURICE-JONES, D.S.O., 41st. Bde. R.F.A. Wounded (at duty). O.R. 2 killed, 47 wounded.	
"	20th.		The following draft arrived :- 8 officers 163 O.R. The weather turned quite cold but fine. CASUALTIES:- O.R. 12 wounded.	
"	21st.		A draft of 6 officers arrived for the 4th. Bn. Guards M.G. Regt. CASUALTIES:- O.R. 44 wounded.	
"	22nd.		Heavy rain in the afternoon. CASUALTIES:- Officers. Lt. W.L.N. ARNOLD, 146th. "A" Bde. R.H.A. wounded (gas). Lt. J.W. ADAMS, -do- -do- 2 killed, 30 wounded.	
"	23rd.		CASUALTIES:- Officers. 2/Lt. H.G. STUDHOLME, 2nd. Bn. Scots Guards. Wounded (gas). Lt. Hon. V.A.C.HARBORD, -do- -do- Lt. H.L. LUNGAIR, 4th. Bn. Guards M.G. Regt. -do- 2/Lt. J.M. NUTTALL, -do- -do- 1/Lt. W.B. EVANS, U.S.M.O.R.C. attd. 1st. Bn. Gren. do-Gas. O.R. 175 wounded.	
"	24th.		The following draft arrived :- 1 officer, 39 O.R. Throughout the day LAGNICOURT and the area all round was intermittently shelled by H.V. guns. CASUALTIES:- officers. 2/Lt. V.E. FOOT, 1st. Bn. Welsh Guards, wounded (gas) at duty. O.R. 1 killed, 17 wounded.	
"	25th.		Administrative Instructions No. 11 were issued (appendix 2). CASUALTIES:- O.R. 4 killed, 5 wounded.	

Army Form C. 2118.

WAR DIARY
or
INTELLIGENCE SUMMARY.
(Erase heading not required.)

Place	Date	Hour	Summary of Events and Information	Remarks and references to Appendices
LAGNICOURT.	26th.		A draft of 2 officers and 31 O.R. arrived for the 4th. Bn. Guards L.G. Regt. CASUALTIES:- O.R. 1 killed, 16 wounded. An Advanced D.H.Q. was opened at 10 p.m. in some dugouts at J.10.a.4.5. The D.A.Q.M.G. went forward.	
"	27th.		The battle opened at 5.20 a.m. By 9.0 a.m. pack transport was going over the CANAL DU NORD. All arrangements worked smoothly. CASUALTIES:- Officers. 2nd.Bn.Grenadier Guards. Lt. R.T. SHARPE, wounded. 2nd.Bn.Coldstream Guards. Lt. C.J.B. SYMON, L.G. " 1st.Bn. Irish Guards. Capt. G.W.W. BENCE-JONES, Wounded. -do- Capt. Hon. B.A.A. OGILVI, " -do- 2/Lt. C.S. O'BRIEN, M.C. " -do- 2/Lt. A.R. BOYLE, " -do- 2/Lt. G.T. MATHIESON, " 1st. Bn.Coldstream Guards. Capt. W.H. GLADSTONE, Killed. -do- 2/Lt. W.N. ROE, Wounded. -do- 2/Lt. C. FITZHERBERT-BROCKHOLES, " (died). -do- 2/Lt. R.D. RITCHIE, Killed. -do- 2/Lt. E.B.C. WOODBURY, Wounded. 1st.Bn.Scots Guards. Capt. H.L.N. DUNDAS, M.C. " -do- 2/Lt. Hon. de B. CORDES, " -do- 2/Lt. R.G. BAKER, " -do- 2/Lt. H.S. HARS[M-TOWNSHEND, " -do- 2/Lt. W.G. DEAN, " 2nd. Guards Brigade. Brig-Gen.G.B.S.FOLLETT, D.S.O.,M.V.O. Killed. 1st. Bn. Grenadier Guards. Lt.Col.J.S.S.P.V.Viscount GORT, D.S.O., M.V.O., M.C. Wounded. 2/Bn. Scots Guards. 2/Lt. E.G. JESPER, Wounded. 75th. Brigade R.F.A. 2/Lt. E.R. NEWDIGGING, " 95th. Brigade R.F.A. Major L. HOLT, " (gas). -do- Lt. H.B. MACPHERSON, M.C. Killed. 4th.Bn.Coldstream Guards. Lt. E.G.C. RICHARDS, Wounded. 4th.Bn.Guards M.G. Regt. 2/Lt. C.H. EILOART, Killed. -do- Lt. A.D. BRADLEY, Wounded.	

Army Form C. 2118.

WAR DIARY
or
INTELLIGENCE SUMMARY.
(Erase heading not required.)

Place	Date	Hour	Summary of Events and Information	Remarks and references to Appendices
LAGNICOURT.	27th.	(contd.)	Lieut. W. REID, 75th. Field Coy. R.E. Wounded (gas).	
			Capt. I.S. CAMPBELL, M.C. 75th. Brigade R.F.A. "	
			O.R. 11 killed, 21 wounded. Total 29.	
"	28th.		The weather fine.	
			The Division came out, and Advanced D.H.Q. returned to LAGNICOURT.	
			CASUALTIES:- Officers.	
			2nd. Bn. Grenadier Guards. 2/Lt. H.C.T. BEVAN, wounded.	
			-do- 2/Lt. P.V. PELLY, "	
			-do- Lt. T.A. COMBE, "	
			2nd. Bn. Coldstream Guards. 2/Lt. E.G. S.C. CHANCE, Killed.	
			-do- Capt. C.P. BLACKER, M.C. Wounded.	
			-do- Lt. L.W.J. BIDDULPH, "	
			-do- Lt. G. STUBLEY, "	
			-do- Capt. C. SUTTON-NELTHORPE, M.C. Wounded, (at duty).	
			-do- Lt. A.D. CROSS, -do-	
			1st. Bn. Irish Guards. Lt. B.S. CLOSE, Killed.	
			-do- 2/Lt. A.R. O'FARRELL, "	
			1st. Bn. Coldstream Guards. 2/Lt. E.A.W. CROSSE, "	
			-do- 2/Lt. G.C.P. Lord BINGHAM, Wounded.	
			-do- Capt. C.H. FRISBY, " (at duty).	
			1st. Bn. Scots Guards. 2/Lt. R.G.M. EDEN, " Wounded.	
			Scots Guards, 2nd. G.B.T.M.Bty. Lt. G. JOHNS, Killed.	
			4th. Bn. Guards M.G. Regt. 2/Lt. E.C.C. GARFITT, Wounded.	
			R.A.M.C. No. 4 Field Amb. Major T. LINDSAY, Died of wounds.	
			U.S.M.O.R.C. attd. No. 4 Field Ambulance. 1/Lt. R. DAVIS, Killed.	
			1st. Bn. Grenadier Guards. Capt. J.S. CARTER, "	
			-do- Lt. A.A. MORRIS, "	
			-do- 2/Lt. A. GRANT, "	
			-do- Capt. W.H. LOVELL, M.C. Wounded.	
			-do- Lt. B.H. JONES, "	
			-do- Lt. A.M. BROWN, "	
			-do- 2/Lt. J.O. BLUNT, " (at duty).	
			-do- Capt. W.A.F.L. FOX-PITT, M.C. "	
			1st. Bn. Welsh Guards. 2/Lt. C.J. WILLOUGHBY, " Total 29.	
			O.R. 139 killed, 637 wounded. 141 missing.	
			Railhead changed to VELU.	

Army Form C. 2118.

WAR DIARY
or
INTELLIGENCE SUMMARY.
(Erase heading not required.)

Place	Date	Hour	Summary of Events and Information	Remarks and references to Appendices
LAGNICOURT	28th.		(Continued).	
"	29th.		A draft of 11 officers 119 O.R. arrived for various units in the Division. Brigadier-General C.P. HEYWOOD, C.M.G., D.S.O., Coldstream Guards, took command of the 3rd. Guards Brigade, vice Brigadier-General G.B.S. FOLLETT, D.S.O., M.V.O., killed. CASUALTIES:- Officers. Major Hon. E.K. DIGBY, M.C. 1st. Bn. Coldstream Guards. Wounded (at duty). O.R. 2 killed, 10 wounded.	
"	30th.		A draft of 3 officers and 25 O.R. arrived for the 4th. Bn. Guards M.G. Regt. Number of War Saving certificates purchased by the Division from week ending 15/6/?18 to week ending 28/9/?18 was 13,528. (75th. Brigade R.F.A. headed the list with 2784). The amount of solder collected by the Division from week ending 11/5/?18 to week ending 28/9/18 was 14,318 lbs. (4th. Bn. Coldstream Guards (Pioneers) headed the list with 3750 lbs.) The weather very cold and rather wet. Continental system of time adopted throughout the British Army from midnight 30th. September/ 1st. October. No. of prisoners captured during the month was 26 officers & 828 O.R. Approximate amount of war material captured during month :- 20 Field Guns, 23 Howitzers, 187 machine guns, and 16 Trench Mortars. CASUALTIES:- O.R. 2 killed, 12 wounded.	

Major-General,
Commanding GUARDS DIVISION.

SECRET.   G.D. Adv.Q./95.

1st. Guards Brigade.
2nd. Guards Brigade.   Divisional Train.
3rd. Guards Brigade.   S. S. O.
4th.Bn. Coldstream Gds.   A. P. M.
4th.Bn. Gds. M.G. Regt.   Div. Signals.
G.D.A.   D.A.D.V.S.
C.R.E.   Rear "Q".
A.D.M.S.   D.A.D.O.S.

GUARDS DIVISION ADMINISTRATIVE INSTRUCTIONS.

Reference G.D. Order No. 218 of 5/9/18.

1. **AREA.**

   Captain W.L. COURTNEY, Welsh Guards, has been appointed Town Major, LAGNICOURT.

2. **BATHS.**

   Baths are being installed in the Large Building at the Cross Roads, LAGNICOURT, and will be ready for use by the evening, 7th September.

   Applications for Baths and Clean Clothing will be made direct to the Divisional Baths Officer, HOMME MORT, B.17.a.8.8.

3. **WATER.**

   Water is being installed at C.28.d.10.5. Troughing 200 feet long. Capacity 3000 gallons per hour.

4. **DIVISIONAL BOMB STORE.**

   Advanced: C.16.b.3.0.   Rear. B.10.b.

5. **TRANSPORT LINES.**

   Brigades and Units will report location of Transport lines.

   Units not in the Divisional Area will move as soon as possible.

   Every effort must be made to obtain cover for both men and horses as soon as possible.

6. **SALVAGE.**

   The Brigades in Support and Reserve will clean up and salve their respective areas.

   Brigade Salvage Dumps will be formed near Roads, locations of which will be notified to this office.

   All Salvage Dumps are to be clearly marked by Notice Boards.

7. **MEDICAL.**

   Separate instructions will be issued by the A.D.M.S.

8. **D.A.D.O.S.**

   The Divisional Ordnance Office is at B.10.b.3.3.

9. **S.A.A. SECTION, D.A.C.**

   The S.A.A. Section is situated at B.10.b.

10. **PRISONERS OF WAR.**

    P. of W. Cage is situated at NOREUIL, C.15.b.5.5.

11. **DIVISIONAL SOLDIERS' CLUB.**

    A Branch has been established at LAGNICOURT. Units will be able to purchase Beer at the same branch on application to D.H.Q.

Lieutenant-Colonel,
A.A. & Q.M.G., GUARDS DIVISION.

S E C R E T.

G.D. No. 1089/94/1/A.

G.D.A.	Camp Commandant.
C.R.E.	S.C.F., D.C.G. Branch.
1st. Guards Brigade.	S.C.F., A.P.C. Branch.
2nd. Guards Brigade.	2nd. Division "Q".
3rd. Guards Brigade.	3rd. Division "Q".
4th.Bn. Coldstream Gds.	62nd. Division "Q".
4th.Bn. Guards M.G. Regt.	52nd. Division "Q".
Div. Train.	63rd. Division "Q".
A.D.M.S.	VI Corps "Q".
D.A.D.V.S.	No. 1 G.C. Coy. Tank Corps.
D.A.D.O.S.	No. 2 " " " "
D.A.P.M.	War Diary.
S.A.A. Section, R.A.C.	"Q".
Offr. i/c Div. Bomb Store.	Officer i/c. Baths & Laundry.
Div. Burial Officer.	

The following amendments to Guards Division Administrative Instructions No. 11., issued under this office No. 1089/94/A of 24/9/18, are issued for information :-

1. PARA. 5.
   1st. Line Transport, 3rd. Guards Brigade will move in such time as to arrive in their new lines by 2.0 p.m. on Zero-day.

2. PARA 15.
   No lorries except those working for the C.E. of the Corps will be allowed, until further orders, to run from HERMIES down to RAMP into the CANAL.

   All other lorries will use the BERTINCOURT- RUYAULCOURT - P.18.c. - HAVRINCOURT WOOD PLANK ROAD - K.32.b. - HERMIES route.

3. PARA 18.
   TRAFFIC REGULATIONS.
   Ammunition wagons (G.S. Limbered and G.S. wagons) of the Guards D.A.C. will have free access to any roads or tracks at any time.

4. PARAS. 18 and 20.
   The C.R.E. will immediately notify both Advanced and Rear "Q" as soon as the CANAL is passable for Transport.

H.Q. Guards Division.
26/9/18.

Lieutenant-Colonel,
A.A. & Q.L.G., GUARDS DIVISION.

SECRET.

G.D. No. 1089/94/A.

G.D.A.
C.R.E.
1st. Guards Brigade.
2nd. Guards Brigade.
3rd. Guards Brigade.
4th.Bn. Coldstream Gds.
4th.Bn. Guards M.G. Regt.
Divl. Train.
A.D.M.S.
D.A.D.V.S.
D.A.D.O.S.
D.A.P.M.
S.A.A. Section, D.A.C.
Offr. i/c. Div. Bomb Store.
Div. Burial Officer.

Camp Commandant.
S.C.F., D.C.G. Branch.
S.C.F., A.P.C. Branch.
2nd. Division "Q".
3rd. Division "Q".
62nd. Division "Q".
52nd. Division "Q".
63rd. Division "Q".
VIth. Corps "Q".
No. 1 G.C. Coy. Tank Corps.
No. 2   "   "   "   "
War Diary.
"G".
Officer i/c. Baths & Laundry.

GUARDS DIVISION
ADMINISTRATIVE INSTRUCTIONS No. 11.

1. **RAILHEADS.**
   Supplies :   VELU.
   Heavy Ammunition   FREMICOURT.
   Light ammunition,
   including S.A.A. etc. HERMIES SLAG HEAP, at P.4.a.7.9.

2. **DIVISIONAL BOMB STORE.**
   A Divisional Bomb Store is being formed at J.9.d. Central.
   This Bomb Store will be common to and available for troops of the 2nd. Division.

3. **SUPPLY TANKS.**
   1 Supply Tank, capacity 9 tons, and 2 supply Tanks, capacity 5 tons, with loads as under will be on Y/Z night, in the vicinity of HAVRINCOURT WOOD, and will proceed at Zero plus 3 hours to establish an Advanced Div. Bomb Store, in trenches near forked roads, K.16.d.4.4.

The 5 ton tanks will carry each:-
S.A.A. rifle	25 boxes.
S.A.A., M.G.	25 boxes.
No. 5 Grenades	50 "
No. 36 "	50 "
V.L.	5 "
S.O.S.	24 signals.
Water.	100 tins.

The 9 ton tank will carry:-
S.A.A. rifle	60 boxes.
S.A.A., M.G.	60 "
No. 5 Grenades	100 "
No. 36 "	160 "
V.L.	16 "
S.O.S.	48 signals.
Water	100 tins.

On arrival, the tanks will remain loaded, each tank will carry a red flag, one of which will be utilized to notify position of dump to troops.
This dump will be fed by S.A.A. Section, Gds. D.A.C., as soon as any crossing over the Canal becomes available.
1st. and 3rd. Guards Brigades will utilize these tanks to take ammunition forward, the tanks returning to K.16.d.4.4. to refill and reloading at once ready to move forward if required.
As soon as the 2nd. Division goes through the Guards Division, this supply of ammunition, etc., will be at the disposal of the 2nd. Division.

/contd.(4)

(2)

4. PACK TRANSPORT.
As no Bridges over the Canal are not likely to be available until zero plus 8 hours, Pack Transport will be the only means of supplying troops EAST of the Canal.

Each Brigade will have 100 pack saddles and 60 water carriers on charge.

5. 1st. LINE TRANSPORT.
First Line Transport will move to the neighbourhood of DOIGNIES, to arrive at their destination not earlier than 5 p.m. on Zero-day. The Brigade Transport Officers and Transport Officers will report exact locations on arrival to both "Advanced" and "Rear" "Q".

6. WATER.
Sources of supply are as follows :-

Drinking:
- (a) Men's water bottles.
- (b) " 2nd. " "
- (c) Water lorries.
- (d) Petrol tins.
- (e) Water points for water lorries and water carts :-
  - (i) DOIGNIES, J.15.b. 20,000 galls. will also be stored there.
  - (ii) SPRING at J.34.d., now open.
  - (iii) Sterilized water storage at K.31.a.0.3., at bottom of canal.
  - (iv) 10,000 gall. tank storage at K.15.a., at bottom of canal, to be pumped up to a similar tank on ground level.
  - (v) 10,000 gall. tank storage at K.27.c., on HERMIES-HAVRINCOURT Road.
  - (vi) MORCHIES, I.5.d.

Note: The filling of these tanks (iv) and (v) will not begin until evening of Zero day.

On relief by the 2nd. Division, Brigades will hand over all water lorries. Care must be taken to prevent delay in handing over and Staff Captains must keep them under their own hand.

HORSES:
- (1) Water troughs in J.36. on both sides of Canal.
- (2) DOIGNIES, J.15.b.

7. RATIONS.
Units will take the necessary steps to ensure that all Iron Rations in their possession are wholly fit for consumption.

8. SURPLUS KITS AND PACKS.
Surplus kits and Packs will be stored at the Baths, LAGNICOURT.

Officer i/c. Divl. Baths will arrange to store everything handed over; all Units will leave one man behind in charge. These may be dumped there as early as desired.

9. TENTS AND SHELTERS.
Instructions as regards the removal of Tentage have been issued under this office No. G.D. No. 1089/93/1/A dated 23/9/18.

/10.

(3).

10. MEDICAL.
Divisional Main Dressing Station, will be formed at J.13.central, WEST of BEAUMETZ at old German Dressing Station.

    A. D. S. before zero: SALMON POST, J.17.a.
                                  TROUT POST, K.7.c.

    A. D. S. after zero: LOCK No. 7.

Further detailed instructions will be issued by the A.D.M.S.

|| As soon as each objective is reached by each Guards Brigade, Brigades will, on demand from the O.C., Divl. Bearers, (Lt.Col. A.D. FRASER, D.S.O.,M.C.) detail 50 O.R. to act as auxiliary stretcher bearers. ||

11. VETERINARY.
An advanced Mobile Veterinary Station will be formed at DOIGNIES, J.16.a.2.3.

12. BURIALS.
The Burial party will be concentrated at DEMICOURT by 7 a.m., Zeroday, and will be responsible as far as the situation allows, for the burial of the men of the Guards Division.
The Divisional Burial Officer will ensure that bodies are collected and buried at a few fixed points, and not buried indiscriminately in ones and twos.

The S.C.F., D.C.G's branch, will detail one Chaplain to live with and co-operate with the D.B.O.

O.C., Guards Div. Train will detail one G.S. wagon to report for duty to the D.B.O. at LAGNICOURT, at 6 p.m. on Y day.

The Camp Commandant will ration the Burial party.

13. PRISONERS OF WAR.
The Div. Prisoners of War Cage will be established at DEMICOURT.
The Corps Prisoners of War Cage is at BEAUMETZ, J.20.a.3.2.

MODE OF EVACUATION.
First phase.
All prisoners will, in the first instance be brought by units to DEMICOURT to be handed over to the D.A.P.M. After examination the Infantry Escort will then conduct all Prisoners to the Corps Cage.

Second Phase.
As soon as the third objective (blue dotted line) is gained, a rendezvous for Prisoners will be formed at the Canal crossing at K.9.b.3.9., where units will hand over all prisoners to the Infantry Escort who will conduct them to the Divisional Cage at DEMICOURT.
In the event of the rendezvous for prisoners being moved forward to the BEETROOT FACTORY, L.13.c.6.6., G.O.C., 3rd. Guards Brigade will be prepared to detail an Escort to conduct prisoners to the Relay Post, K.9.b.3.9., CANAL Crossing, where they will be handed over to the D.A.P.M.

(4).

14. STRAGGLERS POSTS.

The 2nd. Guards Brigade will arrange for Stragglers' Posts to be placed at the Canal Crossings, at K.9.b.2.9., K.9.c.5.0., and at CAUSEWAY, K.15.a.3.4.

The D.A.P.M. will arrange to patrol the HERMIES-MOEUVRES Road from the CAMBRAI Road at K.1.a.8.3. to South of DEMICOURT at J.24.a.7.0.

15. ROADS, TRACKS AND CANAL CROSSINGS, AVAILABLE FOR USE BY GUARDS DIV:

See attached Schedule marked "A".

16. TRAFFIC CONTROL.

RESPONSIBILITY. The D.A.P.M. will be responsible for all traffic in the Divisional Area, NORTH of a Line drawn WEST and EAST through J.24.Central and K.19.central.

17. TRAFFIC ROUTES.

Traffic routes WEST of the road running from K.1.a.8.3. on the Main CAMBRAI Road to DEMICOURT, will be as follows :-

LAGNICOURT-LOUVERVAL Road.	Single, South-East only, except for Motor Ambulances.
MAIN CAMBRAI ROAD.	Double way.
Road from K.1.a.8.3. to DEMICOURT.	Single, South-West only.
Road from DEMICOURT to BOURSIES.	Single, North-West only.
Road from DOIGNIES to DEMICOURT.	East only, except for Motor Ambulances.

18. TRAFFIC REGULATIONS.

(a) No traffic will move EAST of a Line N. and S. through Road junction (BEETROOT FACTORY) on CAMBRAI Road at J.9.b.7.3.- DOIGNIES J.28.a.0.2. until :-
  1. (For Traffic across the Canal): the crossings are reported available, as shown in -para 20.
  2. (For First Line Transport moving to DOIGNIES): 5 p.m. on zero-day.

NOTE: Guards Division R.E. Bridging wagons will pass through all control posts without a pass and will move under instructions received from the C.R.E.
Guns and Limbers Royal Artillery will be given free passage at all times in the Divisional Area.

(b) Precedence of traffic after zero :-

R.E. Bridging wagons and Road repair wagons.
Royal Artillery.
Machine Gun Pack Transport.
First Guards Brigade Pack Transport.
Third Guards Brigade Pack Transport.

NOTE:- Guns and Limbers of the Royal Artillery will be given free excess over the Canal as soon as any crossing is reported available.

(c) Under no circumstances will traffic be permitted to double-bank.

18 (d).

18. Contd.
TRAFFIC REGULATIONS.

(d) Units must arrange for their traffic to be kept together as for a Convoy and an Officer will always be in charge.

(e) Traffic Control Posts have orders to pass Convoys at intervals, the gaps so caused to be utilized to pass Traffic with a right to free movement, i.e., R.E., R.A., Machine Gun Pack Transport, Motor Ambulances.

(f) Traffic EAST of the CANAL will be similarly controlled.

(g) No man, unless a driver of wheeled transport or in charge of a pack animal will cross the canal by the crossings available for guns and wheeled vehicles.
All men on foot will continue to cross by means of the Infantry Crossings shown in para. 15.

(h) A Circuit will be arranged as early as practicable, but no traffic which has passed Eastwards over the Canal will be allowed to cross Westwards, until at least two of the three wheeled traffic Crossings are available.
In case of subsequent breaking of Crossings, by shell fire, no Transport will attempt to cross the Canal until the Control Posts on the Canal intimate that crossings are again available.

19. MOVEMENT OF CONVOYS.
As soon as any crossing is available, Transport Officers will arrange for their pack animals to go forward in "Convoys", the Officer-in-Charge riding forward to the Canal Bank to ascertain from the Traffic Officer that the crossing is available. In the event of temporary breakdown or of a block occurring, convoys will at once clear the track and park until further movement forward is possible.

20. TRAFFIC CONTROL POSTS.
Traffic Control Posts will be established at :-

(1) Cross Roads, DOIGNIES, J.16.a.5.45.
(2) Cross Roads (BEETROOT FACTORY) on Main CAMBRAI Road at J.9.b.3.2.

N.C.O's in charge of Posts 1 and 2 will NOT allow any traffic to proceed EASTWARDS as shown in para. 18 (a).

(3) DEMICOURT at J.18.b.
(4) DEMICOURT at J.12.d.
(5) BOURSIES, J.5.d.3.3.
(6) Main CAMBRAI Road at K.1.a.9.3.

N.C.O's in charge of Posts 3 to 6 will not allow any traffic to move Eastwards until the crossings over the Canal are reported available. Each Post will be provided by the R.E. with a Flag, which is to be flown, when a flag of the same colour is shown at the crossings over the Canal.
The Traffic Control Post at (6) must keep in touch with the situation at the crossing at E.27.c.2.4., under construction by 52nd. Division.

/20.Contd.

20. **TRAFFIC CONTROL POSTS. (Contd.).**

Crossings will be marked by flags as follows :-

Field Guns ... Red and Yellow with black bands.
Pack animals ... Red and Green.
Infantry ... Black and yellow.

Care is to be taken to lower the flags immediately whenever a crossing is out of action.

(7) CAUSEWAY at K.15.a.4.6.
(8) BRIDGE at K.15.a.7.9., Lock No. 7.
(9) BRIDGE at K.9.b.3.9.
(10) At all crossings for pack animals :-
K.15.a.3.4. UP.
K.15.a.4.5. DOWN.
K.9.b.1.0. UP.
K.9.b.3.3. DOWN.

These posts, in addition to the above instructions, will receive orders from the D.A.P.M. or Advanced "Q" by means of Runners and mounted patrols, and will halt if necessary, on receipt of orders, all traffic proceeding Eastwards, should the passages of the Canal be interrupted at any time: even if only temporarily.

The personnel for Posts Nos. 1 to 6 will be in position by 3 p.m. on Y night, those for Posts 7 to 10 will take over not later than Zero plus 4 hours.

The D.A.P.M. will arrange to establish control Posts EAST of the Canal as soon as practicable.

21. **DUTIES OF CONTROL POSTS.**

The Divisional Traffic Officer will be responsible for all crossings over the CANAL.

The Officers attached to the D.A.P.M. will be responsible for the Control Posts WEST of the Canal.

The duties of the officers and N.C.O's in charge of Control Posts will be :-

(a) To prevent blocks in the traffic.

(b) To prevent unauthorized crossings of the Canal until the R.E. officer in charge of construction work on the crossing has given permission for traffic to proceed.

(c) To keep D.A.P.M. informed of any occurrences affecting the traffic.

(d) To keep in touch with the Officer R.E. in charge of construction and to receive orders from that officer as to whether the crossings may be used by traffic.

(e) To give precedence to passage of units in the order shown in para. (18.(b)., or in accordance with orders given by D.H.Q.

(f) To be always fully cognisant of the situation at the Crossings and of any change which may take place and to keep Advanced "Q" fully informed.

(7).

21. **DUTIES OF CONTROL POSTS. (Contd.).**

    (g) To give every assistance to officers in charge of convoys.

    (h) To notify D.A.P.M. by runner as soon as any crossings are available or become out of action at any time. The D.A.P.M. will at once inform all Control Posts in rear and will cause the flags at Control Posts to be raised or lowered as circumstances demand.
Advanced "Q" will be frequently notified of any change in the Traffic situation.

    Communication from the Canal Control Posts to the D.A.P.M's office at DELICOURT, J.18., will be by runner.

22. **PATROLS.**

    Dry weather tracks will be patrolled by mounted police.

23. **FLAGS.**

    The D.A.P.M. will arrange to draw the flags from the C.R.E. on Y day.

A C K N O W L E D G E.

[signature]

H.Q. Guards Division.   Lieutenant-Colonel,
24th. September, 1918.   A.A. & Q.M.G., GUARDS DIVISION.

SCHEDULE "A".

ROADS, TRACKS, and CANAL CROSSINGS, AVAILABLE FOR USE BY THE
GUARDS DIVISION.

ROADS.	TRACKS.	CANAL CROSSINGS.
MOTOR ROADS. (A) VELU – BERTINCOURT – RUYAULCOURT – HAVRINCOURT Wood. (B) K.31.a.1.3. along bed of CANAL to K.15.a.7.2. The Ramp at K.15.a.3.2. out of the CANAL and a plank ROAD thence to K.15.b.5.0. will be constructed by the Guards Division. (C) VELU-BEAUMETZ – DOIGNIES – HERMIES – Ramp into Canal at K.31.a.1.3. – out at CULVERT at K.32.a.1.3. or at K.15.a. (D) MAIN BAPAUME-CAMBRAI Road when Crossing at E.36.d.9.3. is completed. NOTE: The Canal Bed will be available for double lorry traffic from the Ramp at K.31. a. to the Lock in K.15.a. Should the Ramp at K.31.a. become impassable, then the Guards Division will send lorries via Route A.	DRY WEATHER TRACKS. (E) DEMICOURT (J.12.d.8.5. – K.8.cent. – K.9.b.3.9. – K.3.d.6.1. thence road to BRAINCOURT. or road to HAVRINCOURT. (F) DEMICOURT (J.12.d.5.1.) – K.14.a.1.1. – K.14.b. 0.6. – LOCK 7 – K.9.d.55.00.	CROSSING FOR FIELD GUNS AND G.S. WAGONS. (G) Bridge or Causeway at K.9.b.2.9. (H) Bridge at Lock 7 at K.15.a.7.9. CROSSING FOR PACK ANIMALS. (I) K.15.a.3.4. UP. (J) K.15.a.4.5. DOWN. (K) K.9.b.1.0. UP. (L) K.9.b.5.3. DOWN. NOTE: It may be found that the labour absorbed in constructing these crossings will be better employed in pushing on the crossings under "G. & H" which pack animals can use as well as guns – in this case, pack animals crossings will not be undertaken. CROSSINGS FOR INFANTRY. (M) It is proposed to improve existing Infantry Crossings and provide new ones (ladders) up to a total of 12 on the Divisional Front. Ropes will be provided on either side of the ladders.

War Diary.
Administrative Staff.
Guards Division.
October 1918.

ADMINISTRATIVE STAFF,
H.Q., GUARDS DIVISION.

INTELLIGENCE SUMMARY. MONTH OF OCTOBER, 1918.

(Erase heading not required.)

Place	Date	Hour	Summary of Events and Information	Remarks and references to Appendices
LAGNICOURT.	1st.		Casualties, O.R. wounded 6.	
"	2nd.		The weather fine and cold. All the Details at BERLES were moved by train to FREMICOURT and went into huts at LEBUCQUIERES. First class accommodation both for officers and men. Personnel Railhead for the Division was changed from SAULTY to FREMICOURT. Leave Train from BAPAUME. Casualties - Nil.	
	3rd.		A draft of 30 O.R. arrived for the 4th. Bn. Guards M.G. Regt. Casualties O.R. 1 Killed, 5 wounded.	
	4th.		Telegram received that TURKEY has surrendered. Casualties O.R. 3 killed and 5 wounded. Lieut. (a/Capt.) R.G. HAMMOND, 75th.Bde.R.F.A. wounded.	
	5th.		News about TURKEY incorrect. 1st. Bn. Irish Guards sent in revised list of O.R., Casualties for 27th and 28th. Sept., i.e. Killed O.R. 26, wounded O.R. 159, missing O.R. 1. Other casualties, 3rd. Bn. Grenadier Guards Killed O.R. 4., wounded O.R. 8. and 1st. Bn. Coldstream Guards wounded O.R. 28 on 5/10/18.	
	6th.		Casualties O.R. 1 wounded.	
	7th.		Divisional H.Q. move to FLESQUIERES, 1st. and 2nd. Guards Brigades to area West of MARCOING, 3rd. Guards Brigade move to area West of RIBECOURT.	
FLESQUIERES.	8th.		Casualties, Killed Officers 2. O.R. 1. Wounded Officers 6, O.R. 13. Died of wounds O.R. 1.	
	9th.		Divisional H.Q. move to SERANVILLERS with the exception of "B" Mess which moved to MASNIERES "C" Mess remaining at FLESQUIERES.	
	10th.		Casualties, Killed Officers 1., O.R. 5. wounded Officers 2, O.R. 60. Injured O.R. 2. Supply Railhead moves up to MASNIERES. Lt.Col. FRASER, O.C. No. 9 Field Ambulance brought in to D.H.Q. with a broken leg, having been knocked over by motor bicycle. "B" Mess move from FLESQUIERES to RUMILLY. Casualties, Officers Killed 1, wounded 8, - O.R. killed 8, wounded 98 - Missing 3. The following draft joined Guards Divisional Reception Camp, LEBUCQUIERE today:- Lieut. W.D. Mc. N. PORTER, 2nd. Bn. Scots Guards, Lieut. H.W.E. FERGUSSON, 4th. Bn. Coldstream Guards (Pioneers), 2nd. Lieut. W.G. NORTON, 1st. Scots Guards, and 85 O.R. including 4 for the Employment Co. Major E.C.T. WARNER, D.S.O.,M.C., rejoined 1st.Bn.Scots Guards from 2nd. Battalion Scots Guards.	
BOUSSIERES.	11th.		Divl. H.Q. complete moved into BOUSSIERES, very good billets and two chateaux practically undamaged. Are able to open advanced branches of Soldiers' Club in St.HILAIRE and QUIEVI. It is quite hard, for the first time, to fill English and Paris leave vacancies.	

contd.

Instructions regarding War Diaries and Intelligence Summaries are contained in F. S. Regs., Part II. and the Staff Manual respectively. Title pages will be prepared in manuscript.

INTELLIGENCE SUMMARY.

(Erase heading not required.)

Place	Date	Hour	Summary of Events and Information	Remarks and references to Appendices
BOUSSIERES	11th.		Capt. W.H. WYNNE-FINCH, M.C., Scots Guards, on relinquishing the appointment of Brigade Major, 2nd. Guards Brigade, is posted to 2nd. Bn. Scots Guards, and Lieut. (T/Capt.) O. LYTTELTON, D.S.O., Grenadier Guards, is appointed Brigade Major in his place. Lieut. W.G. HORTON, M.C., and 12 O.R. joined 1st. Bn. Scots Guards Details on 10/10/18. 12 O.R. joined 3rd. Bn. Grenadier Guards Details on 10/10/18. Casualties Killed, Officers 1 and O.R. 13. wounded Officers 8 and O.R. 111 - Missing O.R. 1 and injured O.R. 2.	
"	12th.		Lieut. (a/Capt.) J.M. PETO, Coldstream Guards is appointed Adjutant, 4th. Bn. Coldstream Gds. (Pioneers) with effect from 8/10/18, vice Lieut. (a/Capt.) L. BOOTLE-WILBRAHAM, M.C., who resigned his appointment. Casualties wounded Officers 2 and O.R. 3. - Killed O.R. 1.	
"	13th.		1st. and 2nd. Guards Brigade move their H.Q. from BOUSSIERES to St.VAAST - 3rd. Guards Brigade H.Q. remain at St.HILAIRE. Casualties Killed O.R. 12, wounded Officers 2 and O.R. 58 - missing O.R. 13.	
"	14th.		Capt.(a/Maj.) H.C.E. ROSS, D.S.O., 2nd. Bn. Scots Guards is struck off strength 10/10/18 on transfer to the Reserve Battalion. Bll Brigade H.Q. now in St.HILAIRE. Casualties, Killed O.R. 3. wounded Officers 4 and O.R. 20.	
"	15th.		Supply Railhead moved to CAMBRAI. The following draft joined Guards Div. Reception Camp, LEBUCQUIRRE today. Capt. G. BARRY, 1st. Bn. Coldstream Guards, Capt. F.C.R. BRITTEN, 1st. Bn. Coldstream Gds., Capt. L.W.G. ECCLES,M.C., 2/G.G., Capt. W.L. GREENLEES, 2/S.G.; Lieut. D.R. BROOKE, M.C., 1st. Bn. S.G., Lieut. R.N. MacDONALD, M.C., 1st. Bn. Scots Guards. 2/Lieut. C.T. ALDRIDGE, 1/C.G., 2/Lt. H.N. VINCENT, 2/C.G., 2/Lieut. D. MILLER, 1/S.G., and 308 O.R. including 2 for 4th.Bn. Gds. M.G. Regt. Casualties, Killed O.R. 3. Wounded Officers 4 O.R. 20.	
"	16th.		Casualties Killed, O.R. 11., wounded Officers 6, O.R. 51. Missing Officers 2 O.R. 45. Injured O.R. 2. Personnel Railhead moved to CAMBRAI. 4 Officers and 181 O.R. left Base Depot to join Division.	
"	17th.		Casualties, Killed O.R. 1. Wounded O.R. 10. Missing O.R. 1. Advanced Reception Camp on CAMBRAI - CAUROIR Road.	
"	18th.		Casualties, Killed O.R. 1. Wounded O.R. 2.	
"	19th.		Supply Railhead to AWOINST. Casualties Killed O.R. 3. Wounded Officers 1 O.R. 5. Injured O.R. 1.	

/contd.

INTELLIGENCE SUMMARY

(Erase heading not required.)

Instructions regarding War Diaries and Intelligence Summaries are contained in F.S. Regs., Part II. and the Staff Manual respectively. Title pages will be prepared in manuscript.

Place	Date	Hour	Summary of Events and Information	Remarks and references to Appendices
BOUSSIERES	20th.		Details to CARNIERES. Capt. G. FURZE takes over duties of Staff Capt. 1st. Guards Bde. vice Capt. Hon. A.N.A. VANNECK, to England for Staff Course. 2/Lieut. J.A.L. DUNCAN and 109 O.R. joined 1/S.G. Casualties to 12 noon Killed O.R. 1, O.R. 12m Wounded Offr.s 3., O.R. 92. Injured O.R. 1.	
"	21st.		Casualties, Killed Offr. 2 O.R. 21. Wounded Offr. 1. O.R. 89. Missing O.R. 7.	
"	22nd.		Division in St.HILAIRE - BOUSSIERES - CARNIERES Area. Casualties Killed O.R. 8. Wounded Offr.s 3 O.R. 32.	
"	23rd.		2/Lieut. A.D. ANDERSON and C.A. FITCH and 7 O.R. joined 1/G.G. Lieut. S.S. HARRISON,M.C., (I.G.) joined 4th.Bn. Guards M.G. Regt. Capt. G.F. BLACKER, M.C. joined 2/C.G. Lieut. C.C. NAINBY-LUXMOORE, 2/Lt. H.R. MORETON-HAVELOCK-ALLAN and Lieut. SMITH CUNNINGHAM joined 2nd. Bn. Scots Guards.	
"	24th.		Casualties Nil. 2/Lt. D.F. WOOLLAND rejoined 2/S.G. from Hospital, Capt. D.W. GUNSTON joined 1/I.G. Lieut. W.A. PEMBROKE and Lieut. W.H. FREEMAN-GREENE and 81 O.R. joined 1/G.G.	
"	25th.		Casualties Nil. C.G. Band returns from PARIS.	
"	26th.		2/Lieut. A.E.F.F. STRANGEWAYS ROGERS joined 3/G.G. Casualties Nil.	
"	27th.		Casualties - Nil.	
"	28th.		Major A.F.L. GORDON from 1st. Bn. I.G. to 2/I.G. to command. Capt. D.W. GUNSTON, M.C., to be 2nd-in-Command 1/I.G. Col. Hon. H.R.L.G. ALEXANDER from O.C.,2nd. Bn. I.G. to be O.C., 10th. Corps School. Casualties Nil. 90 O.R. joined Reception Camp for 1st. Bn. Irish Guards. Brig:Genl. WILSON, (C.R.A.) assumed command of Division during temporary absence of Major-General T.G. MATHESON in England, on duty.	
"	29th.		Casualties Nil.	
"	30th.		Lt.Col. RUDKIN, D.S.O., R.A.M.C., took over command of No. 9 Field Ambulance.	
"	31st.		2/Lieut. J.H. SIMPSON and 90 O.R. joined 1/C.G. 2/Lieut. H.W. WILD and 120 O.R. joined 2/C.G. Casualties, Nil.	

signature
Major-General,
Commanding GUARDS DIVISION.

Army Form C. 2118.

WAR DIARY
or
INTELLIGENCE SUMMARY.

Administrative Branch
H.Q., Guards Division.
NOVEMBER, 1918.

(Erase heading not required.)

Instructions regarding War Diaries and Intelligence Summaries are contained in F.S. Regs., Part II. and the Staff Manual respectively. Title pages will be prepared in manuscript.

Place	Date	Hour	Summary of Events and Information	Remarks and references to Appendices
BOUSSIERES	1		31 O.R. joined 3rd Bn. Gren.Gds. Lieut. S.B. DERMAR-MORGAN, 2/Lt. R.S. FERNIHOUGH, 2/Lt. G. FELLOWS, 2/Lt. G.M. OLIVER, 2/Lt. W.R. COLQUHON, 2/Lt. R.J.HEDDERWICK joined 2nd Bn. Scots Gds.	
VERTAIN	2			
VERTAIN	3			
VERTAIN	4		2/Lt. D.K.J. GRAHAM joined 2nd Bn. Scots Guards.	
VELLERS POL	5		G. Staff to PREUX-AU-SART. Brig-Gen. G.P. HEYWOOD C.M.G.,D.S.O. commanding 3rd Guards Brigade, wounded. Railhead to SOLESMES.	
VILLERS POL	6			
VILLERS POL	7			
MECQUIGNY	8		Lt. A.G.B. REAVELEY and Lt. H.C. PINKNEY joined 1st Bn. Scots Guards. Lt.Col.R.C.BINGHAM,D.S.O,Comdg. 4th.Bn. Guards M.G. Regt., wounded. Major F. PENN, M.C. took over command.	
MECQUIGNY	9		G. Staff to LA LONGUEVILLE. Capt. L.G. FISHER-ROWE, M.C., joined 1st Bn. Gren.Gds. 2/Lt.G.W. KENTON-SLANEI and 2/Lt. T.R. MAYS joined 1st Bn. Gren.Gds. 2/Lt. H. BEECHING joined 3rd Gren.Gds.	
MECQUIGNY	10		G. Staff to MAUBEUGE. Lt. A.R. CLARE-SMITH, Lt. W.G. DIXON, M.C., and 2/Lt. J.H.S. LONGE joined 1st Bn. Coldstream Guards.	
MECQUIGNY } MAUBEUGE }	11		Cessation of hostilities 11 a.m. Brig-Gen. J.V.CAMPBELL,V.C.,C.M.G.,D.S.O. takes over command of 3rd Guards Brigade., vice Brig-Gen. HEYWOOD, wounded. Band of Coldstream Guards plays in PLACE VERTE, MAUBEUGE. Lt-Col. J.C. BRAND commanding 1st Bn. Coldstream Guards, wounded, gas.	
MAUBEUGE	12		Band of Coldstream Guards plays in PLACE VERTE, MAUBEUGE. Lt. C.G. HEYWOOD and 2/Lt. V.B. LONGWORTH and 194 O.R. joined 2nd Bn. Coldstream Guards.	
MAUBEUGE	13		Orders received that Guards Division is to form part of Army of Occupation in Germany.	

Army Form C. 2118.

WAR DIARY
or
INTELLIGENCE SUMMARY.
(Erase heading not required.)

Instructions regarding War Diaries and Intelligence Summaries are contained in F. S. Regs., Part II and the Staff Manual respectively. Title pages will be prepared in manuscript.

Place	Date	Hour	Summary of Events and Information	Remarks and references to Appendices
MAUBEUGE	14		MASS and Thanksgiving in Collegiate Church, MAUBEUGE. Mayor of MAUBEUGE presents G.O.C., Guards Division with a flag on behalf of the citizens. Major-General MATHESON presents Mayor of MAUBEUGE with a Silver Cup in commemoration of liberation of Town by Guards Division. Mayor and Municipal officials to lunch at D.H.Q. Massed Drums of the Division play Tattoo in square.	
MAUBEUGE	15		4th Guards Brigade arrives at CAMBRAI en route for Guards Division.	
MAUBEUGE	16		Divisional Thanksgiving Services in Barrack Square. 500 men of Division unfit to march to be left behind under Major DUDLEY-WARD, 1st Bn. W.G. Reception Camp to SOLESMES.	
MAUBEUGE	17		Move to Germany postponed 24 hours. 4th Guards Brigade arrives at Guards Division, Battalions returning to their original Brigades. Brigade Headquarters and Trench Mortar Battery disbanded. Capt. Hon. W.S.P. ALEXANDER D.S.O. joined 2nd Bn. I.G.	
MAUBEUGE	18		Divisional Soldiers Club moves to SOLESMES. Details of Division under Major DUDLEY WARD M.C., 1st Bn. W.G., move to SOLESMES.	
MAUBEUGE	19		Division commences march route to occupy strategical points in Germany, halting for the night at BINCHE. G.O.C., Guards Division, was met by local massed bands and civil authorities, escorted to the Hotel de Ville and received thanks for the liberation of the town. Band of Coldstream Guards played outside the Hotel de Ville.	
BINCHE	20		Division continues march route, halting at CHARLEROI. Division marched past G.O.C. 4th Army, General Sir H.S. RAWLINSON, G.C.V.O., K.C.B., etc., at entrance to the town. 2/Lt. H.G. TALBOT posted to 4th Bn. Coldstream Gds. 2/Lt. E. KNIGHT posted to 3rd Bn. Coldstream Guards. 2/Lt. W. BROWN posted to 2nd Bn. Coldstream Gds. Lt. (a/Capt.) R.J. PINTO, M.C., posted to 2nd Bn. Coldstream Gds. 2/Lt.A.J.B. TICKLE posted to 1st Bn. Coldstream Gds. 2/Lt. A. WHARTON posted to 1st Bn. Welsh Gds.	
CHARLEROI	21		Massed Drums of Division played Tattoo in PLACE DU SUD. Capt. F.G.R. BRITTEN joined 1st Bn. Coldstream Gds. 2/Lt. H.G.S. ROTHWELL-GREEN and 18 O.R. joined 2nd Bn. Irish Guards.	
CHARLEROI	22		Coldstream Guards Band played in the PLACE DU SUD. Capt. & Qmr. J. TEECE joined 1st Bn. Gren Gds.	

Army Form C. 2118.

WAR DIARY
or
INTELLIGENCE SUMMARY.
(*Erase heading not required*)

Instructions regarding War Diaries and Intelligence Summaries are contained in F. S. Regs., Part II. and the Staff Manual respectively. Title pages will be prepared in manuscript.

Place	Date	Hour	Summary of Events and Information	Remarks and references to Appendices
CHARLEROI	23			
CHARLEROI	24		Division continues march route, resting at FOSSE Area. D.H.Q. did not move.	
CHARLEROI	25		D.H.Q. moves to FOSSE.	
FOSSE	26			
FOSSE	27		Capt. (a/Maj.) R.M. WRIGHT, M.G. joined 4th Bn. M.G. Regt.	
FOSSE	28		March continued, D.H.Q. halts at ASSESSE. Railhead moved to CINEY.	
ASSESSE	29		Band of Coldstream Guards played at CINEY.	
ASSESSE	30			

Lieut-Colonel,
A.A. & Q.M.G.,
for G.O.C., Guards Division.

Army Form C. 2118.

WAR DIARY
or
INTELLIGENCE SUMMARY.
(Erase heading not required.)

ADMINISTRATIVE BRANCH
H.Q., GUARDS DIVISION.
DECEMBER, 1918.

Instructions regarding War Diaries and Intelligence Summaries are contained in F.S. Regs., Part II. and the Staff Manual respectively. Title pages will be prepared in manuscript.

Place	Date	Hour	Summary of Events and Information	Remarks and references to Appendices
ASSESSE	1.		Band of Coldstream Guards played at MAILLEN. 2/Lt.C.J.N.ADAMS,2/Bn.Gren: Gds., Lt.I.W.G.GRENFELL Lt.S.R. LORD,2/Lt.G. THOMPSON & 78 O.R. joined 3/Bn.Gren:Gds. Lt.F.M.B. LUTYENS,M.C. joined 3/Bn.Cold:Gds. Lt.D.A.B. MOODIE,M.C. joined 1/Bn.Irish Gds. 2/Lt.I.D. ERSKINE joined 2/Bn. Scots Gds. 1 O.R. joined 1/Bn.Gren:Gds. 1 O.R. joined 2/Bn.Cold:Gds. 2/Lt.T.A. DUFF, 2/Lt. J.H. TALBOT & 21 O.R. joined 4/Bn.Cold:Gds.	
"	2.		Band of Coldstream Guards played at GESVES. 10 O.R. joined 2/Bn.Gren:Gds.	
"	3.		Capt. A.E.F. SELFE,M.C., joined 1/Bn.Coldstream Guards.	
"	4.		Divisional Headquarters moved to OCHAIN.	
OCHAIN.	5.			
"	6.		T/Maj: H.L. AUBREY-FLETCHER D.S.O. M.C. formerly employed, later AA&QMG Sh.Div. proceeds to England to be appointed Dr H-Col F.G. ALSTON D.S.O. Scots Guards, vice in district BG I/c Administration, and in district T/Capt J.N. BUCHANAN, appointed T/GSO 4, Gds.Div?	
"	7.		Railhead moved to BOMAL.	
"	8.		Band of Coldstream Guards played at JENNERET CHATEAU.	
"	9.		Lieut.(a/Major) G.D. TRELOAR, D.S.O.,M.C. joined 3/Bn.Coldstream Guards.	
"	10.		Railhead moved to TROIS PONT. Lt.A.D. BRIDGE,M.C. & 21 O.R. joined 1/Bn.Cold:Gds.	
"	11.		D.H.Q. moved to GRANDE HALLEUX. 2/Lt.W.C.BROWN,2/Lt.W.M.GOODENOUGH & 59 O.R. joined 2/Bn.Cold: Gds. 2/Lt.E.H.KNIGHT & 23 O.R. joined 3/Bn.Cold:Gds. Lt.J.H.JACOBS joined 2/Bn.Gren: Gds.	
GRANDE HALLEUX	12.		Railhead moved to WEYWERTZ. 2/Lt.C.A.P. TUCKWELL joined 1/Bn.Gren:Gds. 2/Lt.A. WHARTON & 2/Lt.D.B. MORGAN joined 1/Bn.Welsh Gds. Lt.H.G. PEARSON joined 4/Bn.Guards M.G. Regt.	
"	13.		D.H.Q. moved to HELLENTHAL, crossing the enemy frontier at POTEAU. 2/Lt.J.B.TICKLE joined 1/Bn. Cold: Gds.	

Army Form C. 2118.

WAR DIARY
INTELLIGENCE SUMMARY.
(Erase heading not required)

Instructions regarding War Diaries and Intelligence Summaries are contained in F. S. Regs., Part II. and the Staff Manual respectively. Title pages will be prepared in manuscript.

Place	Date	Hour	Summary of Events and Information	Remarks and references to Appendices
HELLENTHAL	14		Railhead moved to BLANKENHEIM. 2/Lt.J.R.F.STRATFORD & Lt.O.PEAKE,M.C. joined 1/Bn.Cold:Gds. Lt.A.R.BROUGHTON-ADDERLY & Lt.A.M. Count de CARAMAN CHIMAY joined 1/Bn.Scots Guards.	
"	15		75 O.R. joined 1/Bn.Gren:Gds., 75 O.R. joined 4/Bn.Gren:Gds. 100 O.R. joined 2/Bn.Scots Gds. 2/Lt.C.B.GRABURN & 91 O.R. joined 2/Bn.Cold:Gds. 100 O.R. joined 3/Bn.Cold:Gds. Lt.F.B. WYNNE-WILLIAMS,M.C. joined 4/Bn.Guards M.G.Regt. 2/Lt.E.C.FITZCLARENCE & 97 O.R. joined 1/Bn.Irish Gds. 2/Lt.H.L.TATHAM & 2/Lt.T.GLYNWALTERS & 100 O.R. joined 1/Bn.Welsh Gds.	
"	16		D.H.Q. moved to ZULPICH. C-in-C visits COLOGNE. Guard of Honour provided by 2/Guards Brigade. 2/Lt.G.MISKIN joined 1/Bn.Cold:Gds. 40 O.R. joined 1/Bn.Scots Gds. 2/Lt.G.M.BRUXNER joined 1/Bn.Scots Gds.	
ZULPICH.	17		Railhead moved to EUSKIRCHEN.	
"	18		D.H.Q. moved to COLOGNE. 2/Lt.W.D.LOWE & 35 O.R. joined 1/Bn.Scots Gds. Railhead moved to EHRENFELD. 47 O.R. joined 1/Bn.Cold:Gds.	
COLOGNE.	19			
"	20.		Lt.B.T.M.HERBERT joined 1/Bn.Welsh Guards. 129 O.R. joined 3/Bn.Cold:Gds. Lt.E.J.P.HEFFERMAN & Lt.A.M.HUDSON joined 4/Bn.Gds.M.G.Regt. 2/Lt.R.B.OSBORNE joined 1/Bn.Gren:Gds. Major J.BULLIUGH,M.C., Lt.F.BREWSTER & 59 P.R. joined 2/Bn.Cold:Gds. Lt.M.M.HENDERSON & 155 O.R. joined 1/Bn.Irish Gds. Lt.J.K.EDWARDS,M.C. and 26 O.R. joined 1/Bn.Scots Gds. Lt.R.C.ANDREWS joined 2/Bn.Scots Gds.	
"	21.			
"	22.			
"	23.		Lieut.J.L.ALLEN, Lt.W.G.MAPPIN, 2/Lt.F.H.DINSLEY & 1 O.R. joined 4/Bn.Cold:Gds. Lt.Visc.H.R.GAGE, 2/Lt.G.F.FORRESTIER-WALKER, 2/Lt.A.B.C.REYNOLDS & 13 O.R. joined 2/Bn.Cold:Gds. 2/Lt.J.S.ALLEN & 24 O.R. joined 5/Bn.Cold:Gds. 2/Lt.J.F.R.REYNOLDS joined 2/Bn.Irish Gds. Capt. C.M.C.DOWLING, Lt.R.Y.T.KENDAL, 2/Lt.W.T.WINDHAM, 2/Lt.D.A.RADERMACHER, 2/Lt.F.M.P.IRWIN joined 4/Bn.Gren:Gds.	
"	24.		D.H.Q. moved to LINDENTHAL. 2/Lt.S.V.SHAW joined 1/Bn.Cold:Gds. 2/Lt.B.F.G.CURRIE & 2/Lt.W.R.H.FORREST joined 2/Bn.Scots Gds.	
LINDENTHAL	25.			

Army Form C. 2118.

WAR DIARY
or
INTELLIGENCE SUMMARY.
(Erase heading not required.)

Place	Date	Hour	Summary of Events and Information	Remarks and references to Appendices
LINDENTHAL	26.		Major & Q.Mr. F.T. PRICHARD joined 3rd. Bn. Coldstream Guards.	
"	27.		Capt. C. Keith M.C. S/c 3rd [march] the was appointed A/DAQMG for situ during Major A.M. DARELL's leave	
"	28.			
"	29.		Capt. R.M. SYNGE joined 1/Bn.Coldstream Guards from SOLESMES.	
"	30.			
"	31.			

H.J. Aubrey Fuller
Major,
A.A. & Q.M.G., for
G.O.C., GUARDS DIVISION.

Army Form C. 2118.

WAR DIARY
INTELLIGENCE SUMMARY.

(Erase heading not required.)

ADMINISTRATIVE BRANCH,
H.Q., GUARDS DIVISION.
JANUARY, 1919.

Instructions regarding War Diaries and Intelligence Summaries are contained in F.S. Regs., Part II and the Staff Manual respectively. Title pages will be prepared in manuscript.

Place	Date	Hour	Summary of Events and Information	Remarks and references to Appendices
LINDENTHAL	1			
"	2		Capt. H.F. LAW,M.C., 2nd.Bn. Irish Guards left for XXII Corps. 2 O.R. joined 4/Bn.Coldstream Guards. Coldstream Guards Band left for England, via BOULOGNE. 2/Lieut. G.M. HUME joined 4th. Bn. Guards M.G. Regt.	
"	3			
"	4			
"	5		50 O.R. joined 1/Bn.Coldstream Guards. 45 O.R. joined 1/Bn. Welsh Guards. 2/Lieut. H.C. LUSH & 32 O.R. joined 2/Bn. Coldstream Guards. 2/Lieut. J.C. LANGTON,2/Lieut. A.B. GUILLET & 15 O.R. joined 2nd. Bn. Irish Guards. 90 O.R. joined 3/Bn. Coldstream Guards. 25 O.R. joined 4/Bn. Coldstream Guards. Lieut. Sir A. SLADE,Bt., Lieut. E.T. SOMERSET, 2/Lieut.P.H.NEWBIGGIN, 2/Lieut. P.H. GATT and 56 O.R. joined 2/Bn. Scots Guards.	
"	6		61 O.R. joined 1/Bn. Irish Guards from Base.	
"	7		Lieut. K.A. CAMPBELL joined 3/Bn. Grenadier Guards. Capt. G.L. TYRINGHAM joined 2/Bn. Scots Guards.	
"	8		8 O.R. joined 1/Bn. Irish Guards. Lieut. W.H. LOVELL,M.C. & 40 O.R. joined 1/Bn. Grenadier Guards. 9 O.R. joined 1/Bn. Welsh Guards. 2/Lieut. J.H. MARTIN & 25 O.R. joined 3/Bn. Grenadier Guards. 2/Lieut. A.C. SIMPSON and 20 O.R. joined 1/Bn. Scots Guards. 2/Lieut. J.A. LONGMORE joined 3/Bn. Coldstream Guards. 10 O.R. joined 2/Bn. Scots Guards. 40 O.R. joined 3/Bn. Coldstream Guards. 2/Lieut. A de PASS and 46 O.R. joined 2/Bn. Grenadier Guards.	
"	9			
"	10			
"	11			
"	12			
"	13		1 officer and 85 O.R. joined 4th Bn. Guards M.G. Regt.	
"	14		H.R.H. the Prince of Wales, K.G., etc., presented Colours to 4th. Bn. Grenadier Guards, 4th. Bn. Coldstream Guards, and 2nd. Bn. Irish Guards.	

Army Form C. 2118.

WAR DIARY

(2).

ADMINISTRATIVE BRANCH,
H.Q., GUARDS DIVISION.

INTELLIGENCE SUMMARY.

JANUARY, 1919.

(Erase heading not required.)

Place	Date	Hour	Summary of Events and Information	Remarks and references to Appendices
LINDENTHAL.	15		Lieut. O.H. RUSS joined 4/Bn. Guards M.G. Regt. Major-General T.G. MATHESON, C.B., C.M.G., proceeded on leave. Brigadier-General J.V. CAMPBELL, V.C., C.M.G., D.S.O., took over temporary Command of the Division.	
"	16			
"	17			
"	18			
"	19			
"	20			
"	21		2/Lieut. J.D.G. DUNCAN joined 2/Bn. Irish Guards.	
"	22			
"	23			
"	24			
"	25			
"	26		Railhead (Supply) was changed from EHRENFELD to EIFELTHOR.	
"	27			
"	28			
"	29		Lieut. L.D. MURPHY, M.C. and 2 O.R. joined 1/Bn. Irish Guards. 2/Lieut. C.G. KIMBALL and 1 O.R. joined 1/Bn. Welsh Guards.	
"	30		Captain J.J.P. EVANS, M.C., Welsh Guards took over duties of D.A.A.G., Guards Division.	
"	31			

Brunker
Major,
a/A.A. & Q.M.G., for
G.O.C., GUARDS DIVISION.

Army Form C. 2118.

WAR DIARY

ADMINISTRATIVE BRANCH, H.Q., GUARDS DIVISION.

Month of FEBRUARY, 1919.

(Erase heading not required).

Instructions regarding War Diaries and Intelligence Summaries are contained in F.S. Regs., Part II. and the Staff Manual respectively. Title pages will be prepared in manuscript.

Place	Date	Hour	Summary of Events and Information	Remarks and references to Appendices
LINDENTHAL.	1.			
	2.			
	3.			
	4.			
	5.			
	6.			
	7.			
	8.			
	9.		Major J. BOYD, M.C., joined 1/Bn. Coldstream Guards.	
	10.			
	11.			
	12.			
	13.		Captain C.J.M. RILEY, M.C., joined 2/Bn. Coldstream Guards.	
	14.			
	15.		Lieut. E.R.D. HOARE joined 4/Bn. Grenadier Guards.	
	16.		Orders received for Battalions of Guards Division to be prepared to move to United Kingdom on 24th February. Lieut.-Colonel R.V. POLLOK, D.S.O., assumed duties of G.S.O.I. (acting). Capt. W.P.A. BRADSHAW, D.S.O., joined 2/Bn. Scots Guards. Lieut. W.B.LESLIE, M.C., joined 1st Bn. Scots Guards. 2/Lieut. S.V. SHAW joined 1st Bn. Coldstream Guards.	
	17.		Thaw precautions ordered.	
	18.		Orders issued for following Battalions to be reduced to Cadre, and remaining personnel distributed amongst other battalions of their regiments:- 4/Bn. Coldstream Guards, 4/Bn. Grenadier Guards, 2/Bn. Irish Guards. 5/Bn. Coldstream Guards appointed Guards Divisional Pioneer Battalion.	
	19.			
	20.		2/Bn. Grenadier Guards left for England with part of 4/Bn. Coldstream Guards Cadre. Entrained COLN NIPPES STATION and left 0900 hours. Capt. PERRINS, M.C., Welsh Guards took over duties of Brigade Major, 1st Guards Brigade. Unit of 3rd Division relieved 2nd Bn. Grenadier Guards.	
	21.			
	22.		2/Bn. Coldstream Guards left for England (& part of 4/Bn. Coldstream Guards Cadre) and were relieved by unit of 3rd Division.	
	23.			
	24.			

Army Form C. 2118.

WAR DIARY (2).

or

~~INTELLIGENCE SUMMARY~~

ADMINISTRATIVE BRANCH,
H.Q., GUARDS DIVISION. FEBRUARY, 1919.

(Erase heading not required.)

Place	Date	Hour	Summary of Events and Information	Remarks and references to Appendices
LINDENTHAL.	25.		H.Q., 9th Infantry Brigade relieved and took over quarters of H.Q., 1st Guards Brigade, (move of Brigade complete). 1st Bn. Irish Guards left for England and were relieved by unit of 3rd Division. Thaw precautions ceased.	
	26.		1st Bn. Scots Guards left for England (with part of 2/Bn. Irish Guards Cadre).	
	27.		Brig: General C.R.C. de CRESPIGNY, C.M.G., D.S.O. to England. 3/Bn.Grenadier Guards left for England (with part of 2/Bn. Irish Guards Cadre).	
	28.		350 surplus horses evacuated to ROUEN by rail.	

(sd.) Major-General,
Commanding GUARDS DIVISION.

Army Form C. 2118.

WAR DIARY

INTELLIGENCE SUMMARY

(Erase heading not required.)

ADMINISTRATIVE BRANCH.

GUARDS DIVISION.

MARCH, 1919.

Instructions regarding War Diaries and Intelligence Summaries are contained in F.S. Regs., Part II. and the Staff Manual respectively. Title pages will be prepared in manuscript.

Place	Date	Hour	Summary of Events and Information	Remarks and references to Appendices
LINDENTHAL.	1 to 9.		No diary.	
	10.		Nos. 3, 4 and 9 Field Ambulances moved to billets in DUREN.	
COLOGNE.	11.		Battalion Headquarters and 1 company Guards M.G. Regiment left for England. Major J.J.P. EVANS, M.C., D.A.A.G., returned from DUNKERQUE. 1st. Bn. Welsh Guards embarked for England.	
GERMANY.	12.		3rd. Bn. Coldstream Guards sailed at 1900 hours from DUNKERQUE.	
	13.		Last train with M.G. Company left COLOGNE for DUNKERQUE.	
	15.		Orders received for 40 Officers and 150 O.R's. from Guards Division Troops and Cadres to take part in march through LONDON. 18 officers left by BOULOGNE-COLOGNE Express.	
	16.		10 Officers and 150 O.R's. left by leave train on 16th. Last sailings reported from DUNKERQUE. 23 Officers 499 O.R's. 4th. Bn. Guards M.G. Regiment - 1400 horses - details 2 officers and 112 O.R's.	
	17.		Second Army wire (A883) ordered Brig.General J.V. CAMPBELL, V.C., C.M.G., D.S.O., to report to Southern Division to take over command of 86th. Infantry Brigade.	
	22.		Leave of officers and other ranks taking part in march of Guards Division through LONDON extended from 25th. to 31st.	
	23 to 30		Units reduced to Cadre on following authorities :-
55th. Field Coy. R.E. to Cadre B. VIth. Corps A 12 of 24/3/19.
Divisional Signal Coy. R.E. to Cadre A. VIth. Corps A 12 of 24/3/19.
Divisional Train to Cadre A. VIth. Corps Q. 1553.

M.T. Company warned to move to ABBEVILLE on 5th. April.

No authority or instructions received with reference disposal of Field Ambulances - D.A.D.V.S. D.A.D.O.S. | |

Army Form C. 2118.

WAR DIARY

ADMINISTRATIVE BRANCH.

INTELLIGENCE SUMMARY.   GUARDS DIVISION.

(Erase heading not required.)

MARCH, 1919.

Instructions regarding War Diaries and Intelligence Summaries are contained in F. S. Regs., Part II. and the Staff Manual respectively. Title pages will be prepared in manuscript.

Place	Date	Hour	Summary of Events and Information	Remarks and references to Appendices

LINDENTHAL. COLOGNE. GERMANY.	30.		Arrangements made for disposal of all "X" horses in units authorized to reduce to cadre.
			
			  To London Division. 201 H.D. 70 L.D. 3pack mules
			
			  To. Northern Division. 54 riders.
			
			It has not been possible to reduce personnel of units while the full establishment of horses are left.
			
			            [signature]
			            Major,
			          D.A.AG., for
			       G.O.C., GUARDS DIVISION.	

Army Form C. 2118.

WAR DIARY

"CADRE" "A" & "B" H.Q. Guards Division

INTELLIGENCE SUMMARY

(Erase heading not required.)

APRIL, 1919.

Instructions regarding War Diaries and Intelligence Summaries are contained in F. S. Regs., Part II. and the Staff Manual respectively. Title pages will be prepared in manuscript.

Place	Date	Hour	Summary of Events and Information	Remarks and references to Appendices
LINDENTHAL, COLOGNE	April 1st to 22nd	—	Cadre awaiting entraining instructions.	
"	23rd	—	Cadre left at 10am by Motor Lorry for DUREN. Billeted for night in Barracks, DUREN.	
DUREN, Germany.	24th	—	Cadre entrained at DUREN for ANTWERP. Strength 2 offrs. 24 O.R. 6 vehicles.	
ANTWERP.	25th	—	Detrained at ANTWERP at 10 am.	
"	26th	—		
"	27th	—	Embarked per S.S. PRETORIAN at 3 pm.	
Tilbury	29th	—	Disembarked at TILBURY at 10 am. Entrained at TILBURY at 6 pm. for BARNES. Conveyed in motor lorries to Chelsea Barracks. Opened D.H.Q. at Room 59, Whitehall.	
Whitehall, London.	30th	—		

R.M. Whittall
Captain,
V.A.A.G.; Guards Division.